POSTCARD HISTORY SERIES

The Hocking Hills
1900-1950

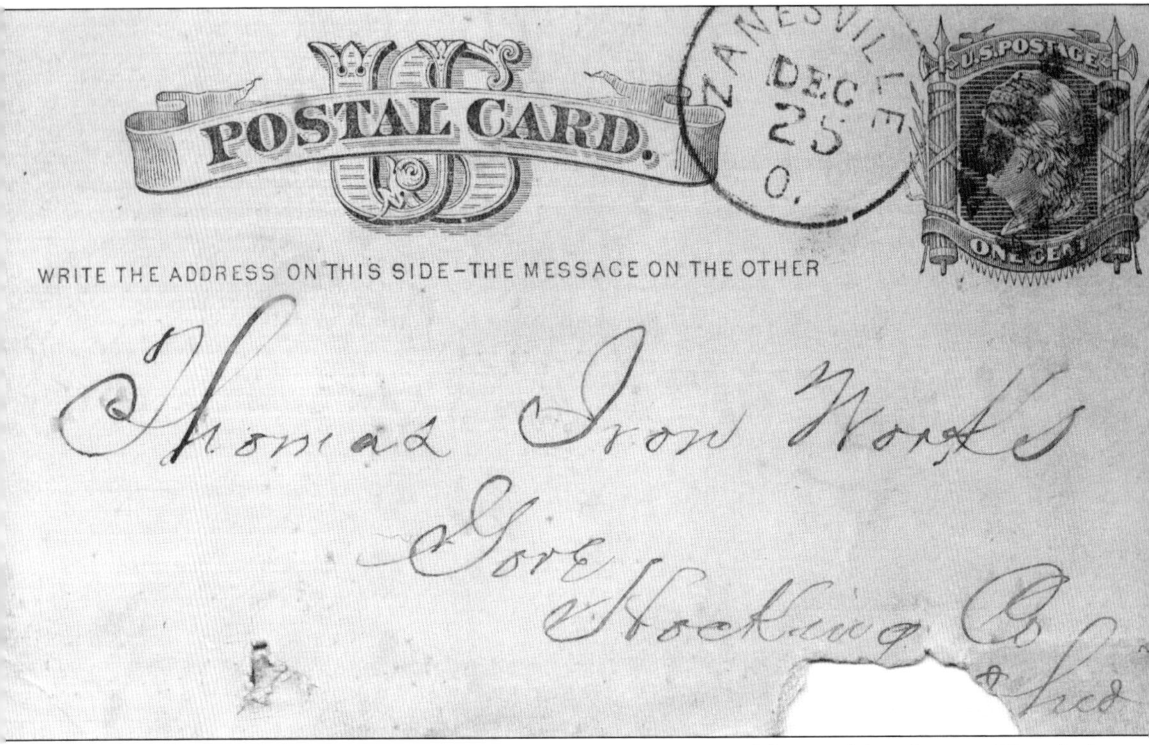

One of the oldest post cards (or postcards) in the collection of the Hocking County Historical Society and Museum is dated November 2, 1876. It is a US Postal Card, stamped with a 1¢ image (indicia) that was preprinted on the card itself. This buff-colored postcard is from the pioneer era of postcard collecting. It was sent to the Thomas Iron Works, Hocking Co. in Gore, Ohio, from the Ohio Iron Works in Zanesville. Note the directions on the postcard explaining how to address the correspondence. Writings were not permitted by law on the address side of any postcard until March 1, 1907. (Courtesy of the Hocking County Historical Society.)

On the Front Cover: Logan, Ohio, is the county seat of Hocking County and the center of the Hocking Hills region. This postcard is a view from the intersection of Main and Market Streets looking east. This "real" type postcard image was taken about 1938. (Courtesy of JM.)

On the Back Cover: The heart of the Hocking Hills cave area is Old Man's Cave. This is a vintage postcard that shows the breathtaking view of the Upper Gorge. As many as three million visitors come to the Hocking Hills each year, just as many who visit Yellowstone National Park. (Courtesy of JM.)

POSTCARD HISTORY SERIES

The Hocking Hills 1900-1950

Judith Stoltz Maniskas

ARCADIA PUBLISHING

ISBN 978-1-4671-1327-4

Published by Arcadia Publishing
Charleston, South Carolina

Printed in the United States of America

Library of Congress Control Number: 2014944624

For all general information contact Arcadia Publishing at:
Telephone 843-853-2070
Fax 843-853-0044
E-mail sales@arcadiapublishing.com
For customer service and orders:
Toll-Free 1-888-313-2665

Visit us on the Internet at www.arcadiapublishing.com

For Steven

Contents

ACKNOWLEDGMENTS

I am indebted to the Hocking County Historical Society for giving me access to their archives. Both the written and photographic files were invaluable to me. Every effort was made to not duplicate previously printed images. This was a challenge, however, and perhaps readers will have seen certain views of old buildings.

The following individuals contributed part or all of their postcard collections to enhance this book. I am grateful for their willingness to share and their sincere interest in the success of this publication. The initials seen at the end of each caption throughout the book will identify the owner of the postcard. Alphabetically, they are DB, David Brown; WD, Willis Dicken; GRF, Gretchen Rochester Fugitt; PNG, Paul and Norma Geiger; PG, Pamela Goss; CCH, Charlotte Crawford Harlow; JWH, Judie Woltz Henniger; HH, Hocking County Historical Society; GBJ, George B. Johnson; KK, Karen Kornmiller; JBL, Judy Buntz Lanning; GM, Georgia Miller; HM, Helen Mowrey; TP, Dr. Thomas Price; BCS, Betty Carpenter Schultz; SS, Sue Smith; MT, Michael Thompson; and NV, Nyla Vollmer. All other postcards are from my personal collection and are labeled JM.

I wish to thank two members of the society, computer gurus Malei Morgan Stewart and Cheryl Edwards Griffin, who worked many hours scanning the postcards.

My research base included information from *Historical Ramblings-Hocking County, Ohio* by Charles R. Goslin; *Haydenville, Ohio's Last Company Town*, published in 2005, by Nyla Vollmer and the Haydenville Preservation Committee; *Union Furnace–New Cadiz*, by David V. Stivison; *Historical Collections of Ohio, 1846* (centennial edition), by Henry Howe; The Ohio Division of State Parks; "The Dew House, 31st Parade of the Hills Booklet, 1980"; "Logan Centennial Souvenir Booklet, 1916"; articles from the *New York Times*, the *Ohio Democrat*, the *Logan Republican*, the *Democrat-Sentinel*, and the *Logan Daily News*; and Greta Huls, Huls Printing Company (Arizona). All information from the Internet and other historical websites included Camp Sherman, Ohio; "History of Picture Postcards" from the *Emotions Greeting Cards & Photography* website; Franklin University, Columbus, Ohio; US Postal Service; US Census Bureau; Hocking County; and hauntedhocking.com.

My sincere appreciation is extended to my friend and editor, Julia Simpson, of Arcadia Publishing, for her encouragement, patience, and kind suggestions.

Royalties from the sales of *The Hocking Hills: 1900–1950* will benefit the Hocking County Historical Society and Museum.

Introduction

The passion of postcard collecting (deltiology) knows no bounds. Collectors will travel to faraway places to seek out the one card they want to add to their collections. Vintage postcards can be found at flea markets, antique malls, and on the Internet for as little as $1 up to any price one is willing to pay for that single, unique card.

The distinct periods of time that follow the progress of postcards are the pioneer era (1870–1898), private mailing card era (1898–1901), undivided back era (1901–1907), divided back era or golden era (1907–1915), early modern era or white border period (1915–1930), linen card era (1930–1945), and the modern photochrome (real) era (1939 to the present). These early eras established the popularity of postcards. According to the US Postal Service data, the fiscal year ending June 30, 1908, tabulated over 677 million of them mailed. Americans were in a frenzy over postcards.

Locating over 200 different postcards, all from the Hocking Hills, was not as easy as one may think. The ever-popular images of Main Street, the Ambrose Hotel, and the Hocking County Court House were plentiful; however, finding the unusual card that may not have been published was challenging. Eventually, as word of mouth circulated, a variety of vintage postcards from the Hocking Hills were submitted. Chapter 1, "Head for the Hocking Hills," is a term our family uses to indicate that after a long day elsewhere, we want to head back to southeastern Ohio for our peace and tranquility. In this instance, the "Hills" refer to the Hocking Hills area called the Caves. They are spectacular and always beckon us home. Chapter 2, "Just Folks," is a compilation of the ordinary or maybe not so ordinary people who were shaped by the Hocking Hills and used their background for the basis of a better world. There is a mix of genealogy, local involvement in three wars, and a promise of peace. Chapter 3, "Times To Remember," details events that made an impact on the Hocking Hills and the lives of its residents. Devastating floods and horrible train wrecks perhaps bring back memories. Chapter 4, "Booming Business," is a walk throughout the Hocking Hills and features the independent business owners and the mom-and-pop stores that were popular back in the day. Most have gone the way of progress, but postcards allow us to renew old memories. Chapter 5, "Friends and Neighbors," includes a five-county area that touches the Hocking Hills. By postcards, we will briefly look at areas in Fairfield, Perry, Athens, Vinton, and Ross Counties. All are at least a small part of the Hocking Hills region. Chapter 6, "The Forgotten Few," came about because of the many postcards that were void of any information. These were real people and families who meant a lot to each other, and now the photographs lie in a drawer or shoebox forgotten by all. Chapter 7, "Hocking Hills Holidaze," celebrates the wonderful cards shared during holidays to let people know that someone cared about them. To those of us who are fortunate to have older postcards handed down in the family, enjoy them. These are just a few chosen for this volume. It is also interesting to note that the postage rates for postcards was still just 1¢ in 1926 and remained at that rate until January 1, 1952, when it was raised to 2¢. Today it costs 34¢ to mail that same card.

Postcards are a method of tracking the progress of an area. The reader of this volume will be able to follow how the Hocking Hills, Logan, and the surrounding areas changed over time. The events of the world around us from 1900 to 1950, including two world wars, changed our way of living forever. This publication is a collection of postcards and photographs that will help document that change.

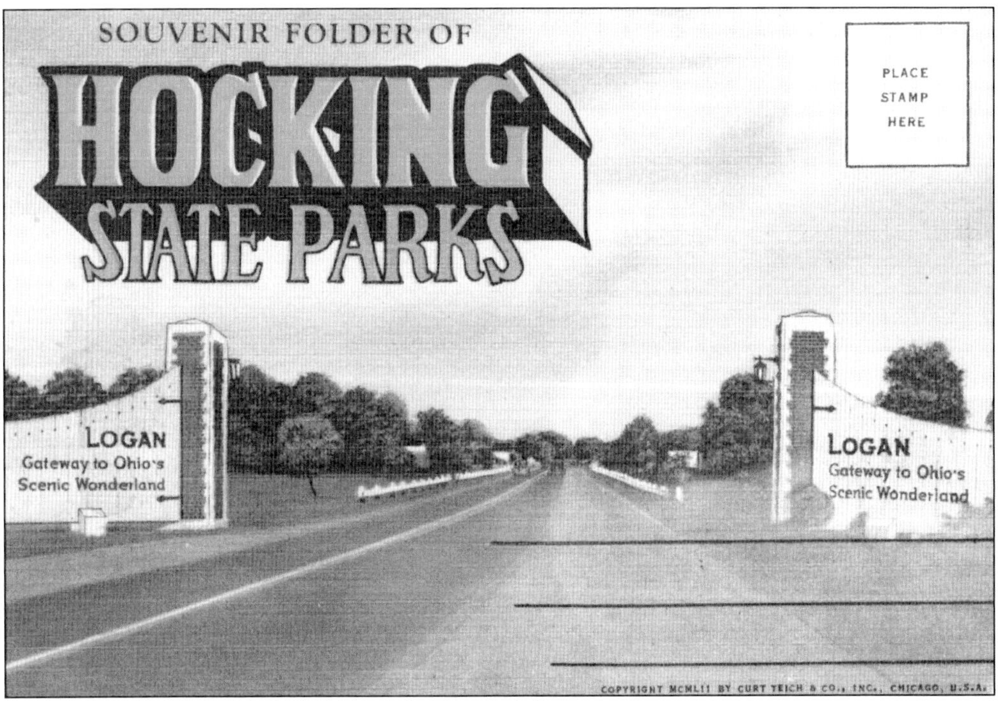

This souvenir postcard from the 1940s is an accordion-type design in the popular linen format. Pictured on the front side are the historical Gates of Logan. When opened, eight postcards unfold with color images on both sides of the card. It also included a map and brief history of the Hocking State Parks. (Courtesy of JM.)

One

Head for the Hocking Hills

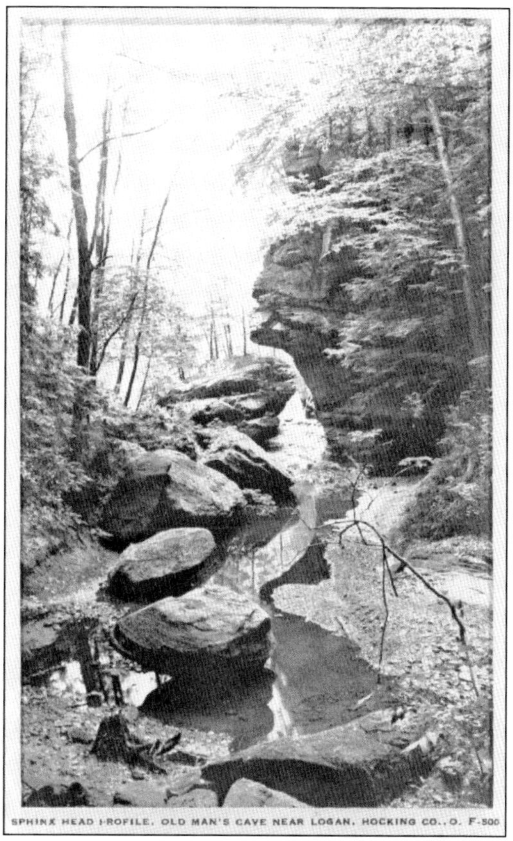

The Sphinx Head Profile, at Old Man's Cave, is perhaps the most well-known natural rock formation in the Hocking Hills State Park. It is a must-see spot for the three million visitors who vacation in the Hocking Hills area each year. This 1945 postcard image of the famous face is a black and white "real" postcard. (Courtesy of CCH.)

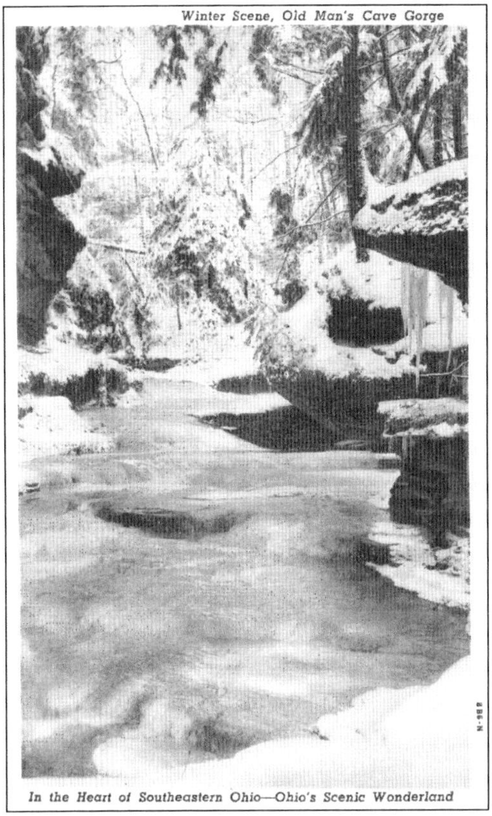

The Hocking Hills Winter Hike is held annually in January. Approximately 5,000 hardy individuals observe the beauty of winter and the fabulous ice sculptures in the parks. January 2015 was the 50th anniversary of the winter hike. These Old Man's Cave images are a "Winter Scene" linen postcard (left) and "Eagle's Rock" (below) real photographic postcard. (At left, courtesy of WD; below, SS.)

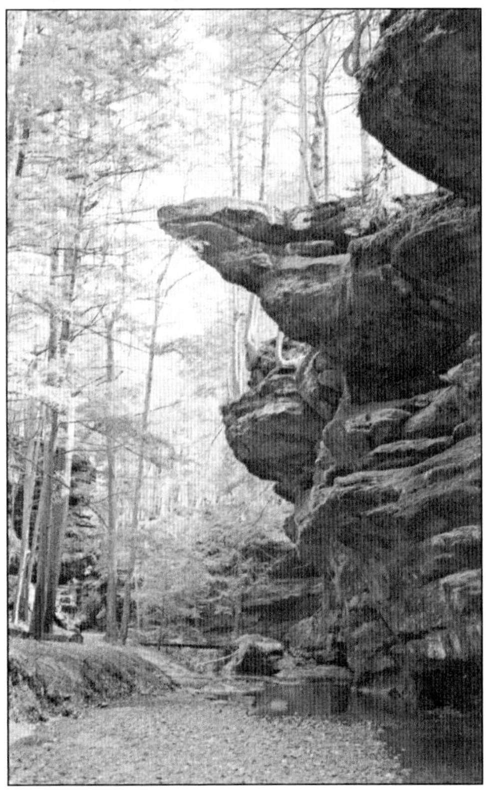

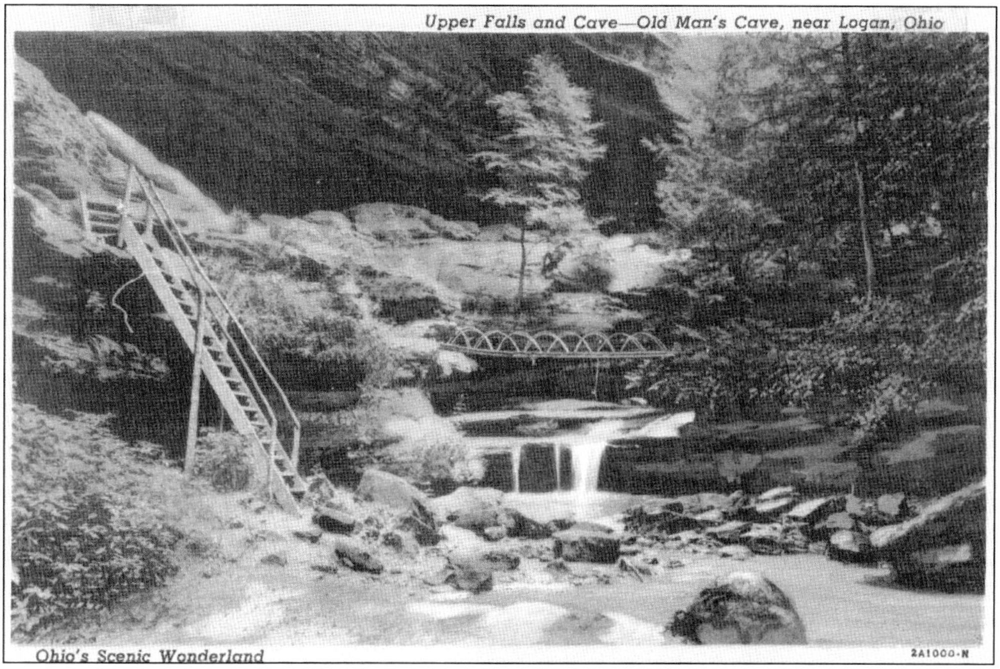

Springtime rains enhance the cave experience for visitors when they see brisk waterfalls. The early-1950s linen postcard (above) shows the upper falls and cave at Old Man's Cave. The steep steps on the left lead to the higher elevations. The lower falls (at right) have a unique beauty. (Above, courtesy of HH; at right, JM.)

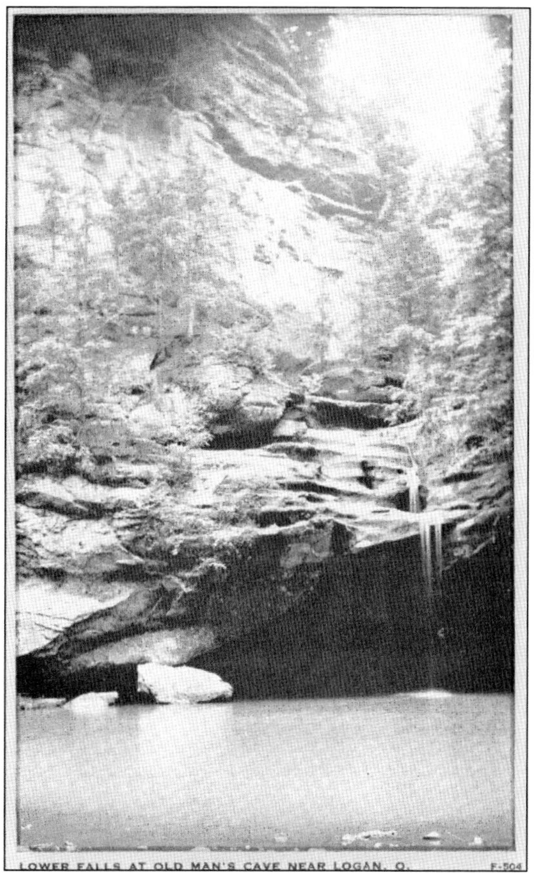

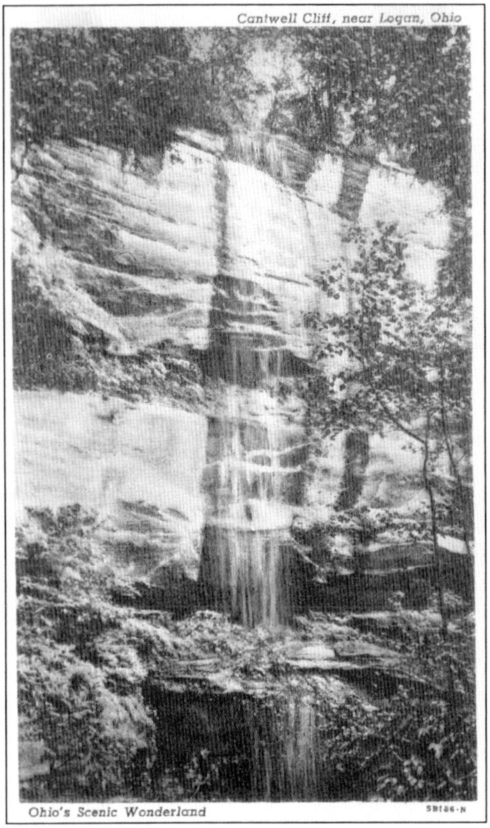

The Cantwell Cliffs are in Good Hope Township and named after early settler Josiah Cantwell. These two linen postcards show the erosion that created the cliffs. The "Fat Woman's Squeeze" (below) is the narrow passage to get to the top of the cliffs, most of which tower 150 feet high (at left). Both postcards are from the 1940s. (Both courtesy of JM.)

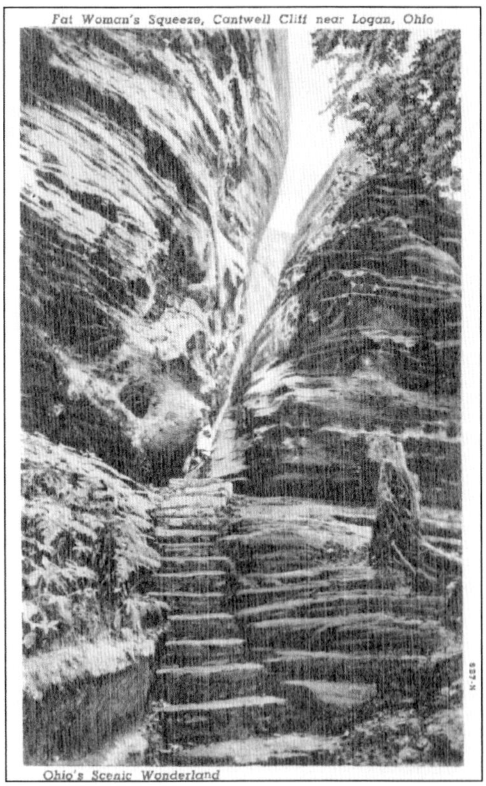

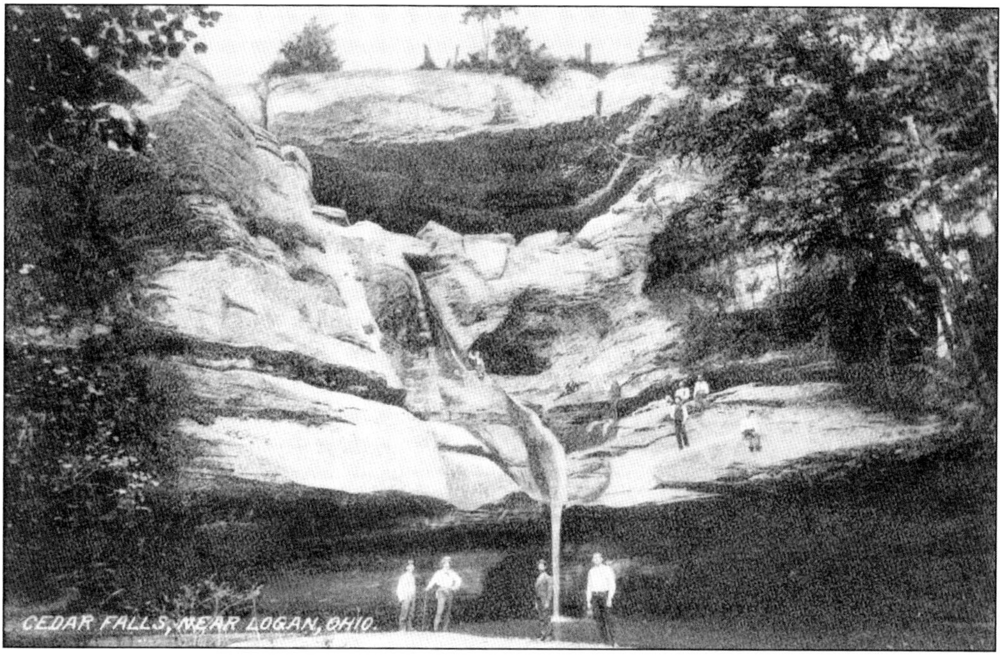

Cedar Falls, in Benton Township, was misnamed by pioneers when they identified the abundant hemlock trees as cedar trees. Cedar Falls has the largest waterfall by volume than any other in the Hocking Hills State Parks. The 1909 postcard above shows men in white shirts and derby hats, rather formal dress by today's casual standards. The image below is a linen card from the 1950s. (Both courtesy of HH.)

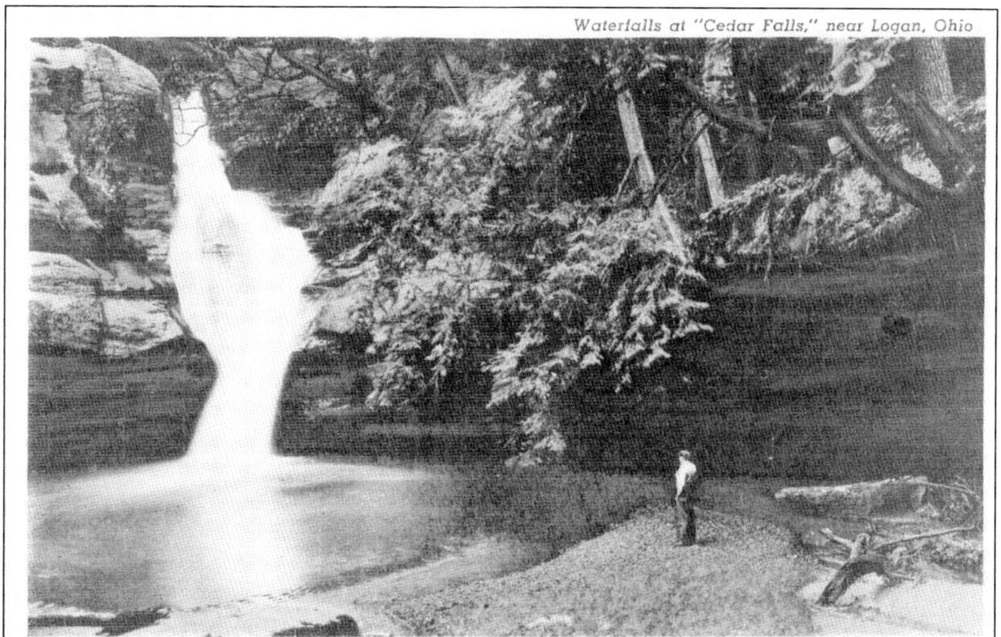

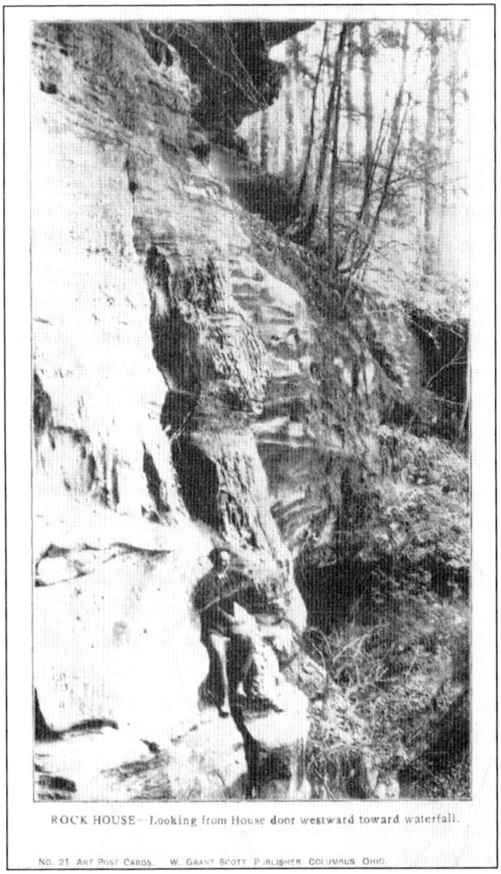

The Rock House is the only true cave in the Hocking Hills State Park. It boasts seven "windows" and a "door." The 1909 real photograph postcard at left shows a visitor outside the cave looking toward the waterfall. The photograph was taken from the Rock House door. The postcard below was made in Germany and imported by F.S. Case Drug Store in Logan, Ohio. The group that is standing on the ledge is dwarfed by the impressive Rock House. (Both courtesy of JM.)

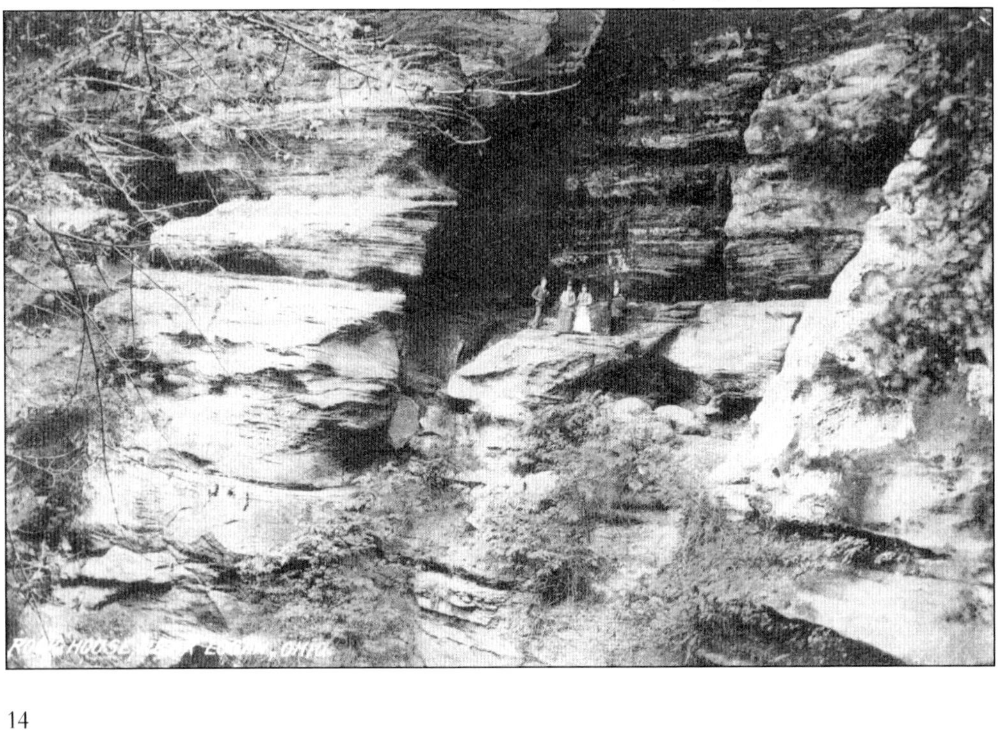

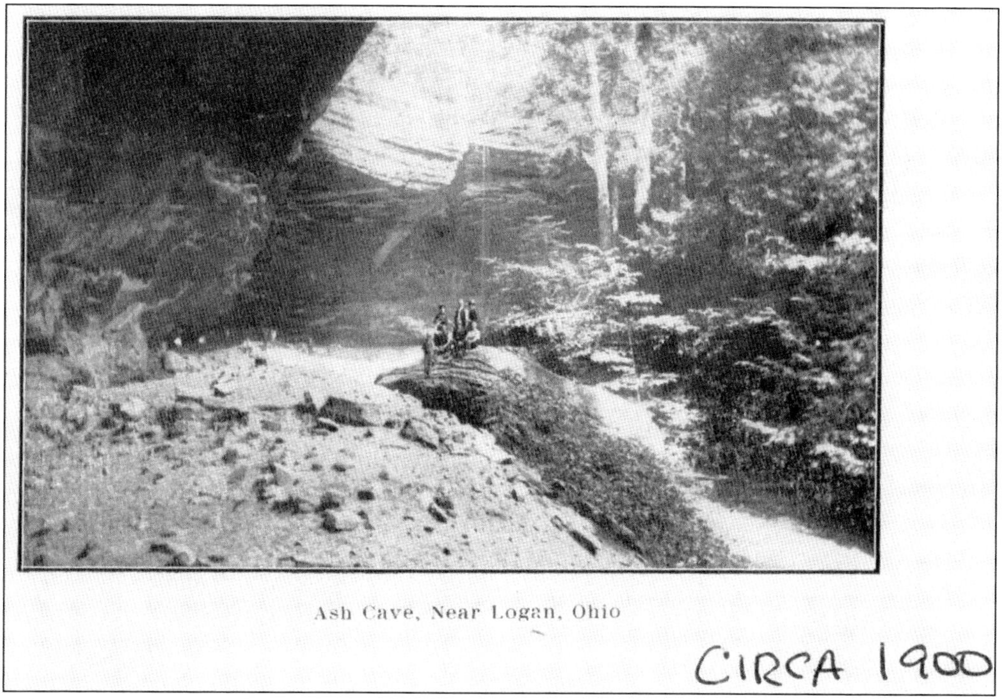

Ash Cave, a truly beautiful formation, has an amphitheater-like recess that is a quarter of a mile long. Its name comes from the dozens of ash piles that were found by early settlers, indicating that Native Americans had long used the cave as protection from inclement weather. The postcard above is dated about 1900 with the area looking very much like it does today. Shown below is an undated linen postcard taken from another angle of the waterfall. Today, a portion of the trails in Ash Cave is handicap accessible. (Both courtesy of HH.)

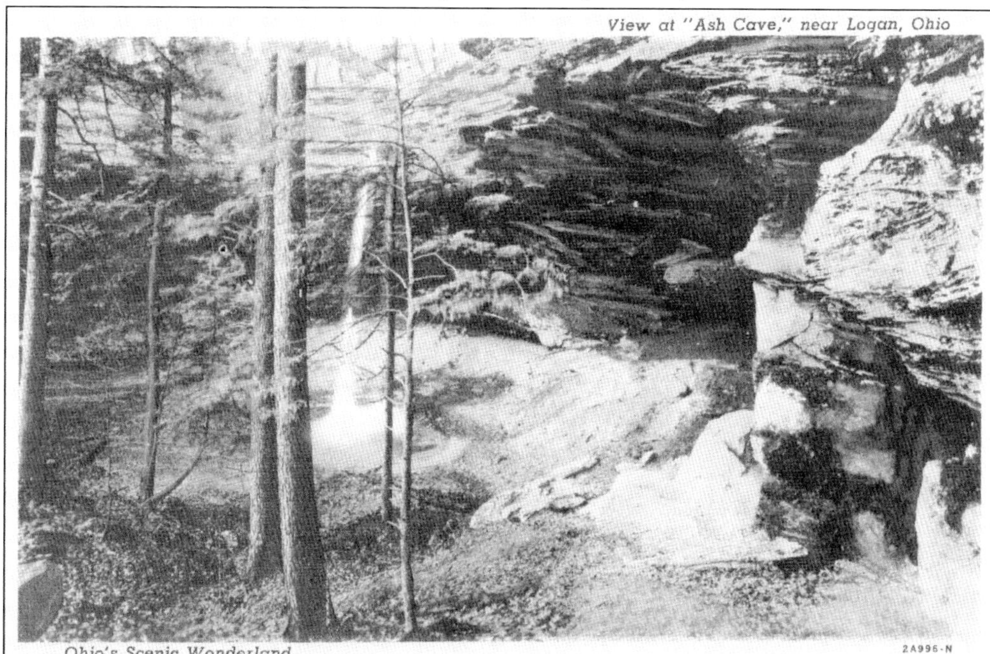

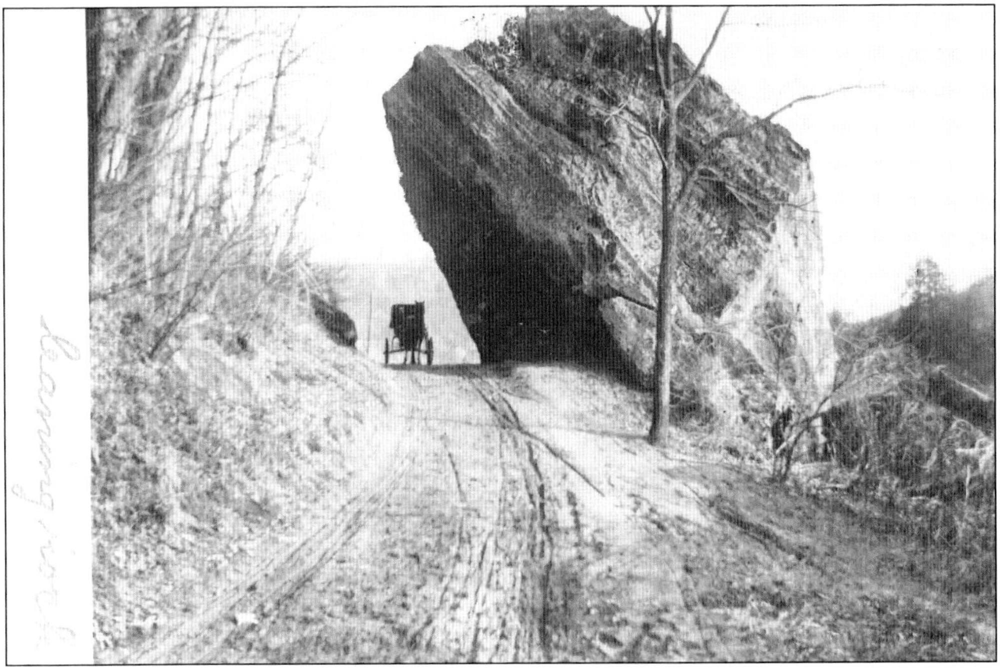

Leaning Rock, or "Leanin' Lena," is quite an interesting rock formation. This large block boulder can be seen at the edge of the Hocking/Fairfield line on Hocking County Road 116, just off US Route 33. It is part of the Clear Creek Metro Park system, also considered part of the Hocking Hills region. Leaning Rock has an interesting history. Legend has it that one can sometimes see long sticks stuck in the ground around the rock, said to be placed there by witches. Fortunately for the buggy driver in this postcard, no witches were seen on the day he passed by. (Courtesy of DB.)

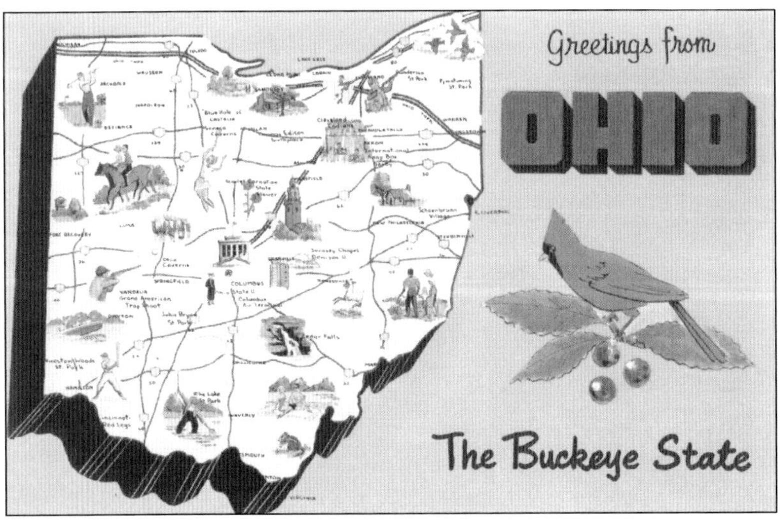

This postcard showing the map of the Buckeye State is unusual because it includes a highlight of Cedar Falls. The Hocking Hills/Logan area has often been bypassed by the postcard maps as they concentrate on other travel spots in the state. (Courtesy of JM.)

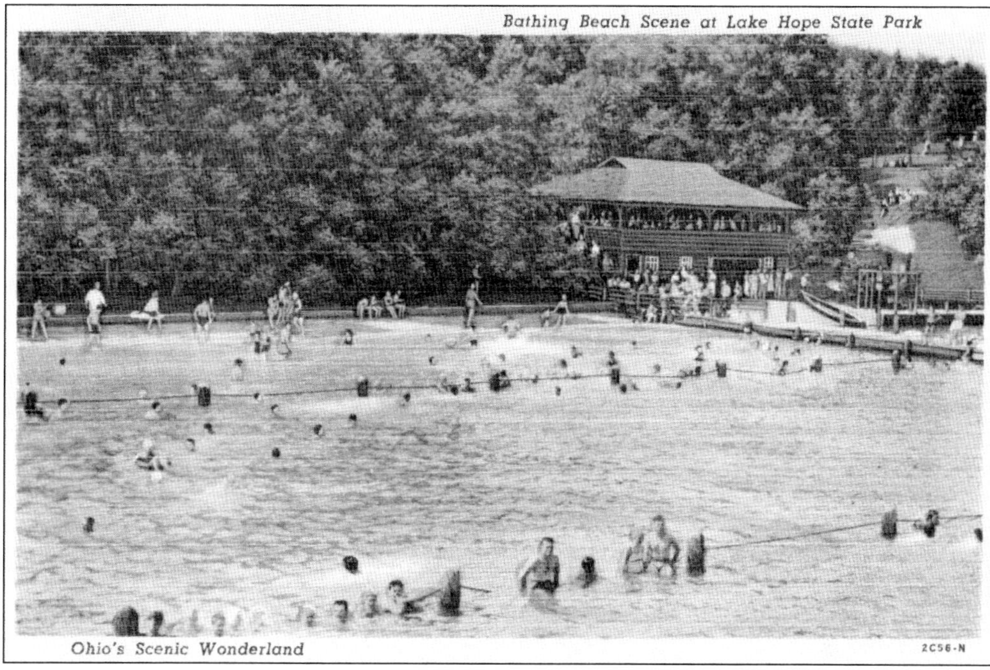

According to the Ohio Division of State Parks, Lake Hope State Park in Vinton County was established in 1949. The 120-acre lake sits in the 2,983-acre Zaleski State Forest in the valley of the Big Sandy Run. The lake is a popular spot for tourists and locals alike. Swimming, boating, and fishing can all be enjoyed at Lake Hope. (Courtesy of JM.)

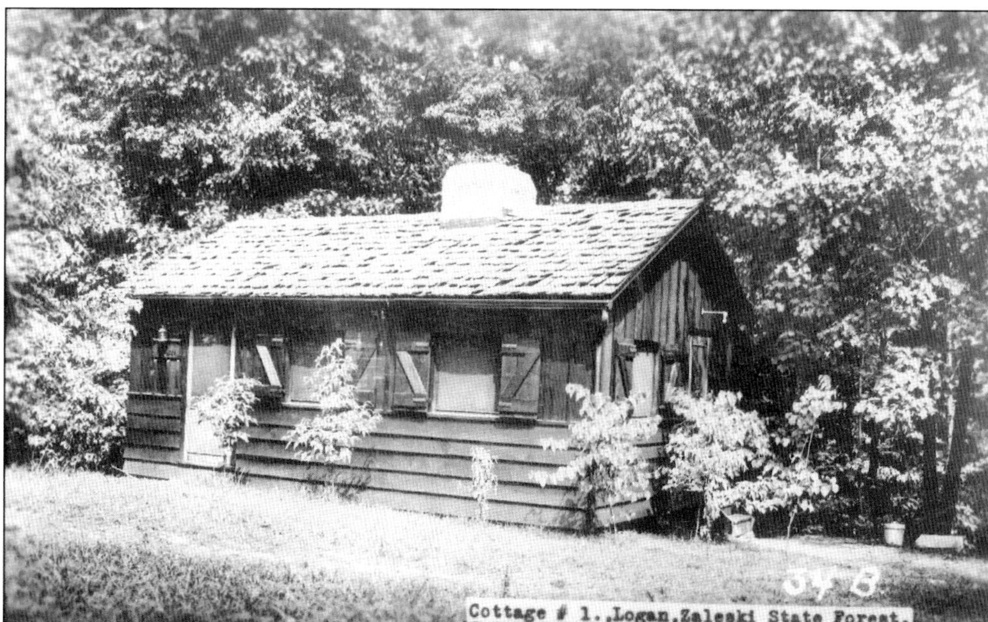

This is one of the first basic cabins to be built in the Zaleski State Forest for guests who wanted to experience nature. This is Cottage No. 1, the Logan. The cabins had a living area, kitchen, bath, bedroom, and a dormitory-style room featuring bunk beds. (Courtesy of JM.)

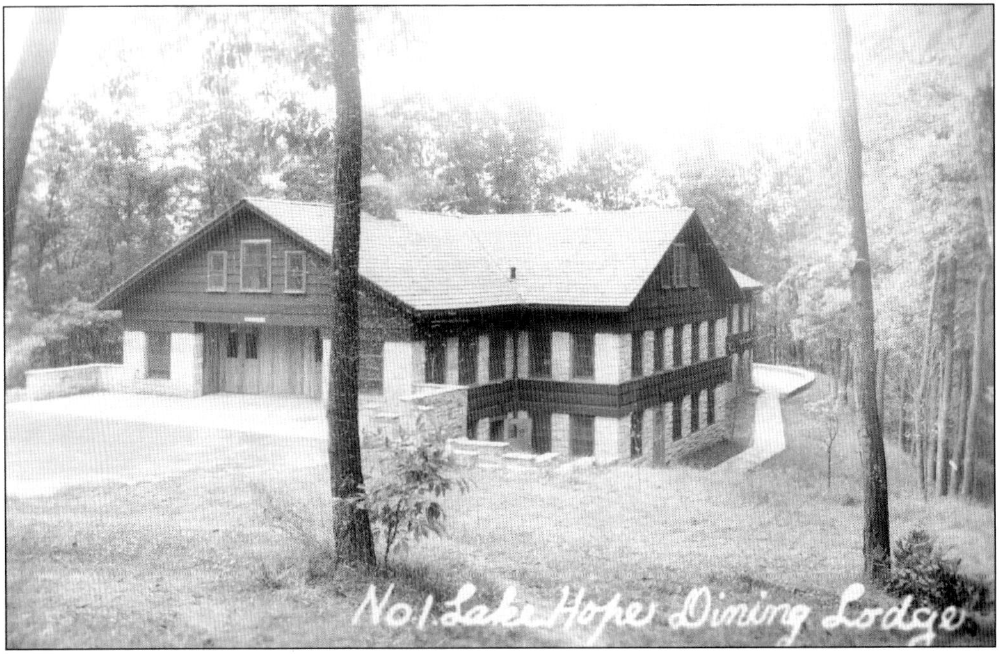

Seen here in this 1950 real photographic postcard is the original Dining Lodge that was home to the Stone Terrace Restaurant. Operated by the Ohio Department of Natural Resources, it was the site of weddings, reunions, and other celebrations. Unfortunately, a fire in 2006 burned the lodge to the ground. In 2014, a new Dining Lodge was opened on the original lodge site. (Courtesy of JM.)

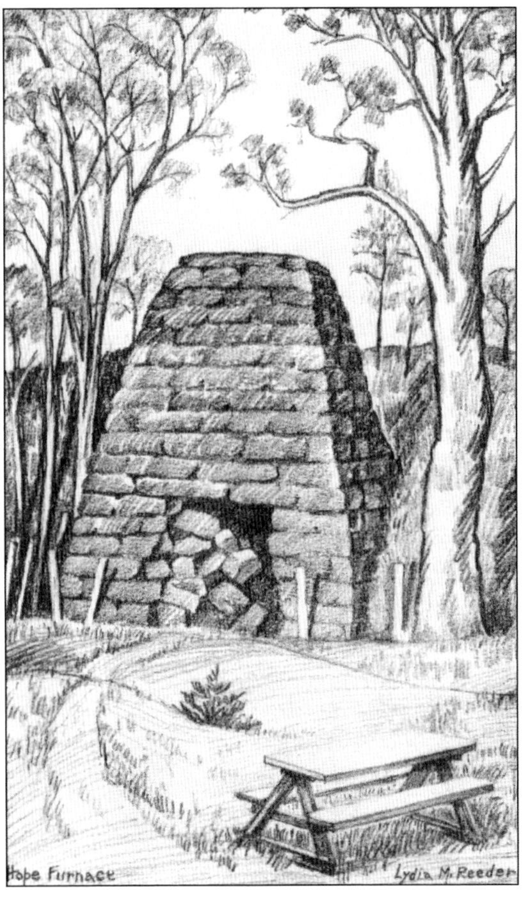

The Hope Furnace shown on this postcard is still standing as a part of the iron ore history in the area. This particular furnace was built over 100 years ago to process the iron ore extracted from the region's sandstone. The iron was used for many items, including ammunition for the Union Army during the Civil War. The drawing of the Hope Furnace is credited to Lydia M. Reeder. (Courtesy of JM.)

Smokey the Bear is the national symbol for fire safety and the prevention of forest fires. First introduced in 1944, Smokey gained instant popularity. This postcard was issued by the Ohio Department of Natural Resources, Division of Forestry. Smokey celebrated his 70th birthday in 2014. (Courtesy of BCS.)

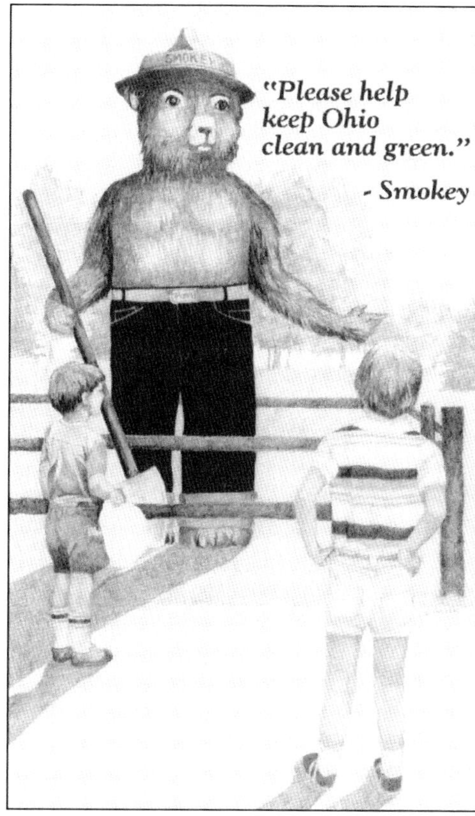

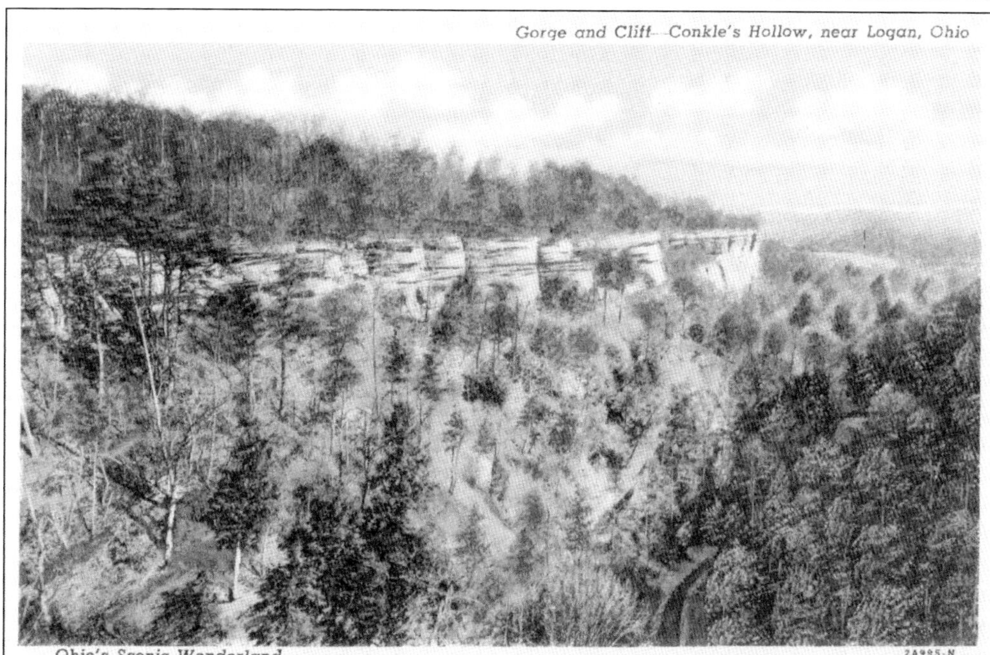

This 1940s view of the lush, green Hocking Hills (Conkle's Hollow) is a reminder to all visitors to heed Smokey's plea, "Please help keep Ohio clean and green." (Courtesy of JM.)

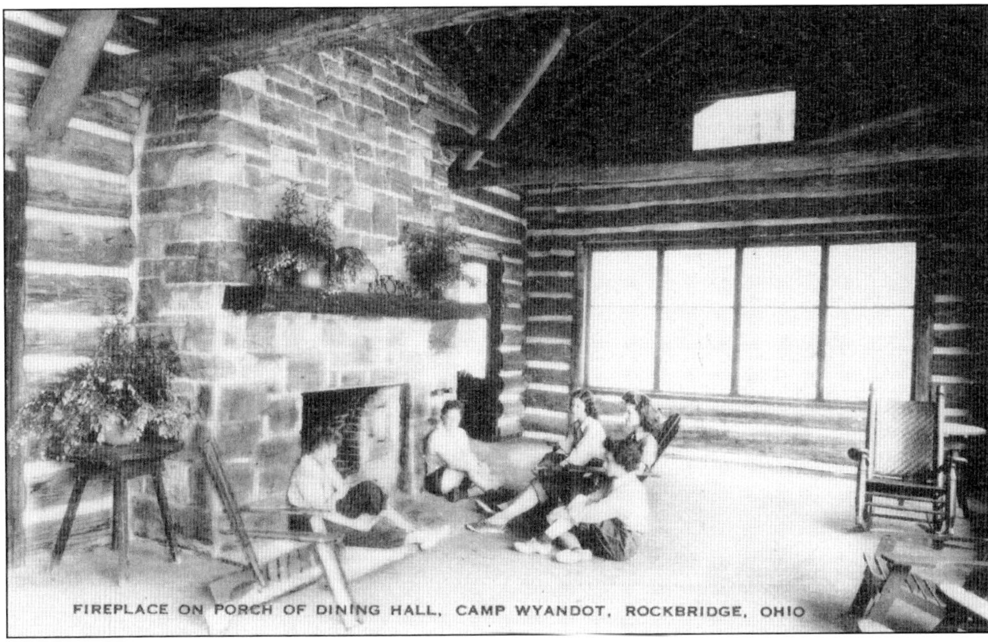

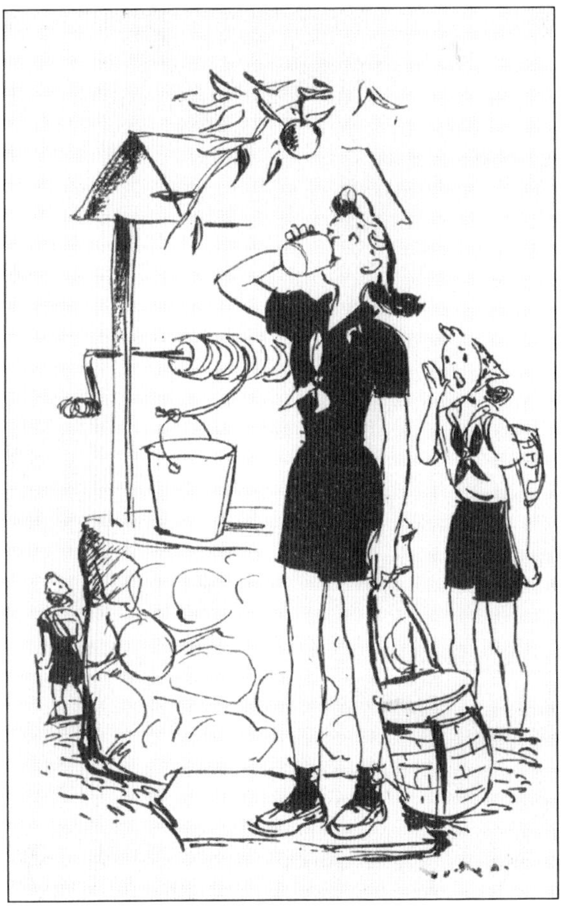

A significant feature of the Hocking Hills is the camping facilities tucked away in the valley. As early as 1928, when Camp Fire Girls retreat Camp Wyandot was opened, youth from urban communities were treated to the great outdoors. Camp Wyandot, pictured above, is located on Clear Creek Road in Rockbridge. Beckoning Trails is a favorite Girl Scout camp near Logan. The 1942 postcard at left is marked as a "Girl Scout Camp Postcard." Camps such as Camp Akita and Camp Otterbein are but two of many faith-based camps throughout the hills. (Above, courtesy of DB; at left, JM.)

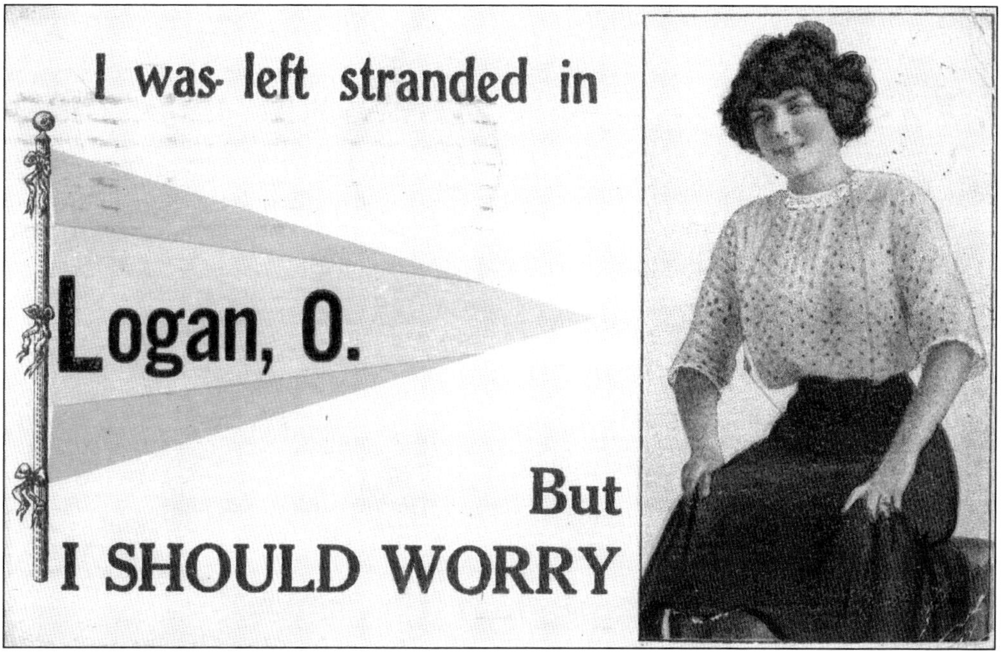

The penny postcard came in a variety of humorous images, as seen above. They were very popular, and this particular card, dated 1913, imagines someone has been "stranded in Logan, O." The serenity of the hills is expressed by the canoeing scene below on the Hocking River. (Both courtesy of JM.)

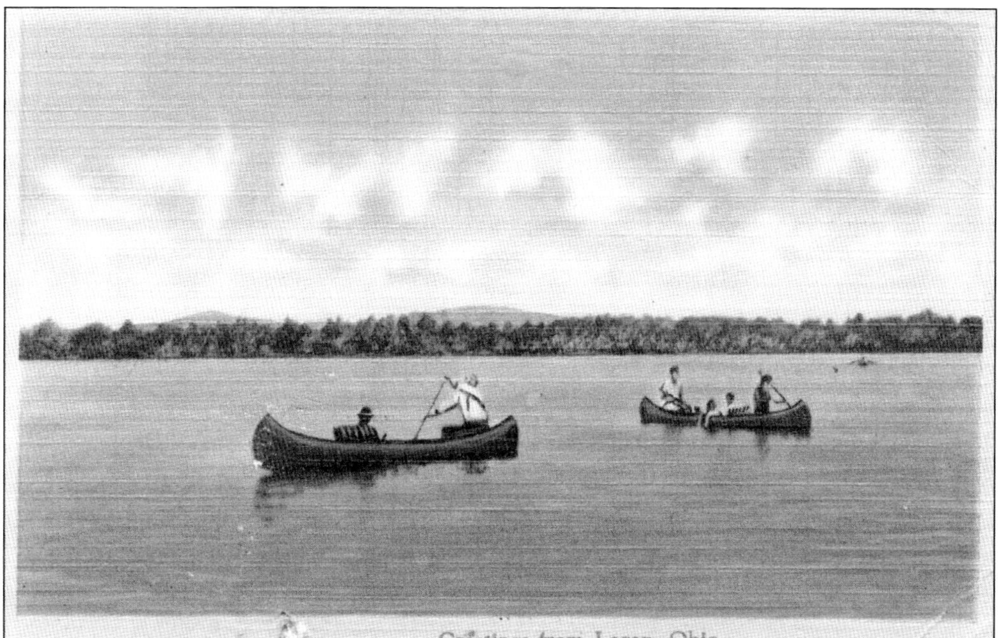

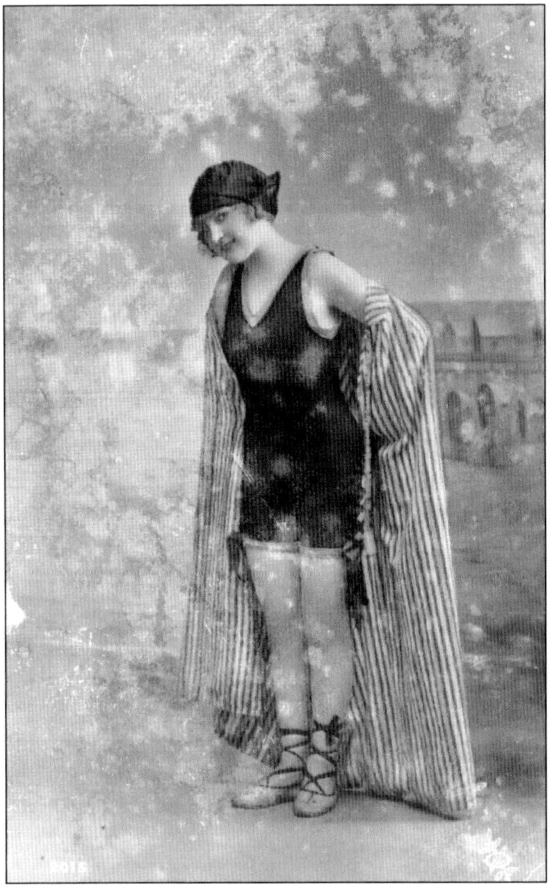

The unidentified bathing beauty at left is wearing the latest beachwear from the 1920s, including swimming shoes. Daring as this outfit was in its day, it is modest compared to the beach scene at Lake Logan below. Opened in the 1950s, the Lake Logan beach covers 400 acres and is a renowned fishing lake. It is a part of the Hocking Hills State Park system. (Both courtesy of JM.)

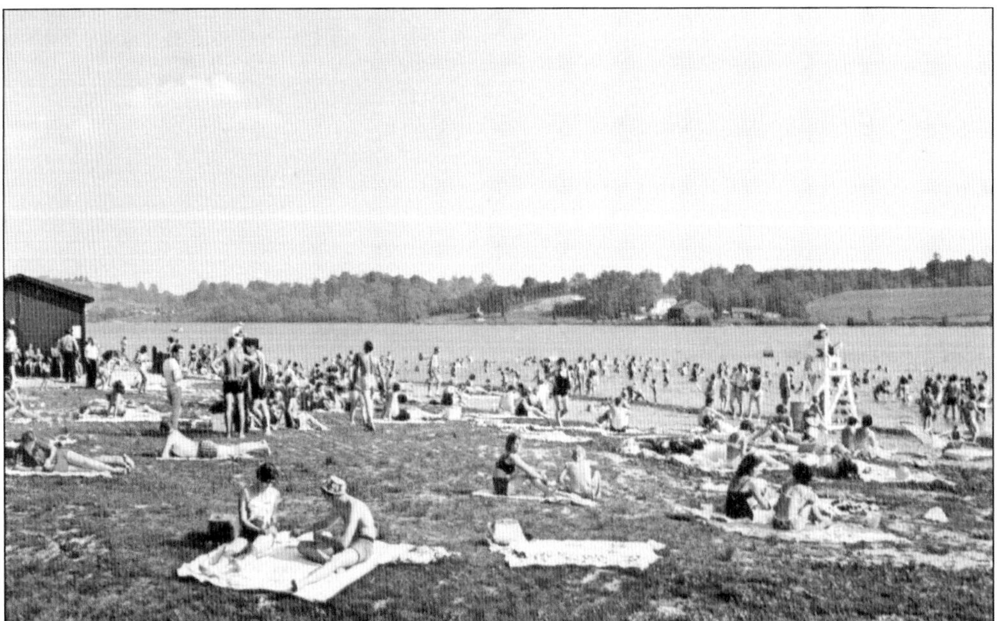

Two

Just Folks

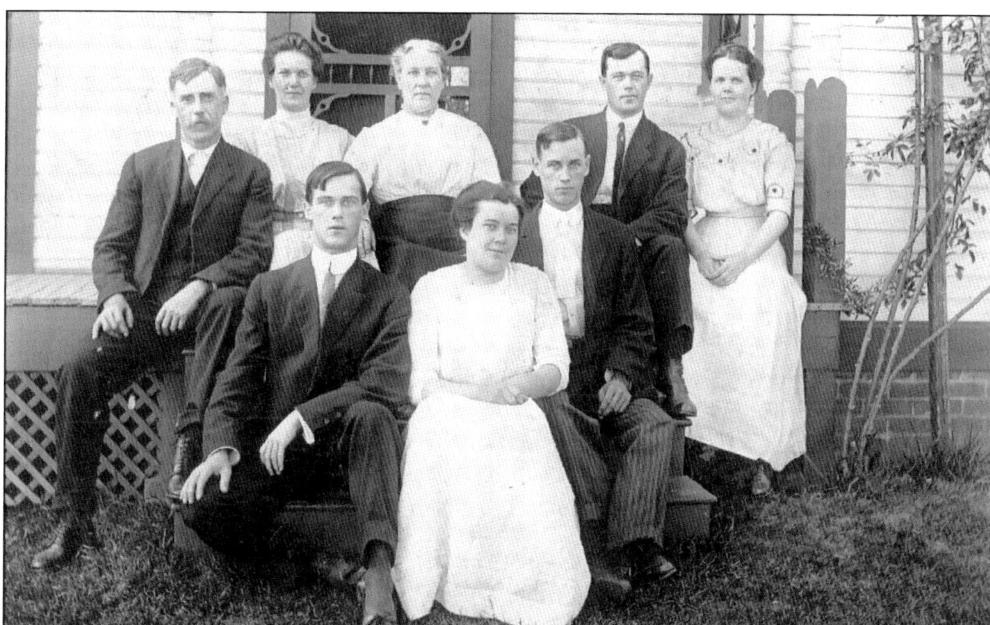

This postcard depicts a typical family in the 1900s. On the reverse side of the card is a message: "This is us, the whole ugly bunch. Laura". (Courtesy of HH.)

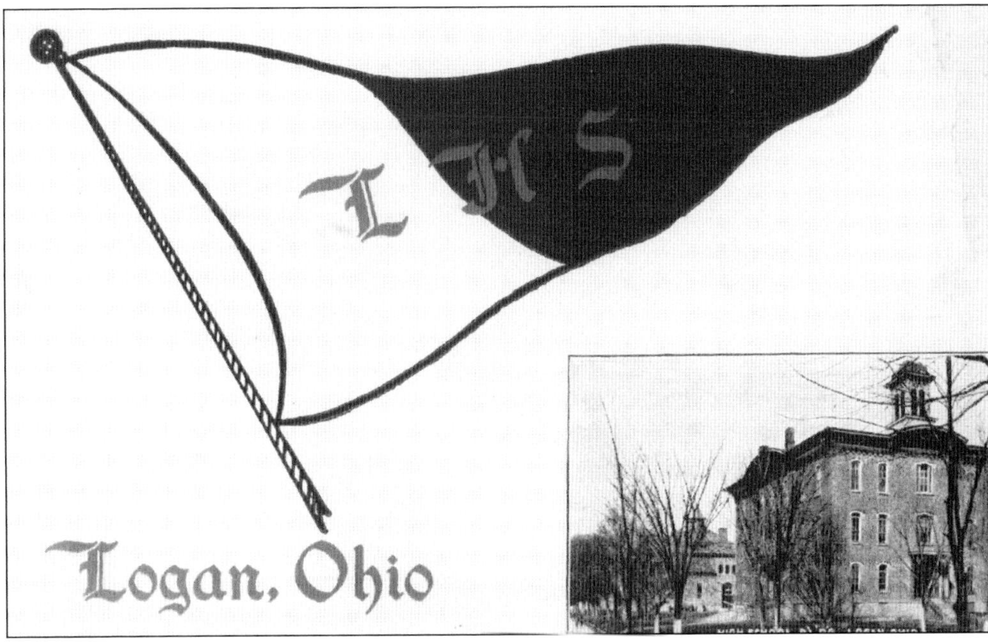

The Logan High School flag is flying high in this penny postcard with an image (inset) of the first high school building. The colors of the flag were purple and white—the school colors to this day. In 1898, this was the first Union (public) school in the city. It was built on the hill opposite what is now called the Old Logan Cemetery. (Courtesy of GM.)

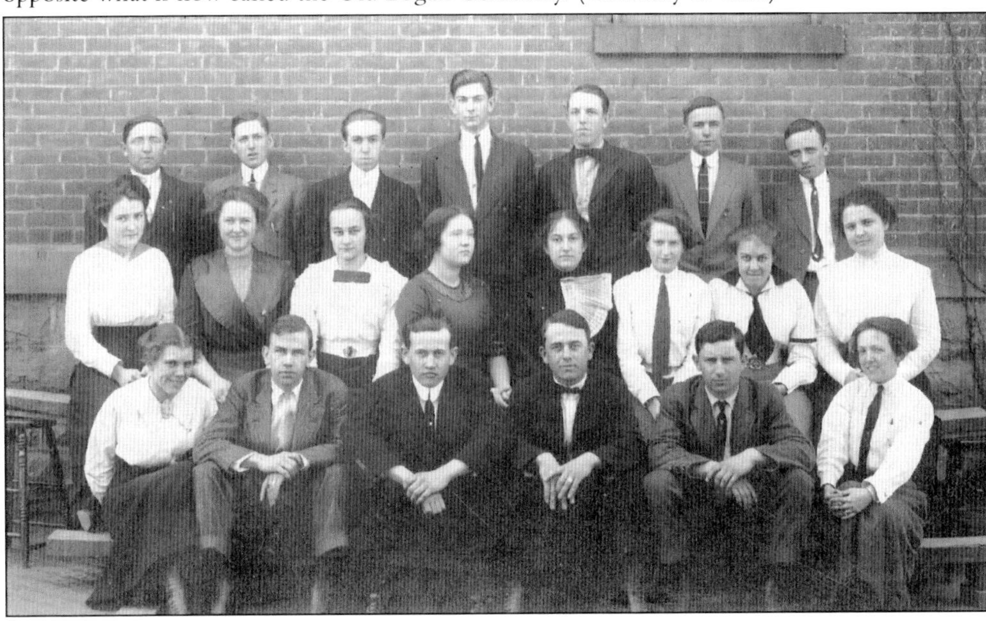

Prior to their graduation, the class of 1912 poses on the east side of the old school building. Pictured here from left to right are (first row) Nancy Easterling, Harry Yontz, Frank Tipton, John McBroom, Robert Green, and Helen Heft; (second row) Arnnel Allen, Esther Tannahill, Mary Francis, Minnie Evans, Winifred Rulon, Florence Robey, Irene Gladman, and Ruth Hillery; (third row) Myron Hansel, Harold Larimer, Donald Bort, Walter Nixon, John Lohr, Carl Lutz, and Rugg H. Brandt. (Courtesy of HH.)

This 1900 portrait shows the Armstrong girls: four-year-old Hazel (left) and seven-year-old Ruth. They were the daughters of C.P. and Wilhelmina Sanderson Armstrong. Ruth is remembered as a longtime schoolteacher, mostly as an English instructor, from 1914 until her retirement in 1954. She passed away in 1988 at the age of 95, having devoted 40 years to the local school system. (Courtesy of HH.)

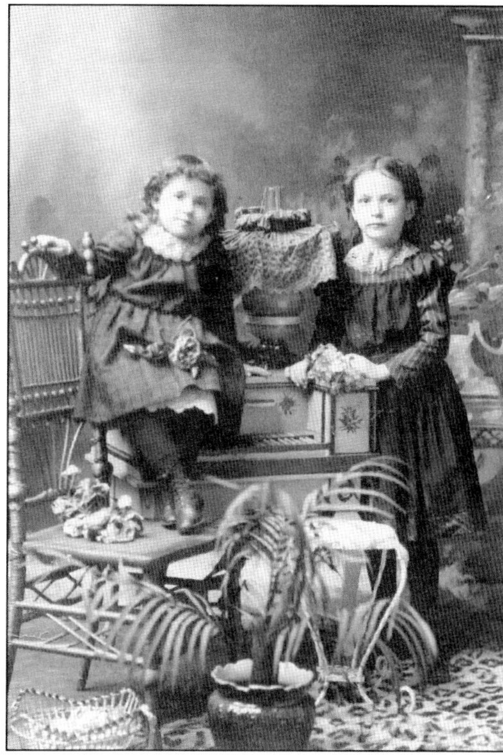

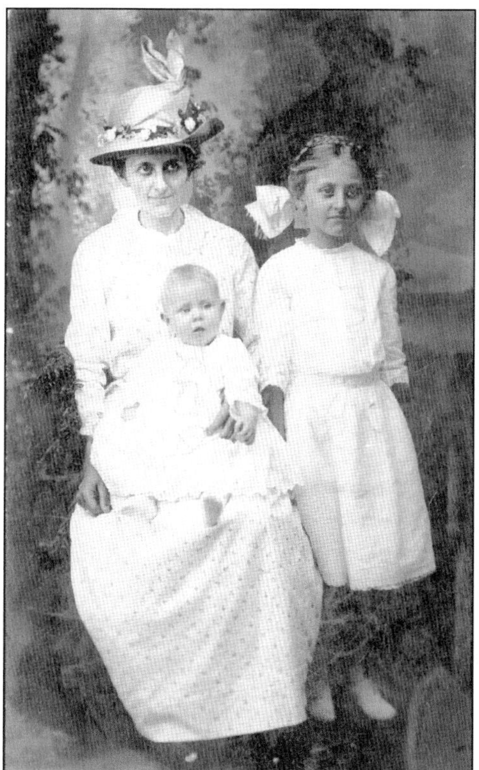

Myrtle (Emmons) Krinn (seated) was the mother of Faith Krinn (standing) and Mary Ruth Krinn (infant). The sisters grew up on a farm on Starr Route Road in Hocking County. The girls attended one-room schools and later received bachelor's degrees in education from Ohio University. Faith taught Latin in Logan schools for 46 years, while Mary Ruth was a home economics teacher for 39 years. Faith was 101 years old in 2010 when she died, and Mary followed in 2012, just two months past her 99th birthday. (Courtesy of HH.)

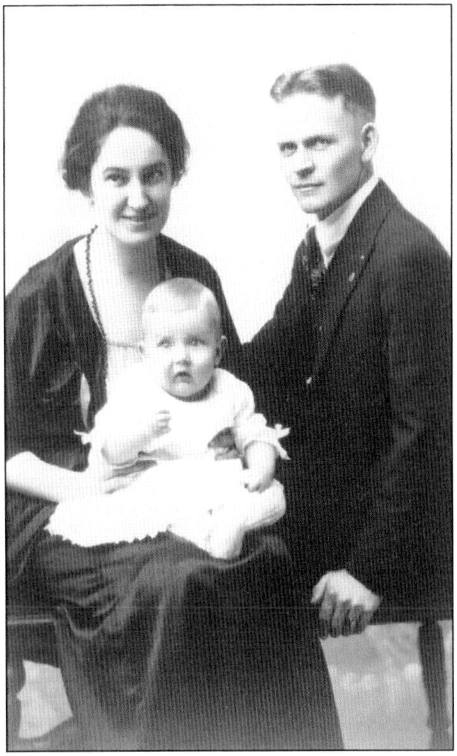

A postcard family scene shows Dale Engle, who was born in 1922 to Carl A. Engle and Winifred Rulon Engle. Dale had a talent for music and drama. He was a 1939 graduate of Logan High School, and in 1943 he received a bachelor's degree from Ohio University in drama, art, and music. Dale moved to New York City and for the next 50 years worked steadily as a versatile actor on the Broadway stage and in Europe. In his later years, he appeared daily as "Smitty" on *Pinwheel*, a children's television program. (Courtesy of HH.)

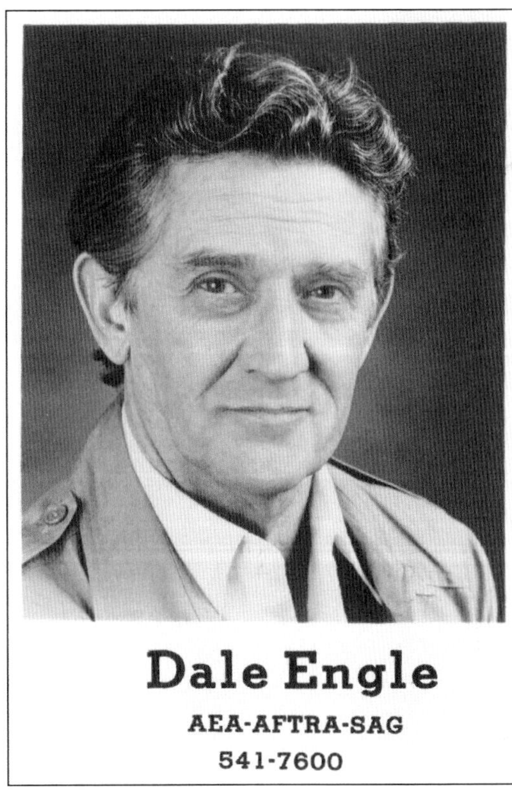

This postcard, which Engle sent to Logan friends, is a list of his professional acting organizational memberships. Engle died in 1990 in New York City. He received the Logan High School Alumni Hall of Fame award, which was bestowed posthumously. (Courtesy of HH.)

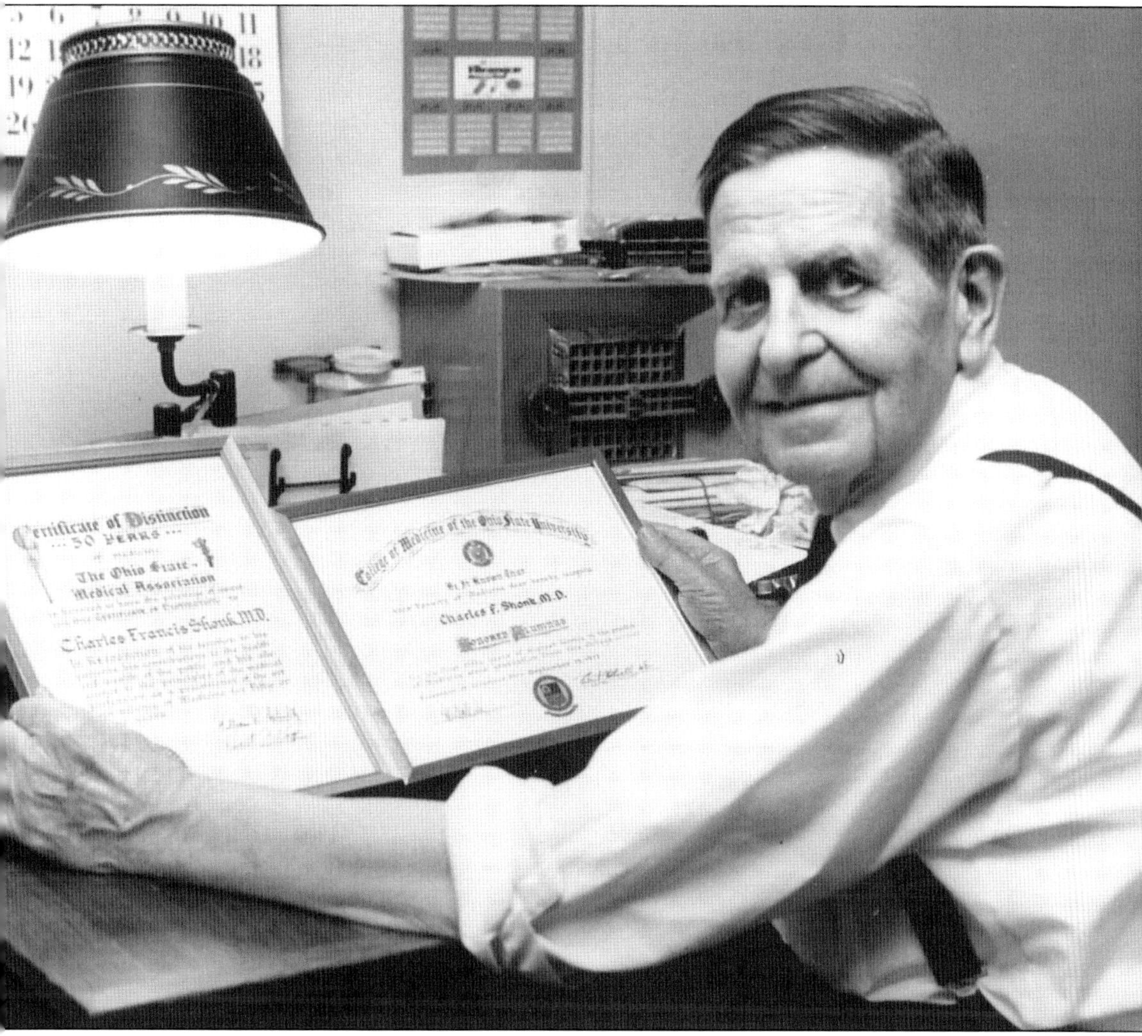

Charles F. Shonk, MD, was a well-known general practitioner in the Hocking Valley for more than 50 years. From his 1922 graduation from Ohio State University's College of Medicine until his death in 1976, he served the community selflessly. Born in 1897, he married Anna Grace Murtha of Logan in 1930. For 49 years, his office was at 64 South Market Street, where Logan Insurance Agency is now located. Dr. Shonk once said that by his count, he had brought 3,086 babies into the world and had signed 779 death certificates. In 1972, he received an honored alumnus award for his first 50 years from OSU. (Courtesy of HH.)

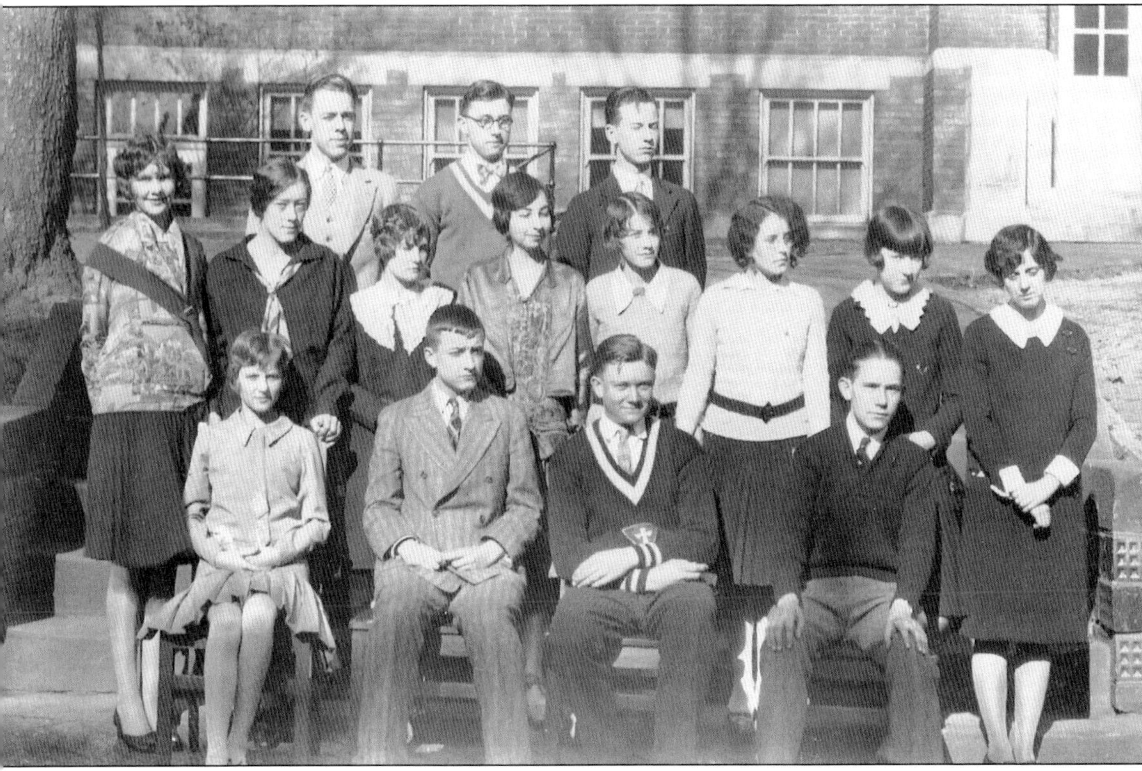

Dr. Joseph F. Frasch Sr., a Logan native, is shown here (top row, far left) as a Logan High School teenager with the English Club. Frasch is known for having served as the first president of Franklin University in Columbus, Ohio. He graduated from high school in 1929 as second honor student. Dr. Frasch continued his education and graduated from Capital University, receiving his doctorate from OSU in 1962. He was named Franklin University's president in 1951. It has been said of Frasch, "He shepherded the university's growth from an institution of fewer than 600 students housed in the YMCA building, to a university of more than 4,000 students." Frasch passed away in 1977, and Frasch Hall, an academic building on campus, is named for him. (Courtesy of HH.)

Monday, in Ward Township, Ohio, was the home to the Joseph Johnson family. Johnson worked in several mines as a pumper. This was a year-round job, pumping out water that seeped into the mines. In the 1930s, he worked in the Goose Run Mine, near the village of Orbiston. His wife, Vica, a descendent of a pioneer Kentucky family, kept the home and children in good order. The names of the children are listed on the postcard. During the early years of the Great Depression, George W. (boy in jacket to the left of Vica) moved from Monday to Logan, where he lived the rest of his life. Many descendants of the Joe Johnson family still live in Hocking County. (Courtesy of GBJ.)

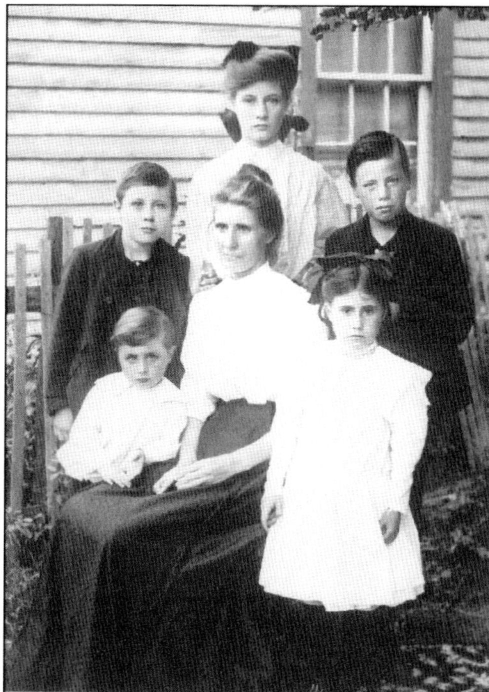

THE JOE JOHNSON FAMILY
Ward Twp. Hocking County, Ohio - 1907
George W. Johnson Nancy Johnson Jacob Johnson
Saul Johnson Vica Harris Johnson Bertha Johnson

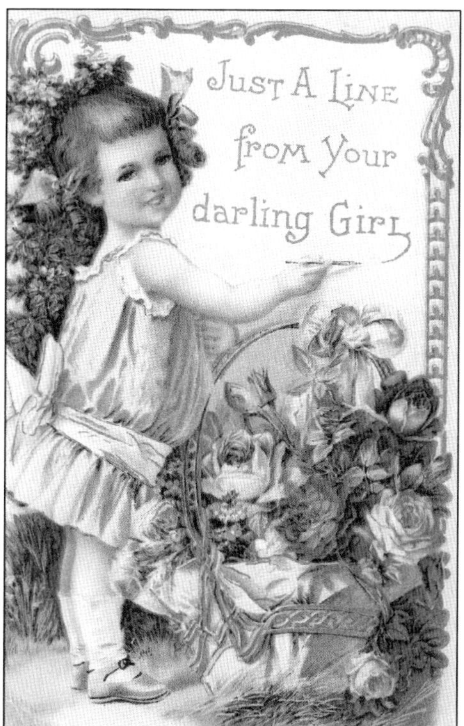

This darling girl is a beautiful example of the artwork on older postcards. (Courtesy of JM.)

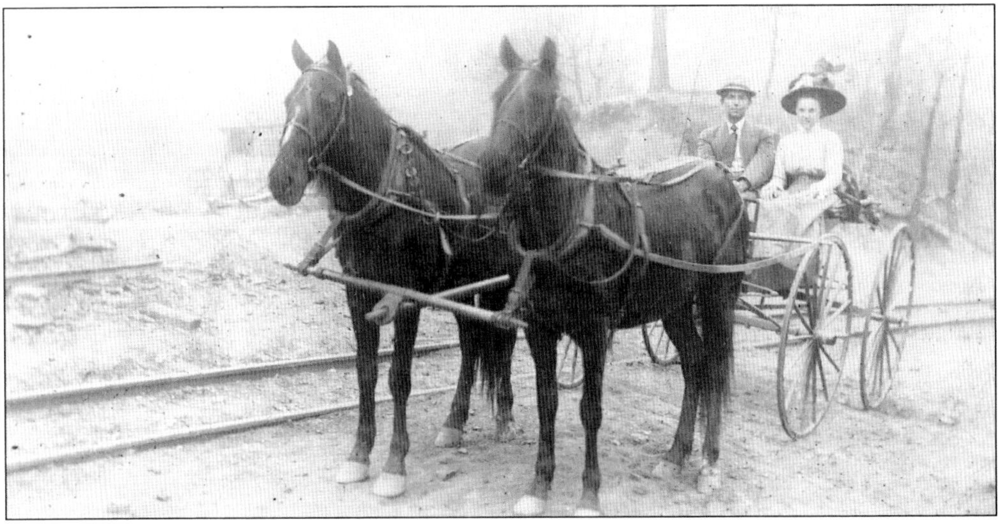

Tena and Simon Bond of Haydenville were photographed taking a Sunday drive in a horse and buggy. The village of Haydenville, founded by Peter Hayden, was a company town, where the entire population was beholden to Hayden's Mining and Manufacturing Company. The laborers were paid in script, not money, and in turn the script was taken to the company store to purchase food and necessities. An Ohio Historical Marker in the village marks Haydenville as the last company town in Ohio. (Courtesy of NV.)

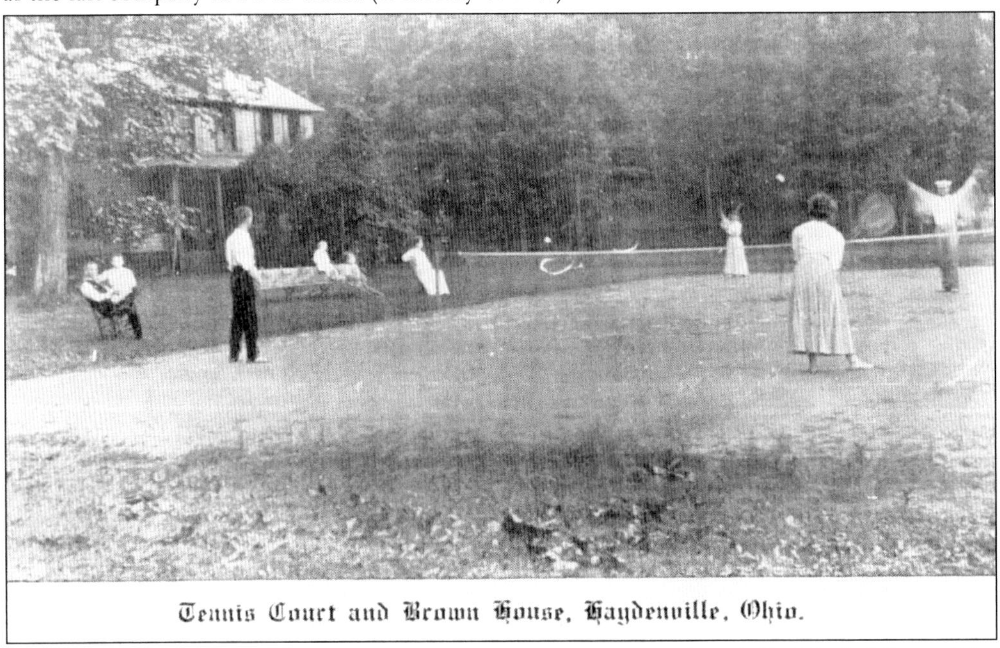

About 1906, the National Fireproofing Company (NATCO) purchased all of the holdings of the Haydenville Mining and Manufacturing Company. Located in Green Township, the purchase included the entire village, mines, kilns, school, company store, and all of the workers' homes. This rare postcard shows the tennis court that was on the front lawn of the general manager's home. It was called the Brown House after T.D. Brown, a former general manager. Supt. Herbert L. Elliot (1906–1911) can be seen at left, sitting in the chair, watching members of his office staff enjoy the game. The home is now owned by Kenneth and Nyla Vollmer. (Courtesy of NV.)

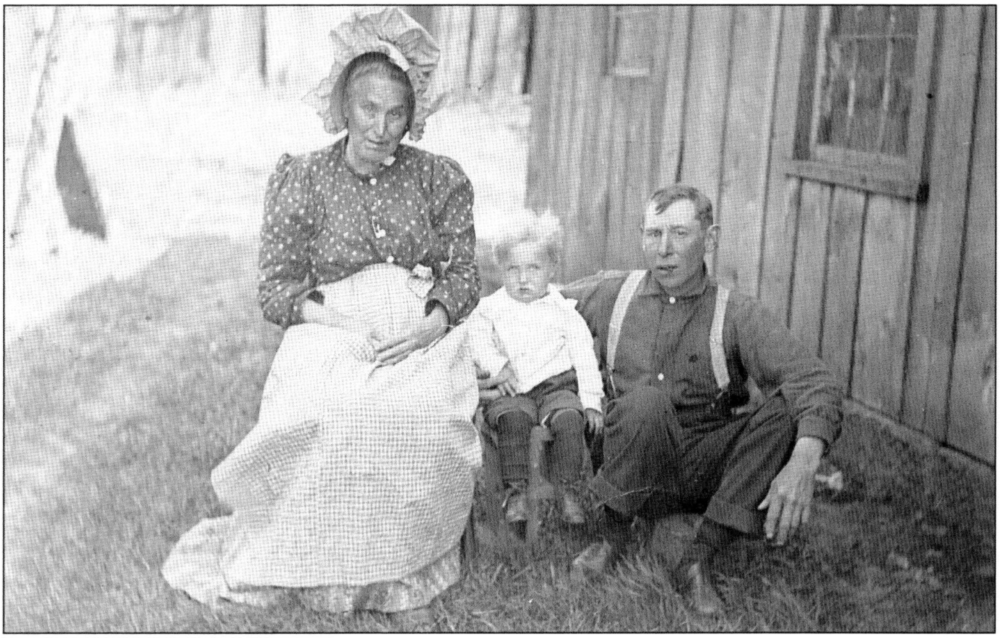

The names of these Haydenville residents are written on the back of this postcard. They are, from left to right, Sarah "Granny" Lusk, James "Jim" Bond, and Henry Schnider. In the 1920 US Census, Hocking County's Green Township lists Sarah Lusk at age 62 with an occupation of umbrella repairer. (Courtesy of NV.)

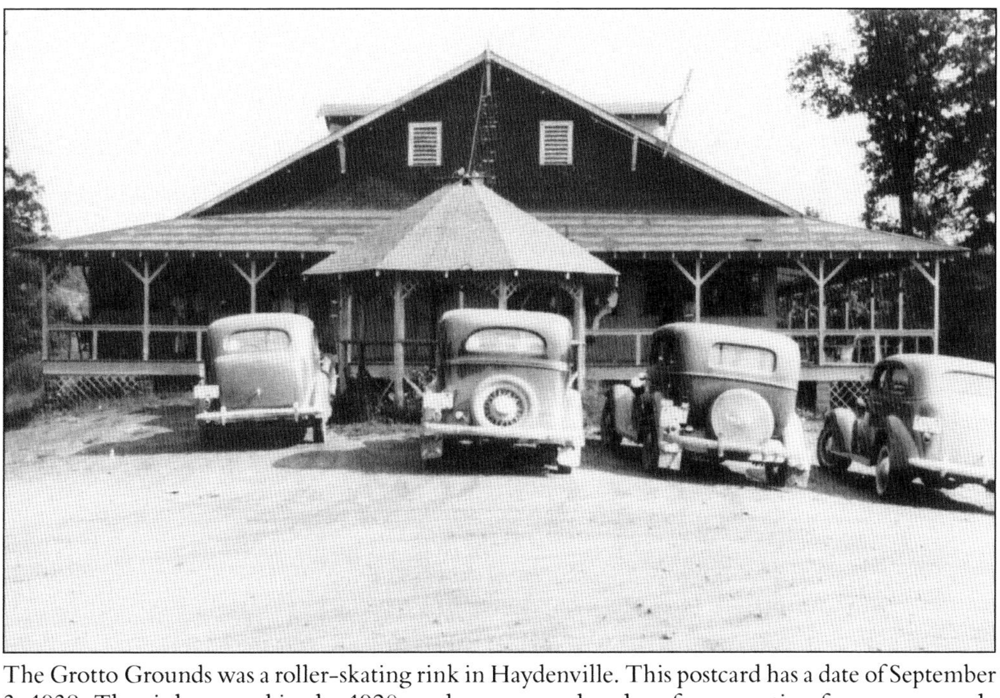

The Grotto Grounds was a roller-skating rink in Haydenville. This postcard has a date of September 3, 1938. The rink opened in the 1920s and was a popular place for recreation for young people and area families. The Grotto Grounds burned to the ground in 1969. (Courtesy of DB.)

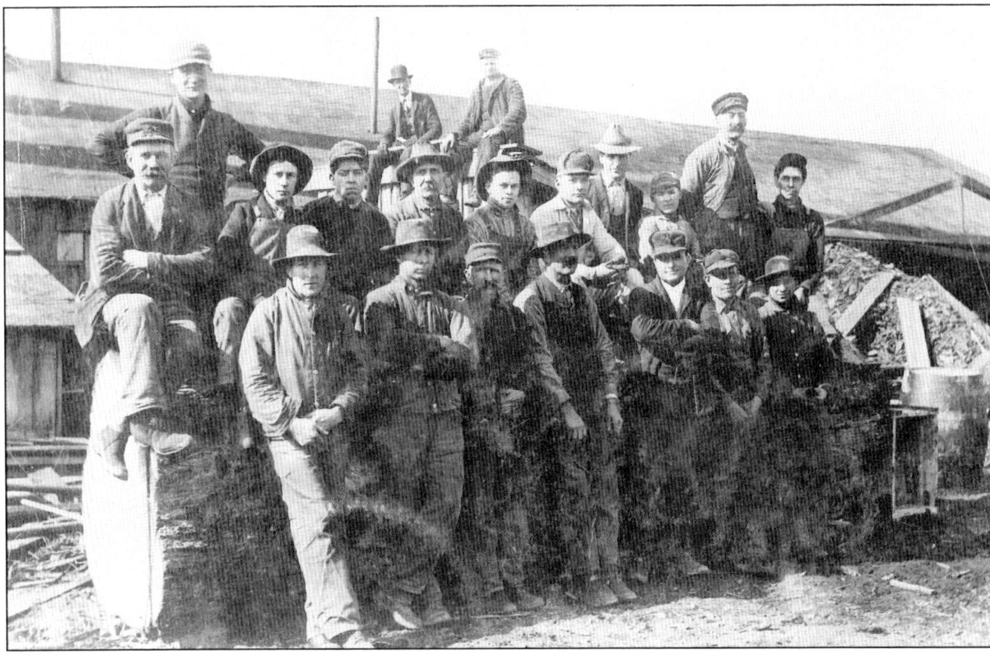

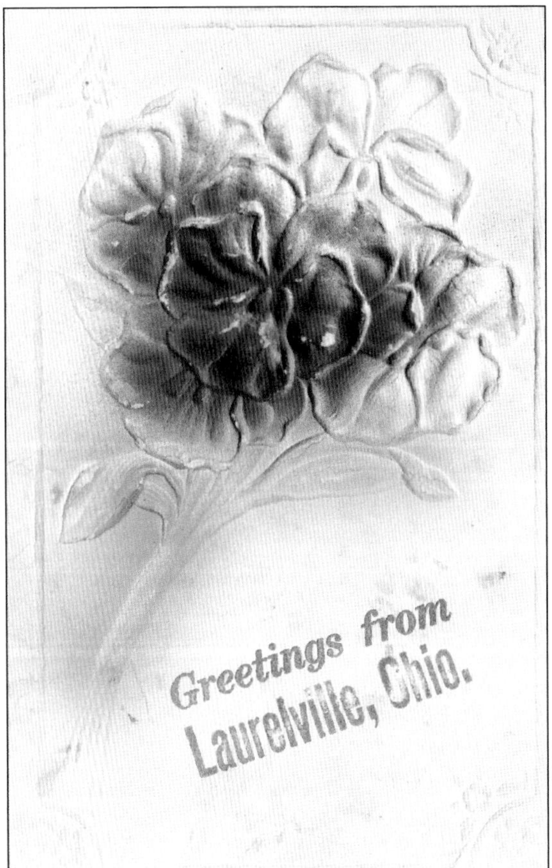

A Laurelville, Ohio, Salt Creek Township postcard features these unidentified sawmill workers lined up by a harvested tree. Dated 1910, forestry is still the main occupation in the Laurelville area. (Courtesy of DB.)

A popular style of postcard was the type emblazoned with "Greetings from . . ." and took many forms. This Laurelville card has an imprint of the design, or in this case the shape of a flower. The postcard was then tinted. (Courtesy of JM.)

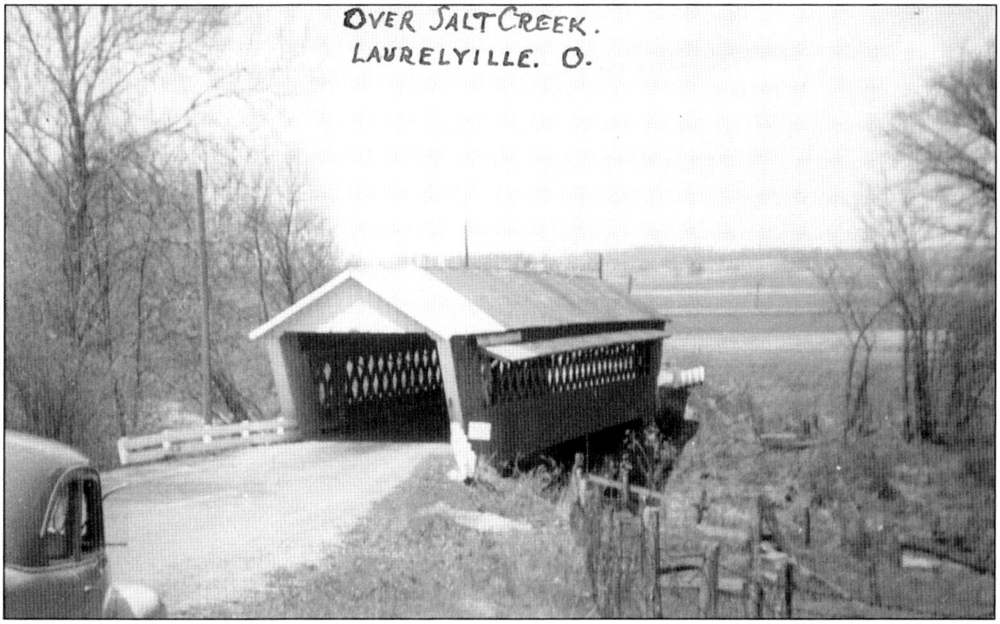

A covered bridge spans the Salt Creek near Laurelville. This is a good example of a real photographic image. At one time, Hocking County had 46 covered bridges, none of which have survived. (Courtesy of DB.)

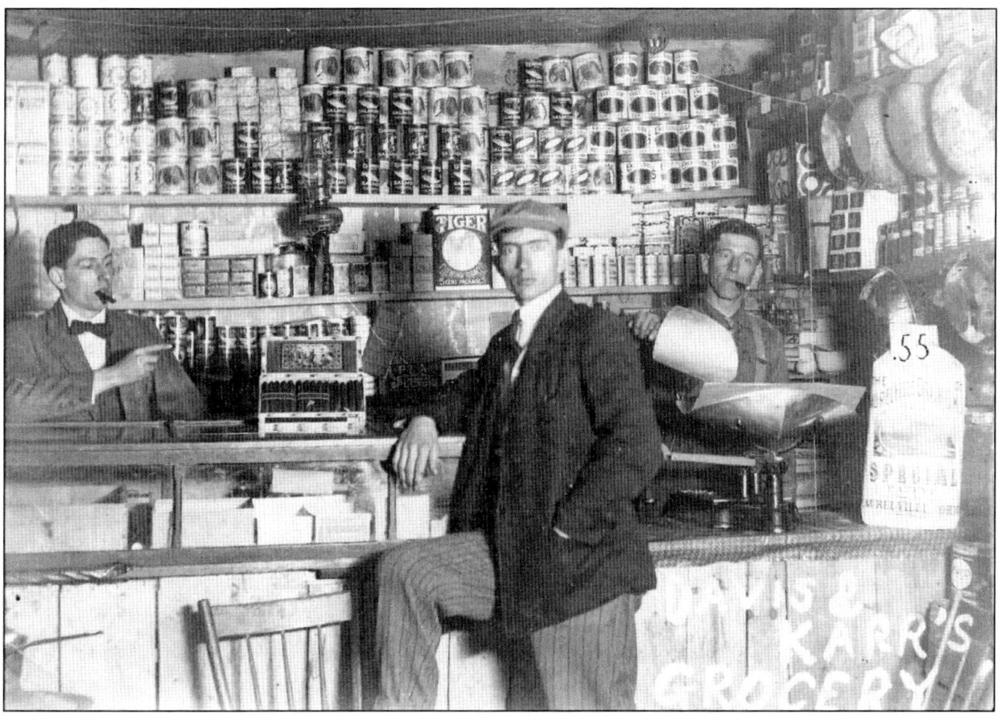

Davis and Karr's grocery in South Perry appeared to be a well-stocked business. This postcard seems to be aimed towards advertising a certain brand of cigar. The two proprietors behind the tobacco humidor display are smoking cigars, and the fellow on the left is pointing at the counter display. (Courtesy of DB.)

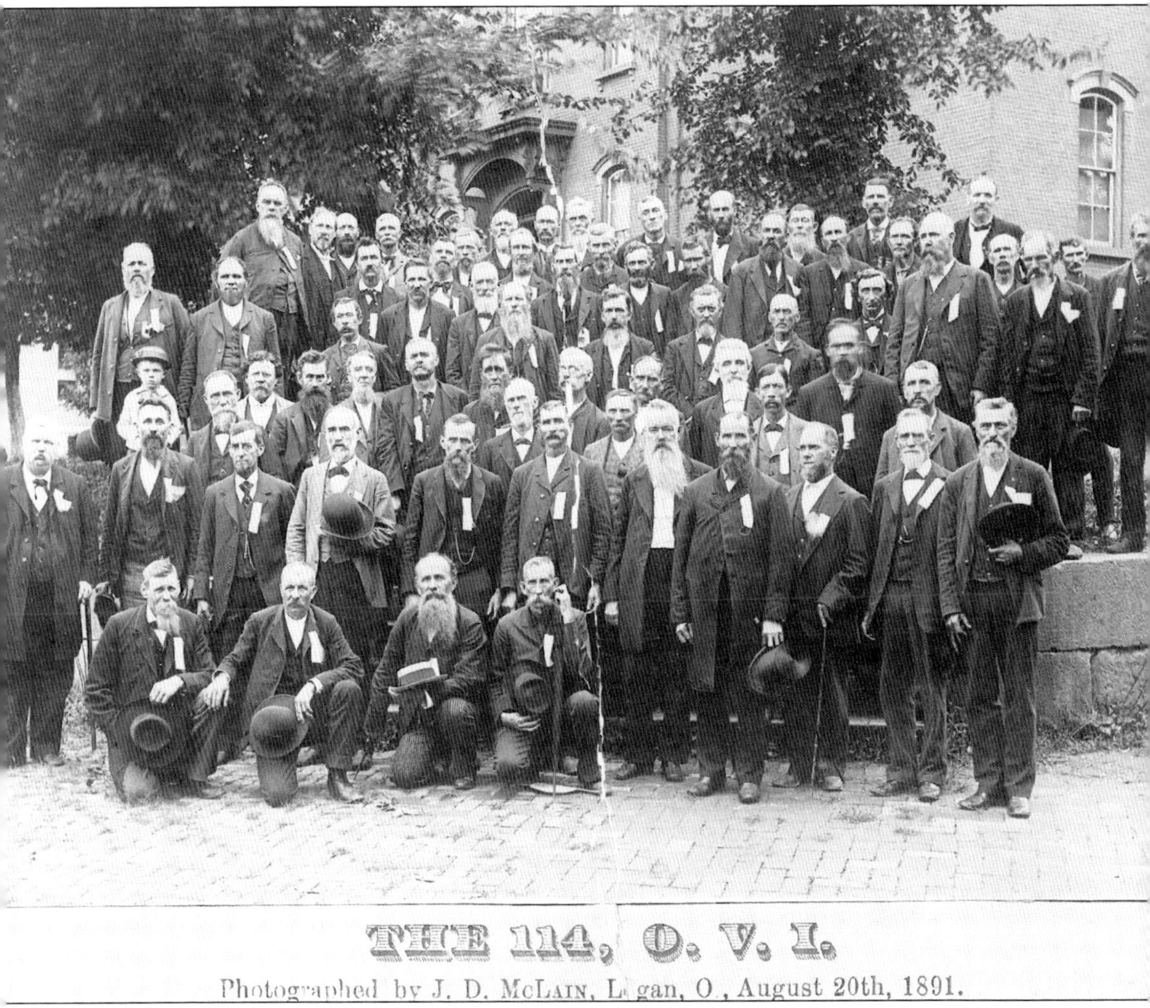

The 114th Regiment, Ohio Volunteer Infantry (OVI) reunion was held in Logan, Ohio, on August 19 and 20, 1891. There were 83 in attendance, representing nine different Ohio infantry companies. According to an August 27 article in the *Hocking Sentinel*, the old soldiers were welcomed to Logan by Mayor J.P. Rochester, who gave a speech on behalf of the citizens of Logan. This group image taken by J.D. McLain, a local photographer, shows the group of Civil War veterans in front of the schoolhouse on Market Street. The newspaper article reported that after the photograph was taken, the comrades marched down the Market Street hill to Main Street and disbanded. It was noted that the veterans voted to meet the next year in Circleville, Ohio. (Courtesy of HH.)

This postcard is an example of how patriotic themes were a favorite remembrance during holidays honoring military forces. On an interesting note, on February 4, 1938, the death of the last surviving member of the J.K. Rochester Post of the GAR (Grand Army of the Republic) was reported. James Allen, age 90, was only a boy when he joined the Gallant 58th; he was stationed in the Mississippi River area during a part of the conflict. (Courtesy of CCH.)

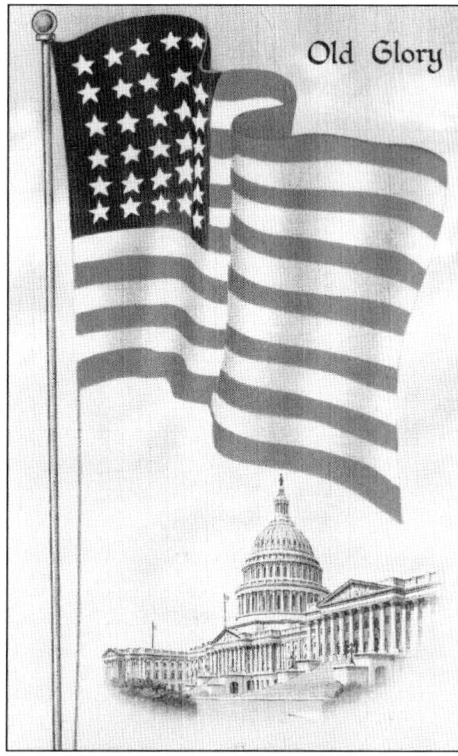

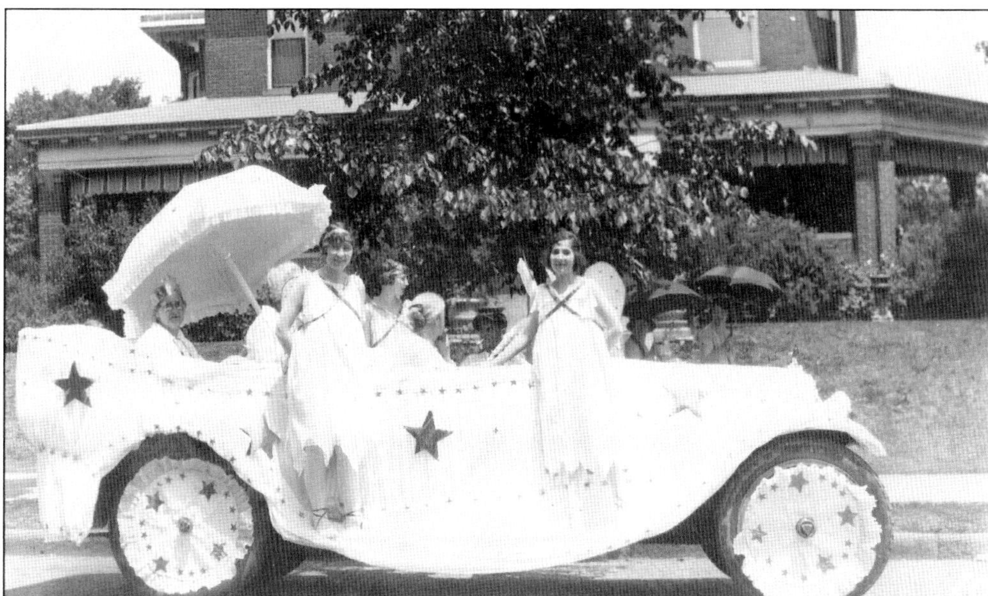

The Gold Star Mothers put a lot of work into decorating their vehicle for this parade. Although the postcard is undated, it is presumed to be in 1925 when the Hocking County Courthouse was dedicated. It was after World War I that then-president Woodrow Wilson suggested an organization to honor mothers who had lost a son or daughter during the Great War. The name came from the flag with a single gold star that hung in the family homes of the deceased. (Courtesy of HH.)

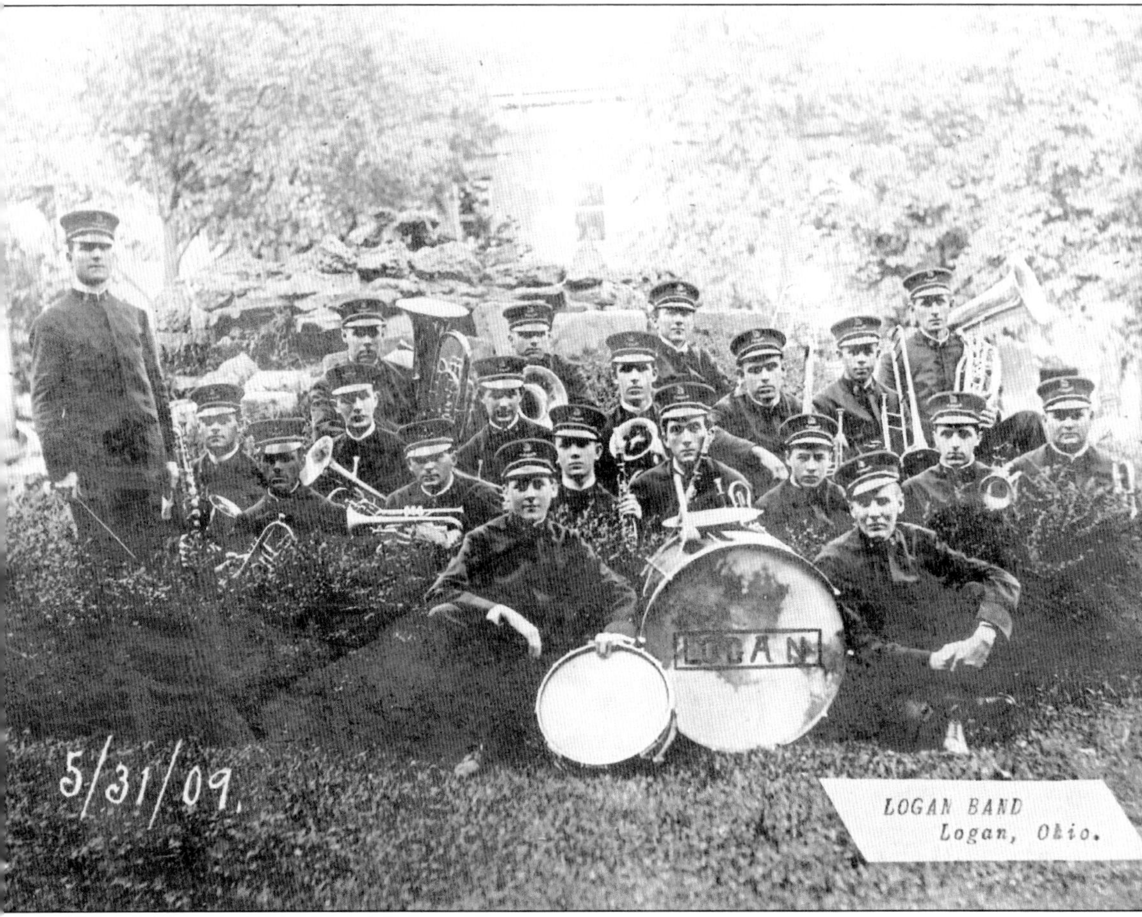

According to the *Ohio Democrat*, an early Logan newspaper, a parade was formed the morning of May 31, 1900, to celebrate Decoration (now Memorial) Day. "The Logan Band, a new organization, and a commendable one, played tunes on the village streets. At two o'clock in the afternoon with the Logan band in the lead, the parade formed to go to Oak Grove Cemetery." Flowers were placed on the veterans' graves, and a rifle salute completed the service. This postcard shows the uniformed band. (Courtesy of JM.)

"Souvenir de France," a French *carte postale* dated August 18, 1918, was sent to Estella Fox by her brother Paul. The card is covered with a silk-like material and embellished with embroidery. The postcard was a thank-you for the letters and newspapers she had sent to Fox and his World War I Army companions. Private Fox was part of the Rainbow Division with Company G, 7th Ohio Infantry, a Logan contingent. Fox returned home safely after the war and was a meat cutter for his father at George Fox's meat market on Main Street for many years. (Courtesy of JM.)

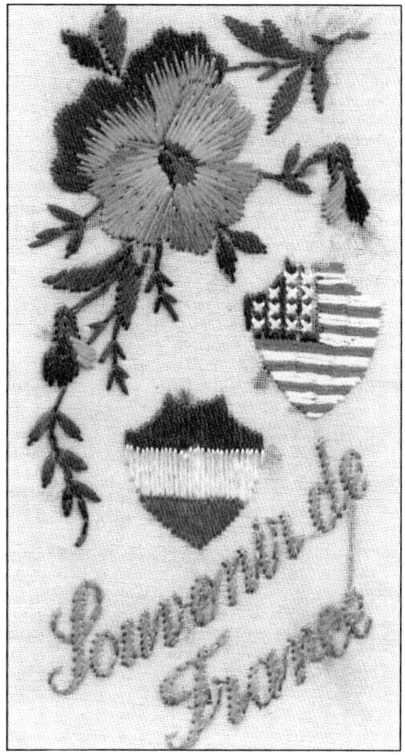

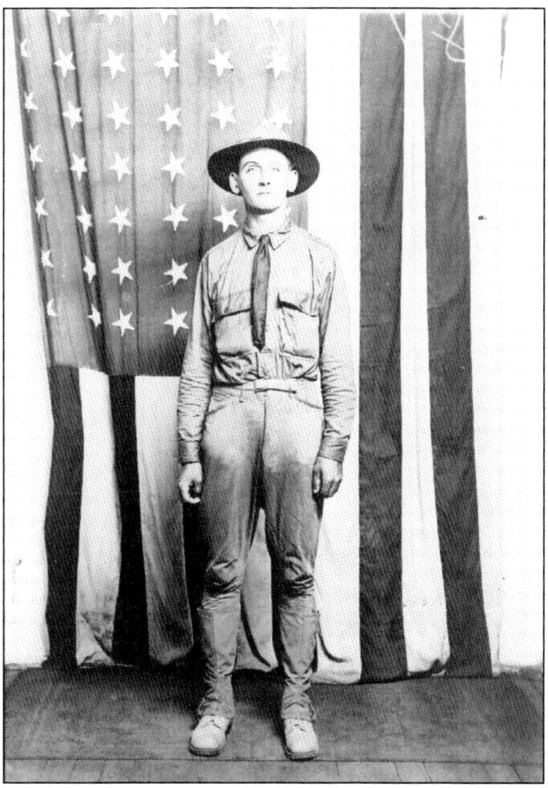

Frederick Alderson Woltz, another native son, is pictured in front of the American flag. These photographic postcards were earmarked to send home to the family as mementos. Woltz joined the US Army on July 18, 1918. He served with the American Expeditionary Forces from September 2, 1918, to March 18, 1919. Fred was the son of George and Lucinda Kline Woltz of Good Hope Township in Hocking County. He died in 1983 at the age of 88. This postcard was found with other articles belonging to Effie A. Woltz, a longtime local newspaper correspondent. (Courtesy of HH.)

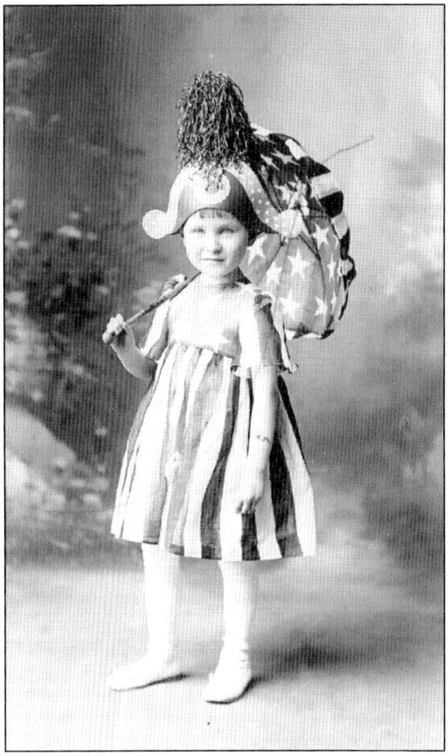

This patriotic little girl with her stars and stripes dress is charming, and the matching parasol completes the picture. Perhaps she is waiting on a parade to begin. The postcard is dated 1914, but she is unidentified. (Courtesy of HH.)

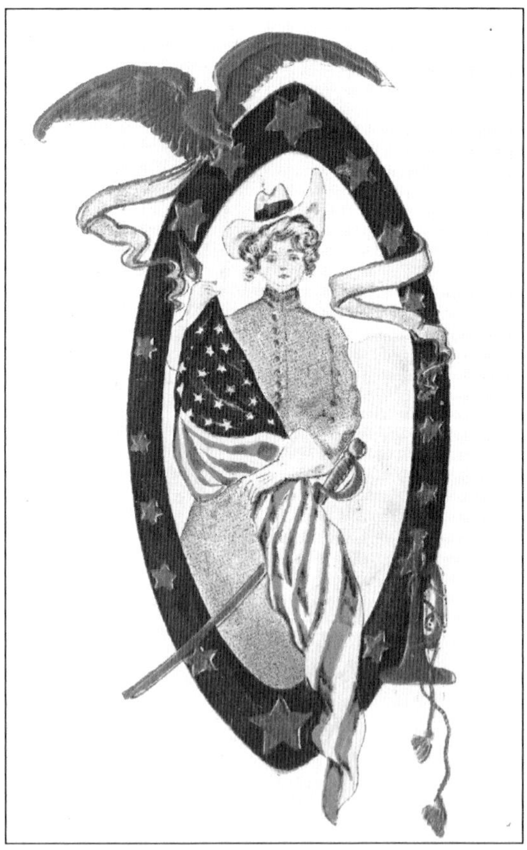

The artwork on this collectible World War I postcard has several symbols possibly representing the cavalry units, including a saber, bugle, and riding gloves. (Courtesy of JM.)

When World War II was declared in 1941, the call to help defend America was answered by millions of young men who enlisted in the military. The postcard at right is dated 1944 and shows the shape of an anchor made up of 2,200 uniformed Navy recruits. Below, "Keep 'Em Flying" was a motto for the US Army Air Corps. The pursuit aircraft, the familiar "V" for victory, and the American eagle complete this 1945 patriotic postcard. (Both courtesy of CCH.)

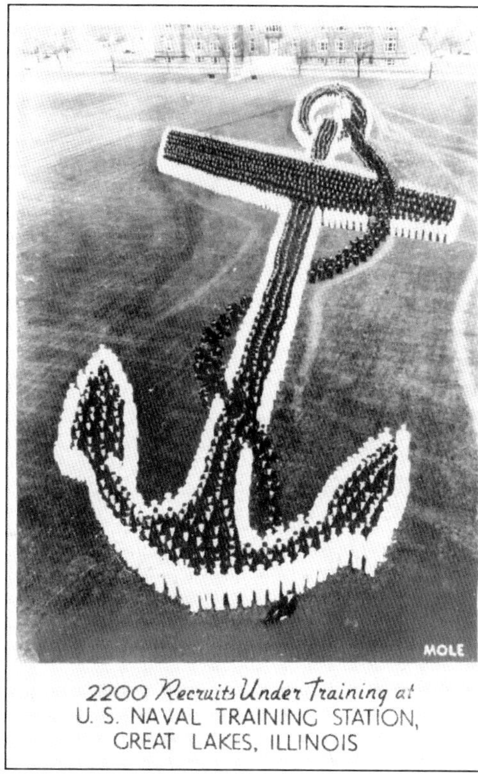

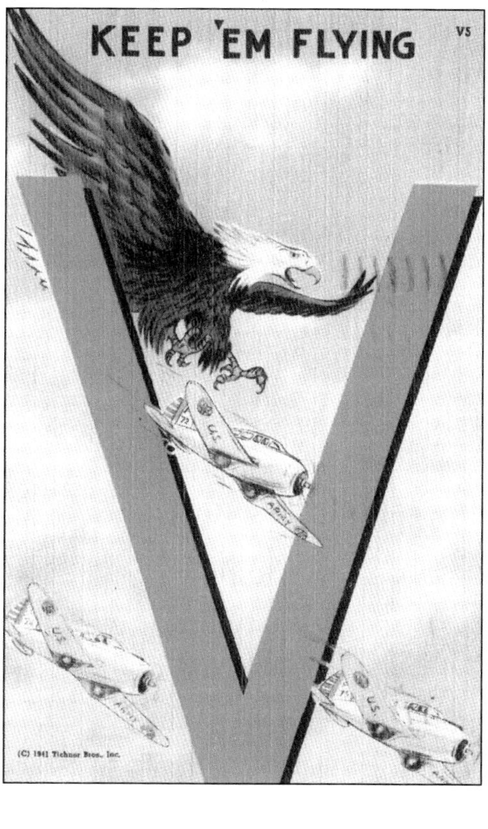

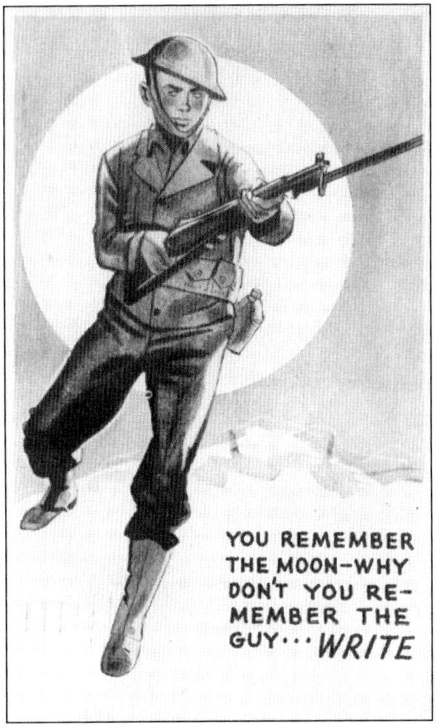

This postcard reminded the girls at home to remember to write to the military men in their lives. Letters from home were important mementos for soldiers on the front lines. (Courtesy of CCH.)

The *New York Times* headline on April 25, 1945, announced, "Conference to form U.N. Meets as Allied Forces Nears Victory over Nazis." Held in San Francisco, Pres. Harry S. Truman attended the opening ceremonies. This postcard is dated June 11, 1945, and was sent from Oakland, California. The Allies intended to form "a United Nations to ensure peace between nations, which they had fought so hard to win." On April 30, 1945, it was reported that Adolph Hitler committed suicide, and the Germans began negotiations to end the war. (Courtesy of CCH.)

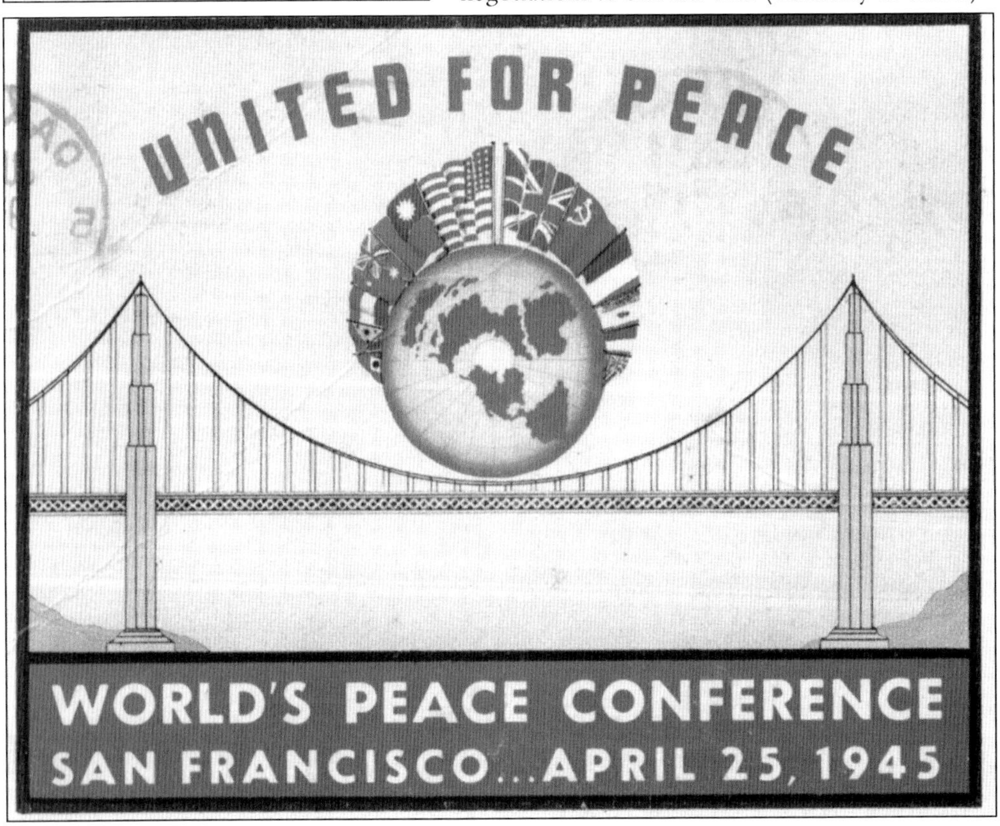

Three

Times to Remember

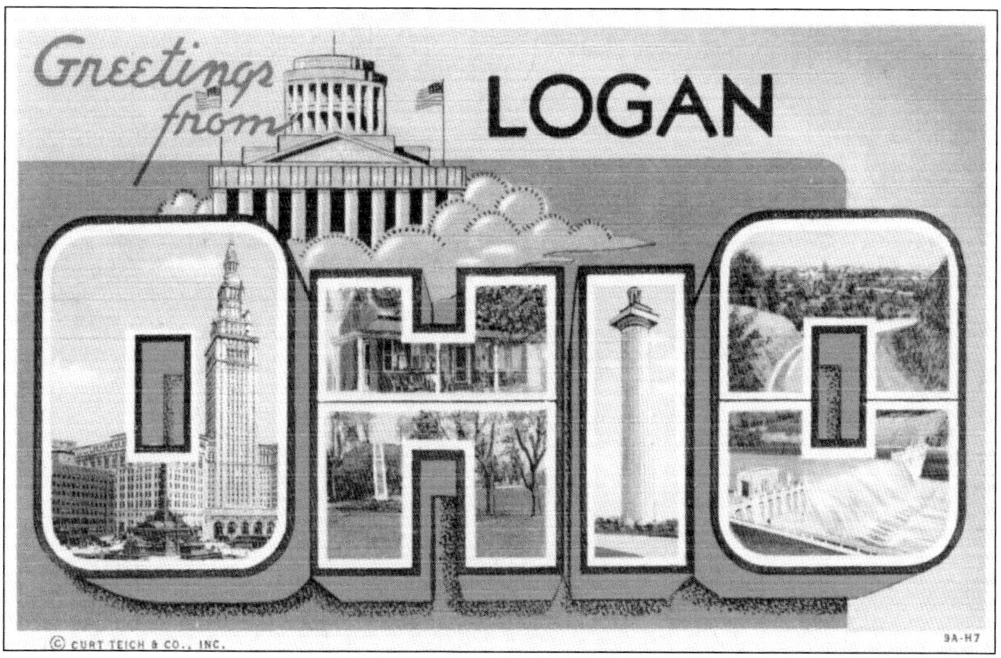

This postcard simply states, "OHIO." It features several well-known places in the Buckeye State, such as Lake Erie and the scene of Columbus, the state capital. Perhaps the Hocking Hills are represented by the drawing in the upper right of the "O" of a dense stand of trees. (Courtesy of JM.)

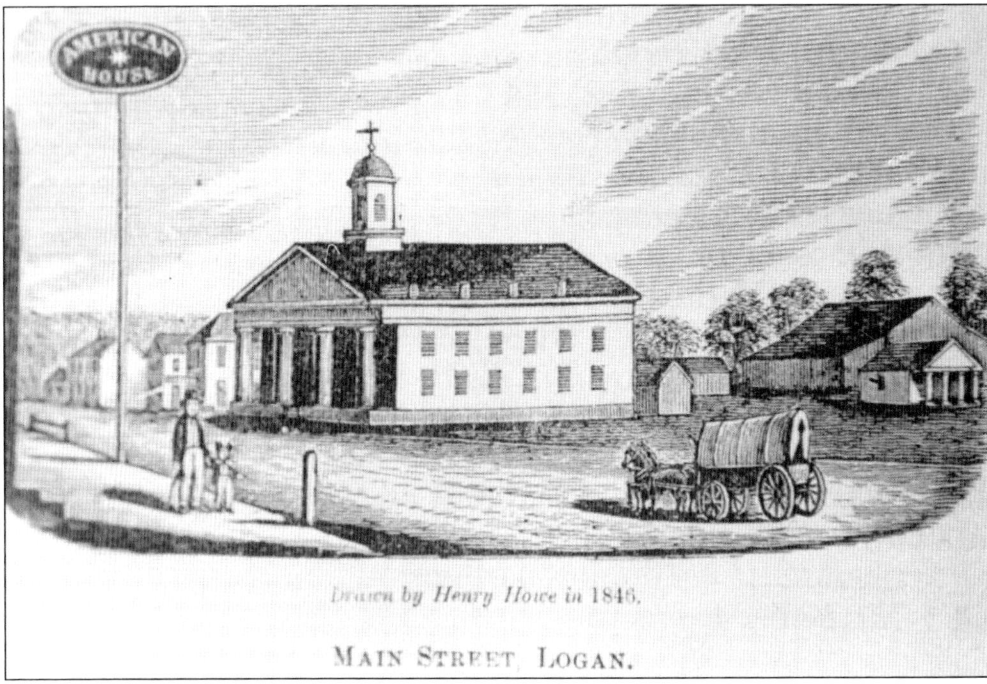

The early court business in the village of Logan was held in a private home for several years. The second Hocking County Courthouse (pictured) was built in 1841 at a cost of $10,000. The two-story frame building was prominently located at the center of the two main crossroads: Main and Market Streets. This image was drawn by author Henry Howe, who in 1846 wrote *Historical Collections of Ohio*. He traveled across Ohio's counties to document each Ohio town's history. A *Columbus Citizen-Journal* column by the late journalist Ben Hayes noted that Howe would borrow a chair and sit in the street drawing on-the-spot sketches of courthouses and public squares. Note the sign on the left, advertising the American House, an early hotel. (Courtesy of JM.)

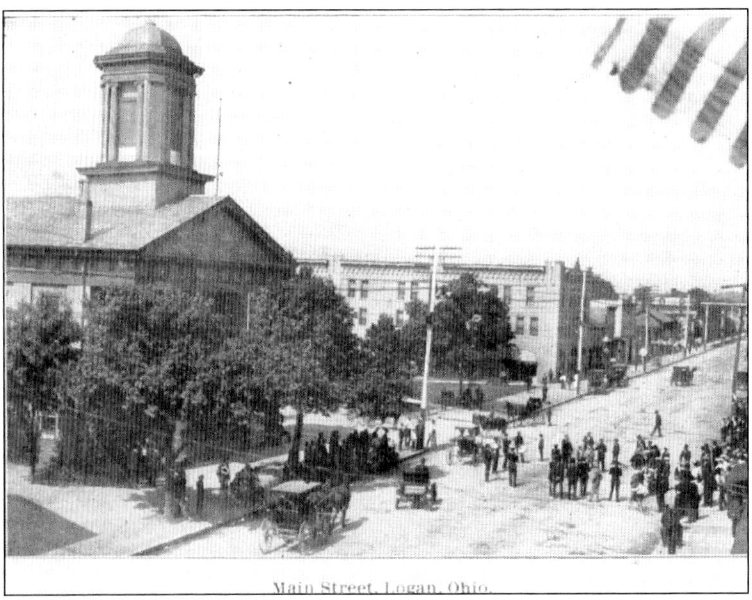

This image, taken about 1909, portrays the courthouse as the centerpiece of the county seat. Electricity had been installed in Logan, as evidenced by the poles and wires strung above the street. This was still very much the days of the horse and buggy. By the 1920s, the old frame building was beginning to show its age. (Courtesy of JM.)

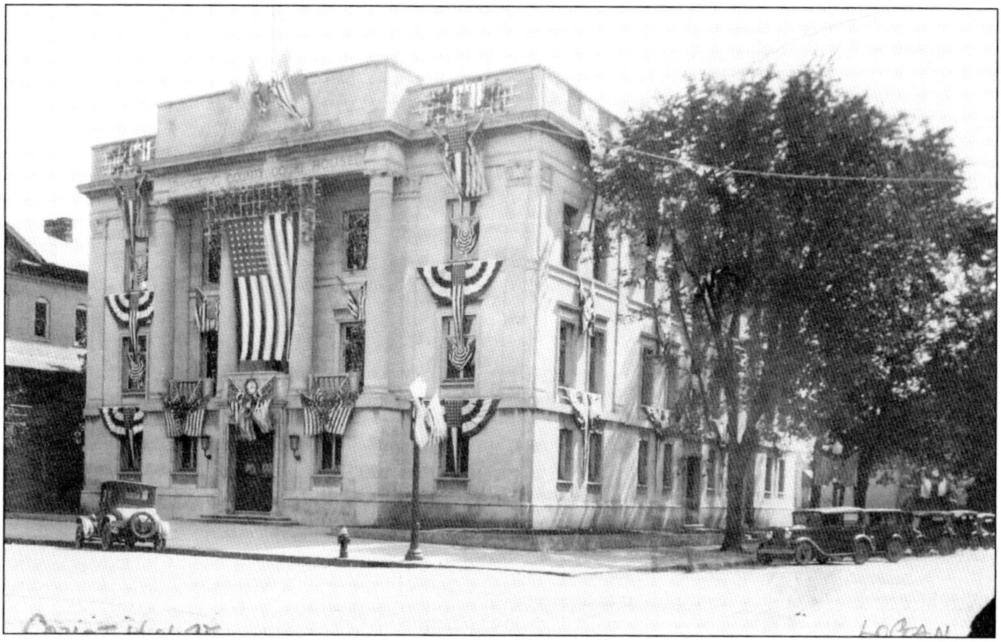

The new courthouse was built in 1924 at a cost of $250,000. Well-known architect Frank Packard designed the structure, and the Logan contractor was William Montgomery. The building's exterior remains the same today, but renovations have been made to the interior. (Courtesy of JM.)

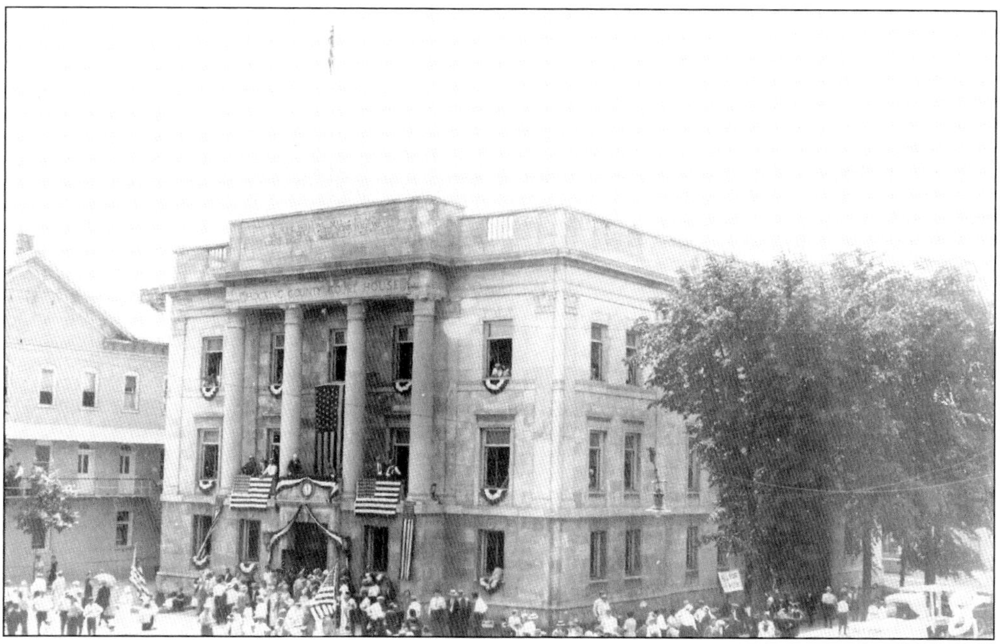

Although these two images of the courthouse seem identical, notice that the patriotic buntings and flags are slightly different, indicating two different events. The Hocking County Courthouse continues to be the center of county activities. (Courtesy of JM.)

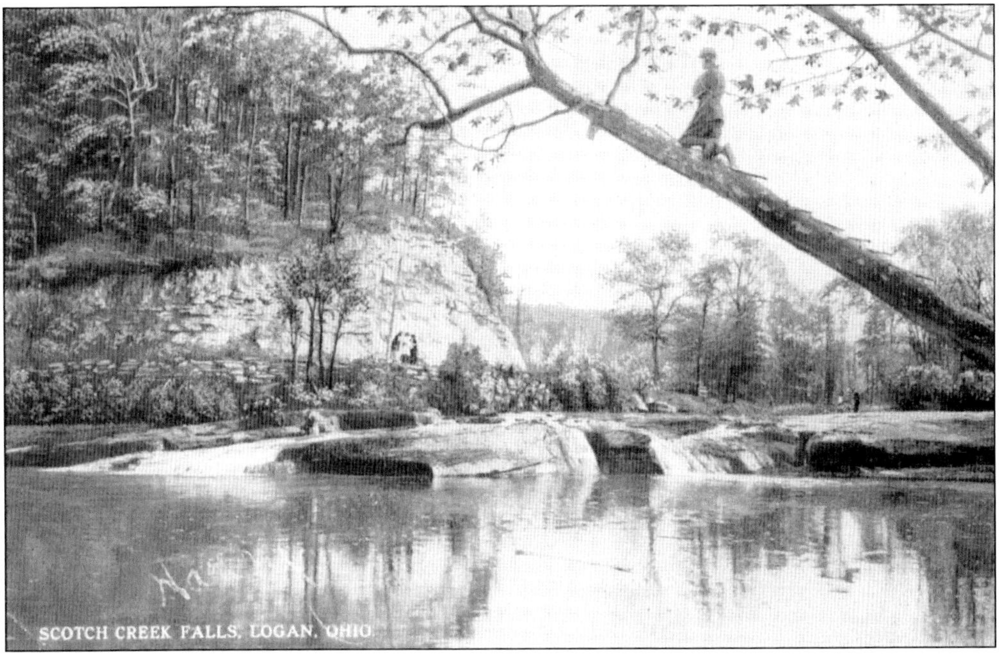

Scott Creek, first known as Scott Fork, is located along Route 93 south of Logan and flows north to empty into the Hocking River. Over time, the name Scott was corrupted to Scotch Creek, as these two postcards clearly indicate. In 1887, the creek swallowed John L. Bensonhaver, his wife Clara, their two horses, and a wagon loaded with 20 bushels of wheat. Eyewitnesses called for help and eventually the two bodies were dredged up from the creek. This incident resulted in the nickname "Death Hole" for many years. In more recent times, professional divers found a precipice that unexpectedly falls approximately 8 to 12 feet from the creek bed, which would be much like jumping off a cliff. (Both courtesy of MT.)

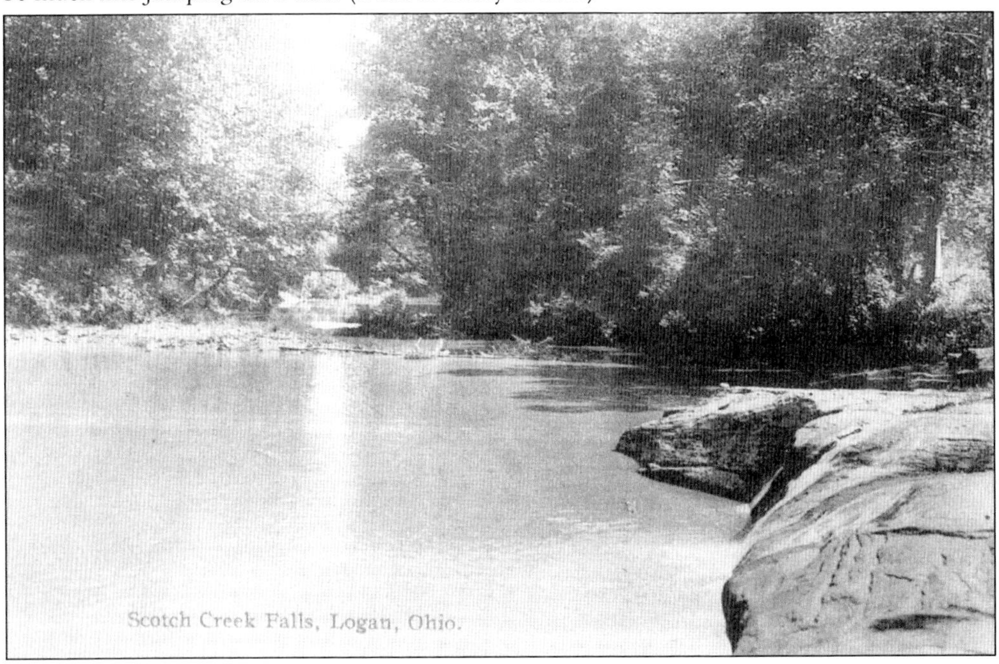

According to the weekly *Democrat-Sentinel*'s March 14, 1907 issue, "Flood and Destruction Lay Waste [to] the Hocking Valley." It was the most devastating flood in the history of the Hocking River to date. In 1873, an earlier flood destroyed 13 miles of the Hocking Canal. Pictured are the Gallagher Avenue and Front Street neighborhoods. It was reported that women and children were rescued by horseback. Note the horses in the photograph. (Courtesy of HH.)

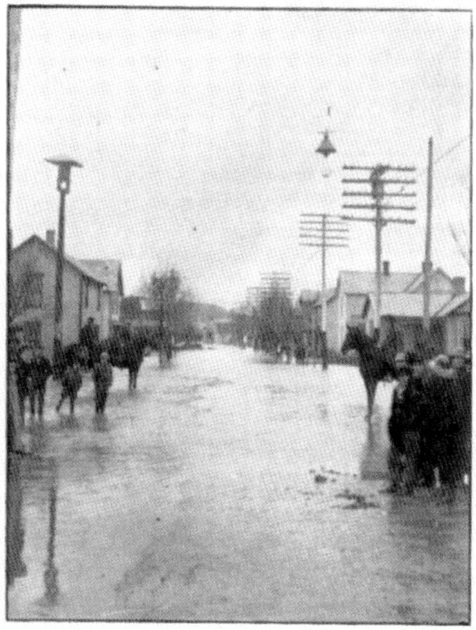

Logan Flood March 1907—Gallagher Avenue Looking toward Depot.

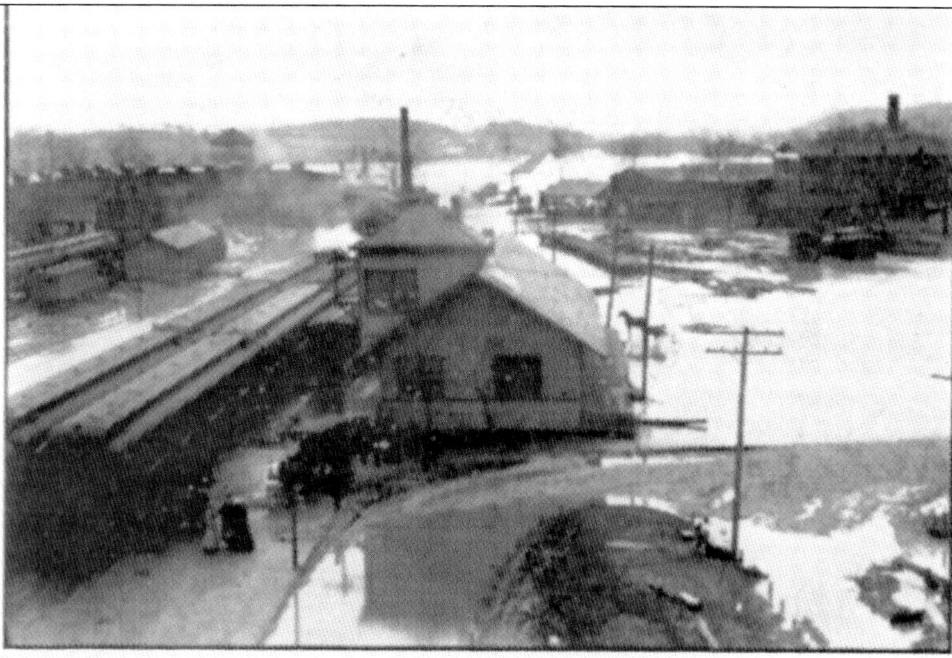

Logan Flood March 1907—From Top of Depot Looking toward R. R. Bridge.

The Hocking Valley railroad depot was also hit hard by the flood, with some 60 stranded traveling salesmen who formed their own relief committee. The Federal Gas Company lines broke, and the rescuers had no light in the utter darkness. Communication to the outside was cut off as both telegraph and telephone lines were downed. Logan lost all mail delivery for several days due to the great destruction of the railroad. When the mail finally did arrive, there were two tons laid down at once in front of the Logan Post Office. (Courtesy of HH.)

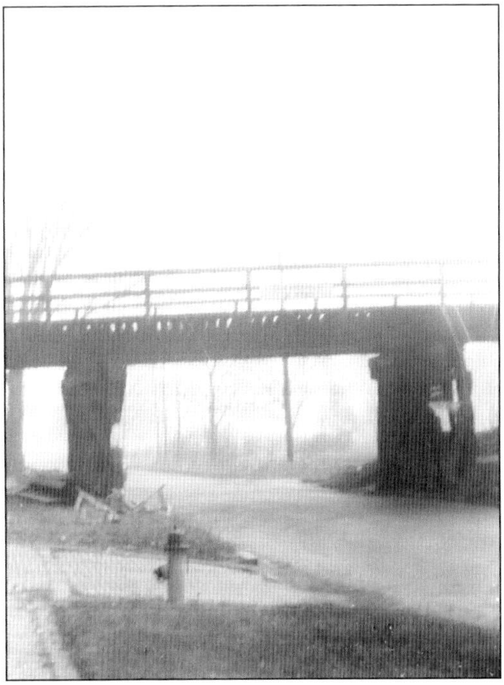

In 1869, this railroad spur track and embankment, known as "the trestle," was constructed when there were heavy rail shipments of coal from the New Straitsville and Monday Creek Mining Company. Also known as the Straitsville Branch, it remained busy until after World War I. The trestle had only a 12-foot clearance, and many a truck driver came to grief attempting to drive under it. The trestle became the subject of an argument between the Logan city administration, the Ohio Department of Transportation, and the Chesapeake & Ohio Railroad as to which was responsible for the removal. About 1950, an agreement was reached that all three entities would share in the removal of the trestle. This allowed for the widening of Front and Second Streets. The embankment removal also increased the value of the RayGerl Allotment and allowed the extension of Main Street. (Both courtesy of HH.)

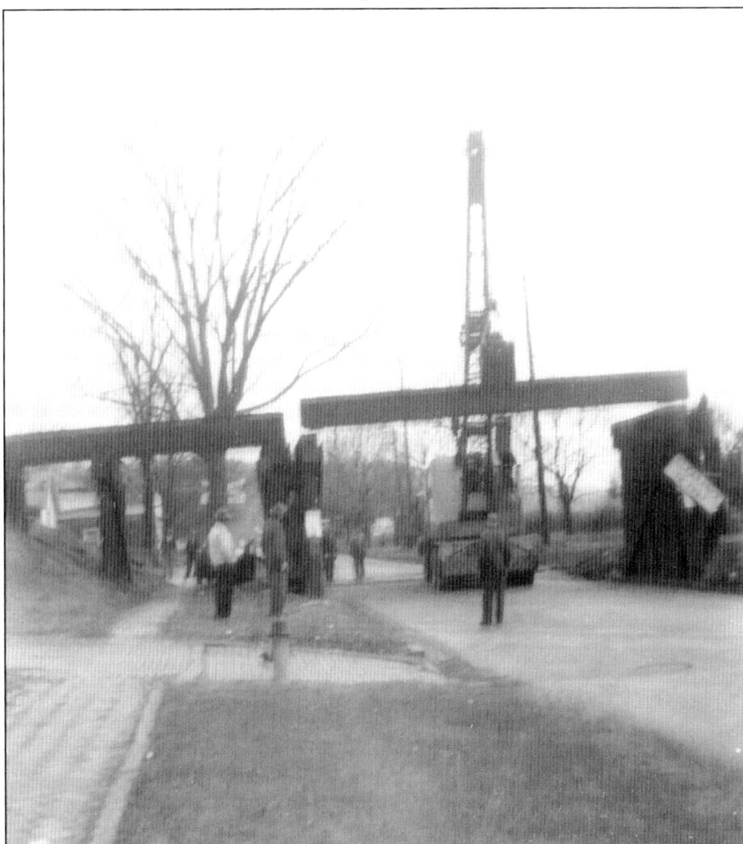

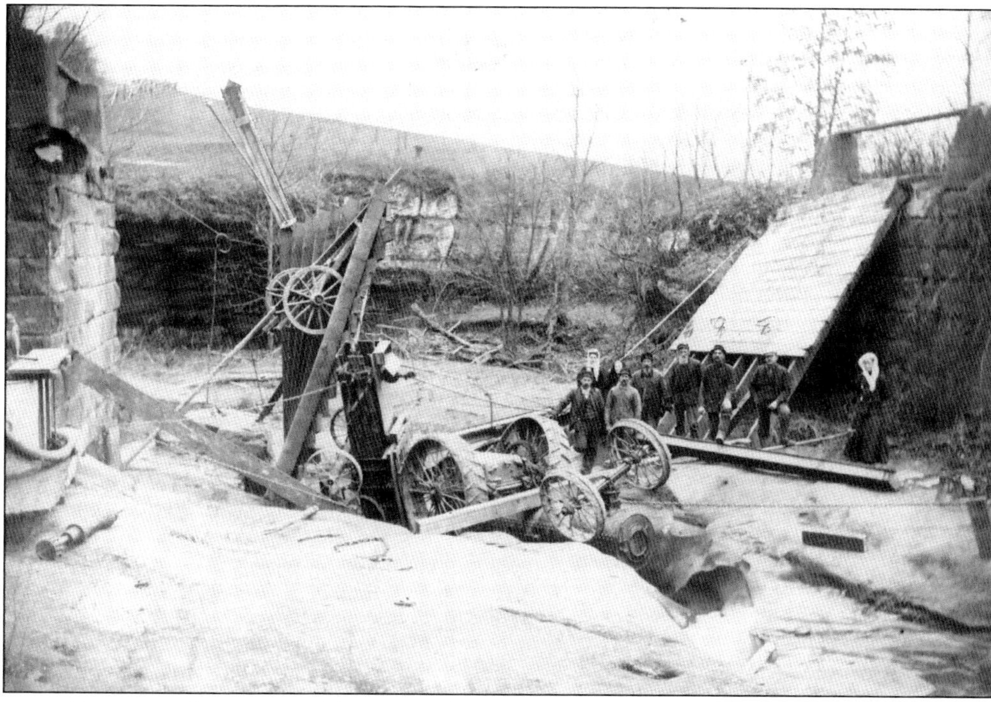

According to the front page of the November 29, 1906, issue of the *Democrat-Sentinel*, an awful accident had taken place at Crockett's Run. Henry Azbell, age 32, was the engineer of the six-ton traction engine. In an attempt to cross the iron bridge near Helber's Rocks, the train broke through and fell into the rocky gulch 30 feet below. Azbell was killed instantly. The article reported that Azbell left a family of four children at home in Enterprise. In this image, the onlookers are, from left to right, George Walker, George Engle, Mary Engle, Ida Engle, Daniel Engle, Louis Ruff, Samuel Helber, unidentified, and Sarah Engle. (Courtesy of HH.)

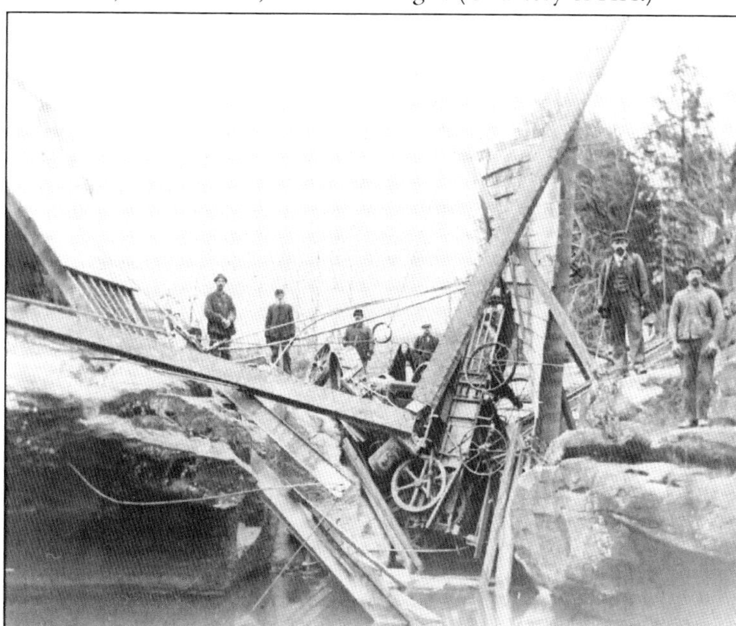

This view shows the mangled iron of the train and the destroyed bridge at Helber's Rocks. From left to right are Samuel Helber, Louis Ruff, Daniel Engle, Ida Engle, unidentified, George Walker, and George Engle. The *Democrat-Sentinel* reported on December 13, 1906, that the contract for rebuilding the bridge had been let to the Mt. Vernon Bridge Company for $581. (Courtesy of HH.)

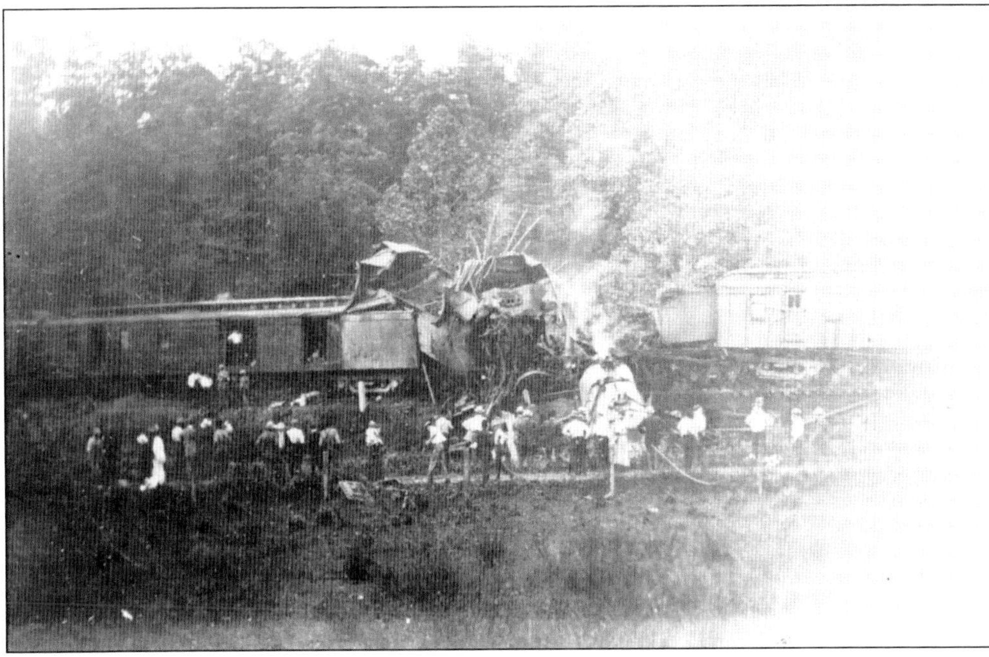

On June 18, 1914, two trains, No. 134 (southbound) and No. 137 (northbound), traveling at full speed, met in a head-on collision on the curve just north of Starr in Hocking County. According to the *Logan Republican*, the disastrous wreck occurred at 5:30 p.m. Due to the curve, the trains could not see each other until it was too late to use the emergency brakes. The engines telescoped into the baggage cars and the passenger coaches, yet no civilian passengers were critically injured. (Both courtesy of HH.)

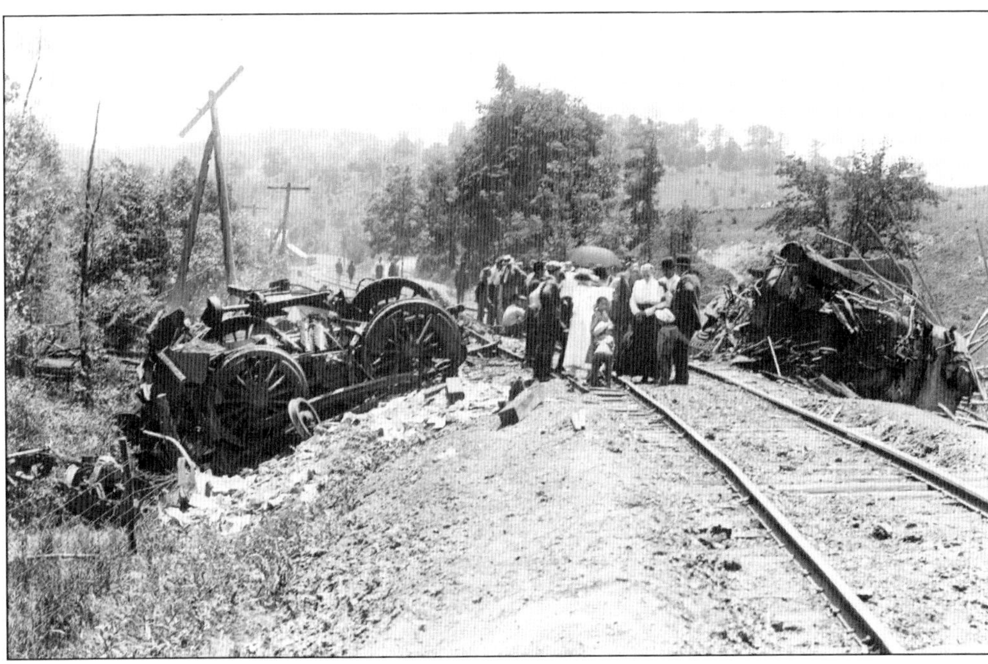

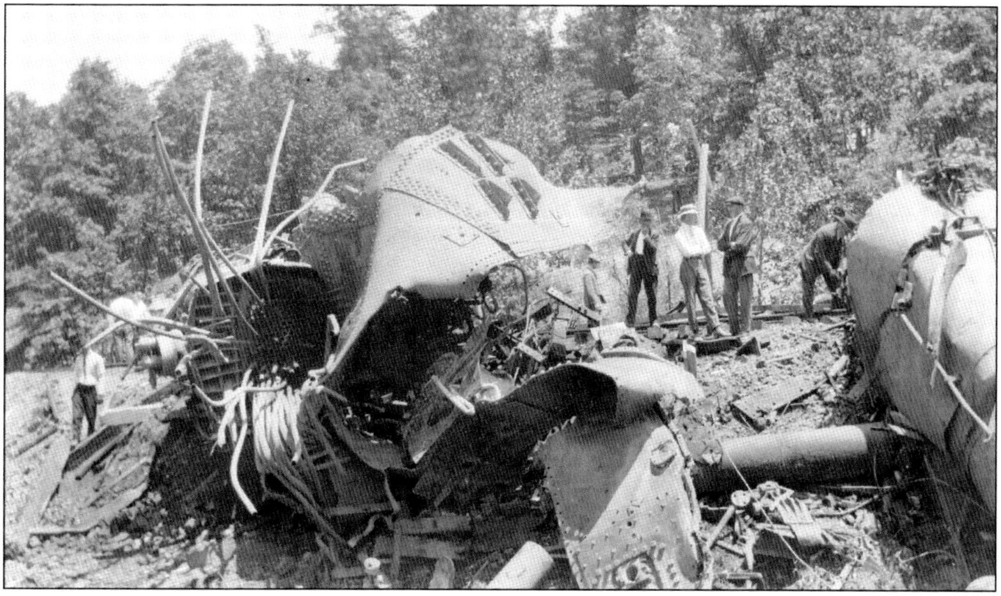

The lives of five trainmen were lost in the Starr train wreck. Killed aboard No. 134 were engineer William Davis of Adelphi, Ohio, and fireman Williams from Pomeroy; on No. 137, fireman Pearl Shaw from Logan, fireman Charles Unkle from Logan, and baggage master Marsh from Columbus. In an investigation, the cause was said to have been the error of the operator at Starr, who failed to pass an order to the trainmen that would have allowed the trains to pass in safety. (Both courtesy of HH.)

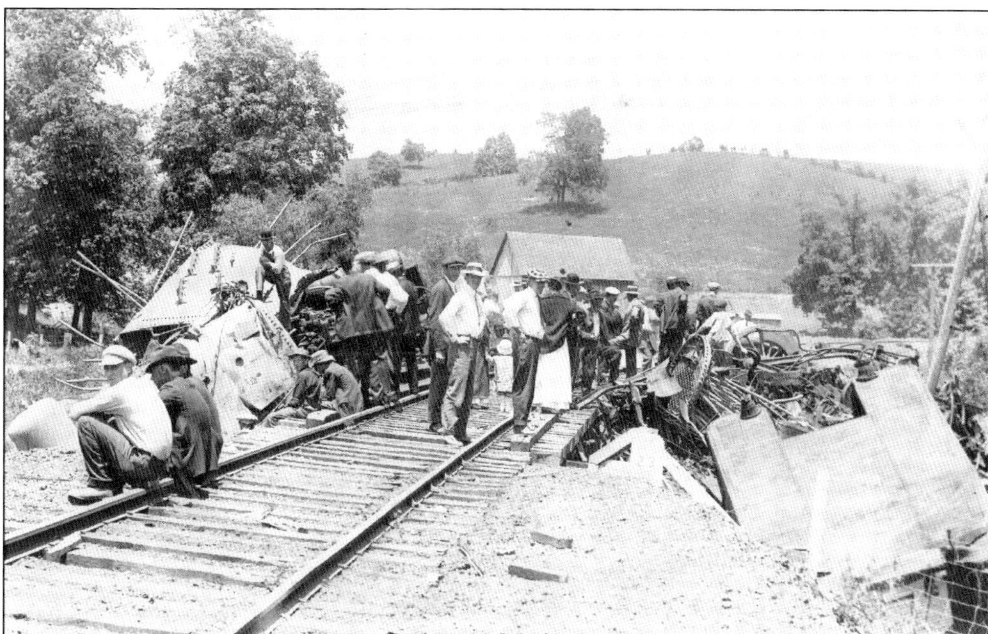

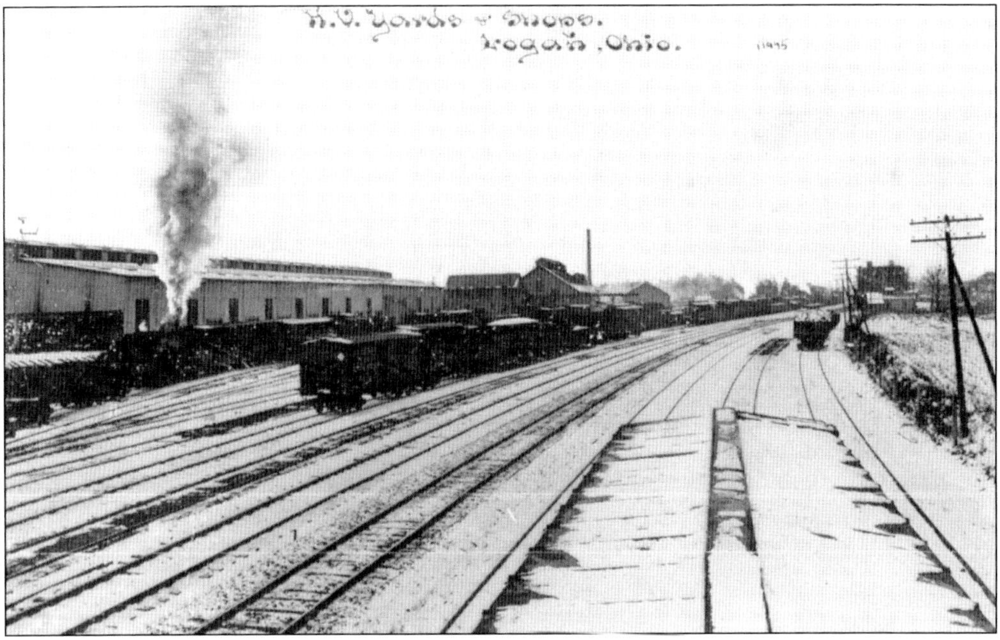

The Hocking Valley yards and shops (above) were a major economic influence in Logan. This postcard shows a winter scene called a "photoette." Hocking Valley Railroad crewmen (below) take a break to pose for a photograph. Only two are identified: in the front row, seated in the center, is freight conductor John Buntz, and standing fourth from the right is W.P. Shaw. (Both courtesy of JBL.)

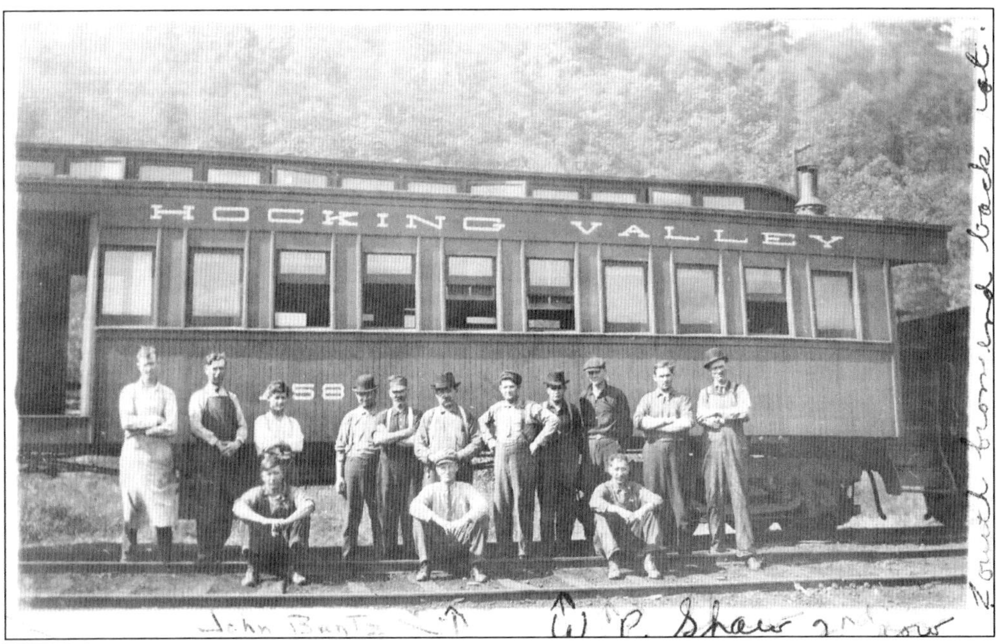

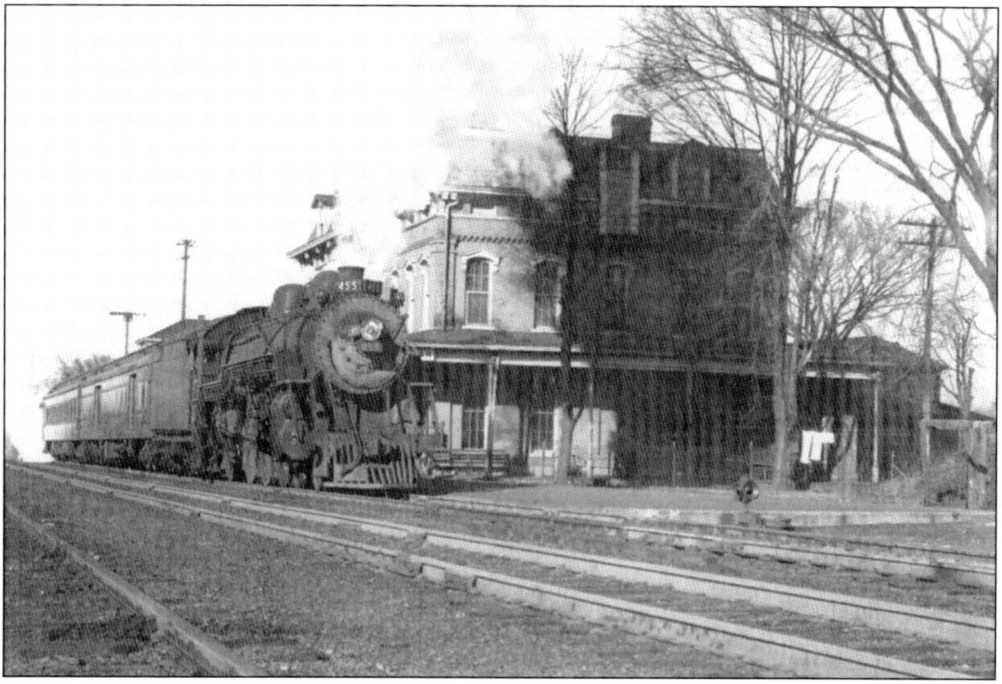

The Chesapeake & Ohio Railway ended 80 years of passenger service to the Hocking Valley on December 31, 1949. According to a front-page story in the *Logan Daily News*, the C&O Railway abandoned two trains, No. 37 and No. 137, claiming heavy losses. The move was authorized by the Ohio Public Utilities Commission. Towns along the route from Logan to the River Division in Pomeroy and Columbus to Logan protested to no avail. To the dismay of historians, the beautiful Depot Hotel above, complete with dining room, was torn down by the C&O in 1950. The 1914 postcard below shows a passenger train much like No. 137, sending thoughts of appreciation and thanks. (Both courtesy of HH.)

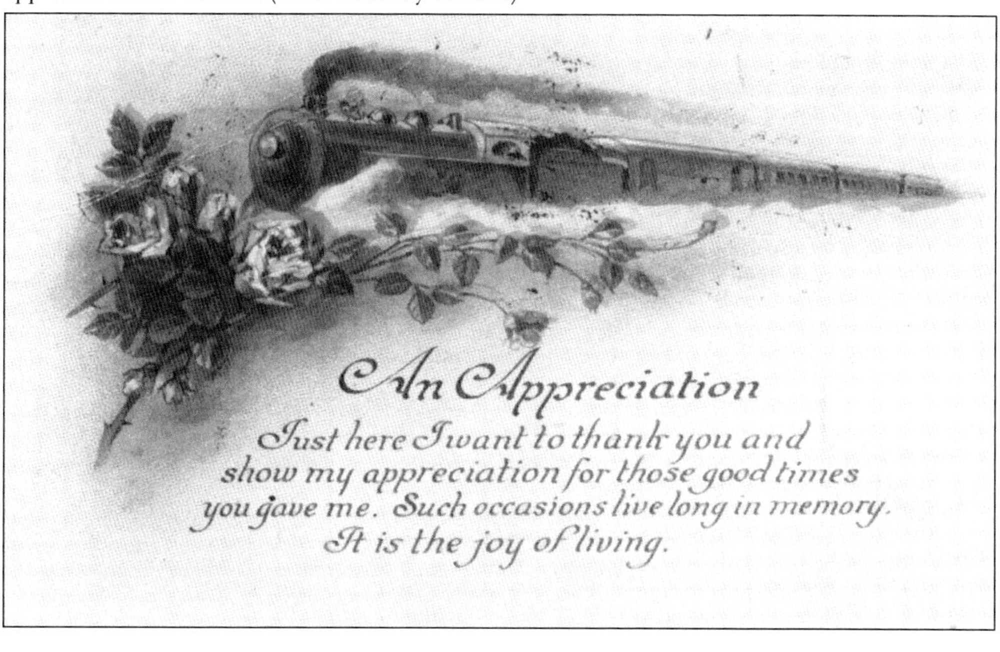

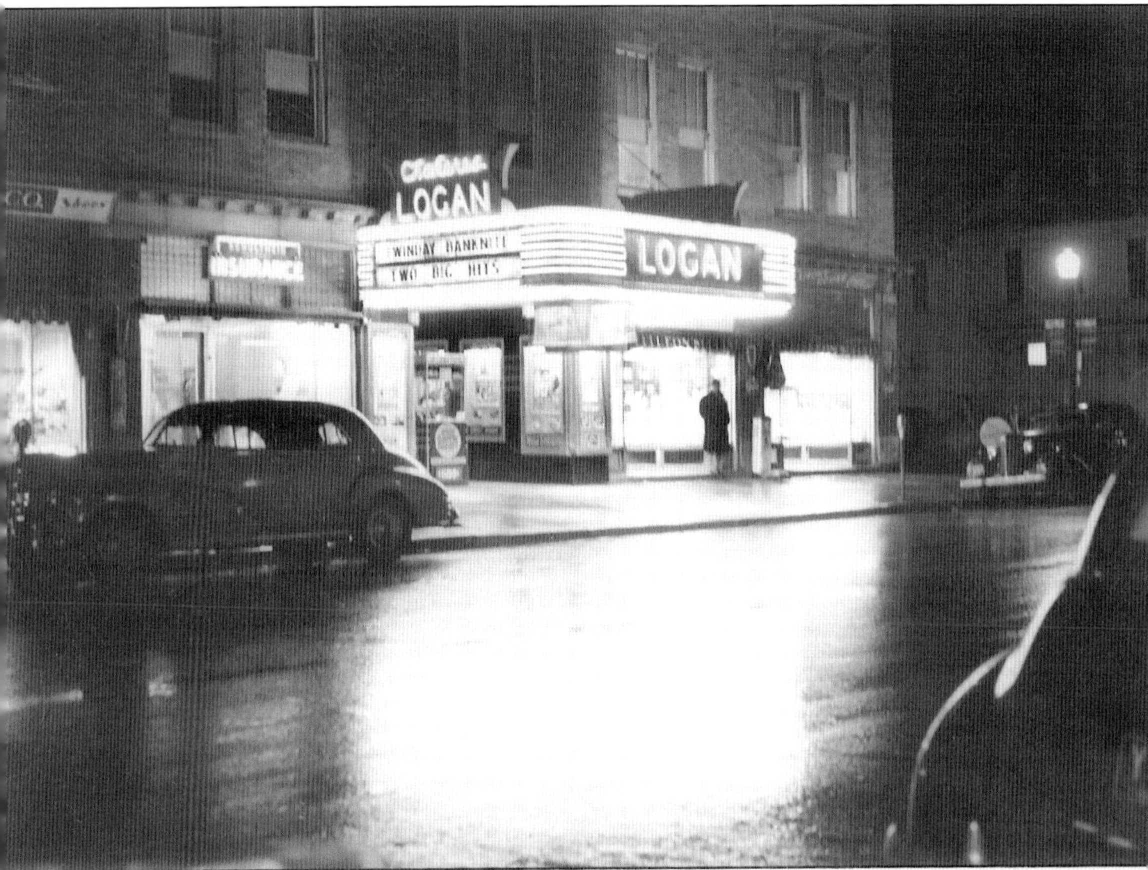

ca 1949 MAIN STREET, LOGAN, OHIO George B. Johns

The Chakeres Logan Theater was opened in 1935 when Phillip "Phil" Chakeres of Springfield, Ohio, purchased and remodeled the existing theater. Members of the theater staff on opening night, August 30, 1935, included Dick Eberst, Floyd Beougher, Ruby Nelle Dollison, Ross Stivison, Jane Walsh, Fritz Ambrose, and Eddie Hamilton. The Chakeres Logan Theater closed in the 1980s, but there is a new interest in renovating and reopening the space as a venue for the performing arts. To the left of the marquee is the Dayton Schultheis Insurance Agency, and to the right is Leon Eichel's Smoke House, a favorite stop to purchase treats before the movies began. (Courtesy of GBJ.)

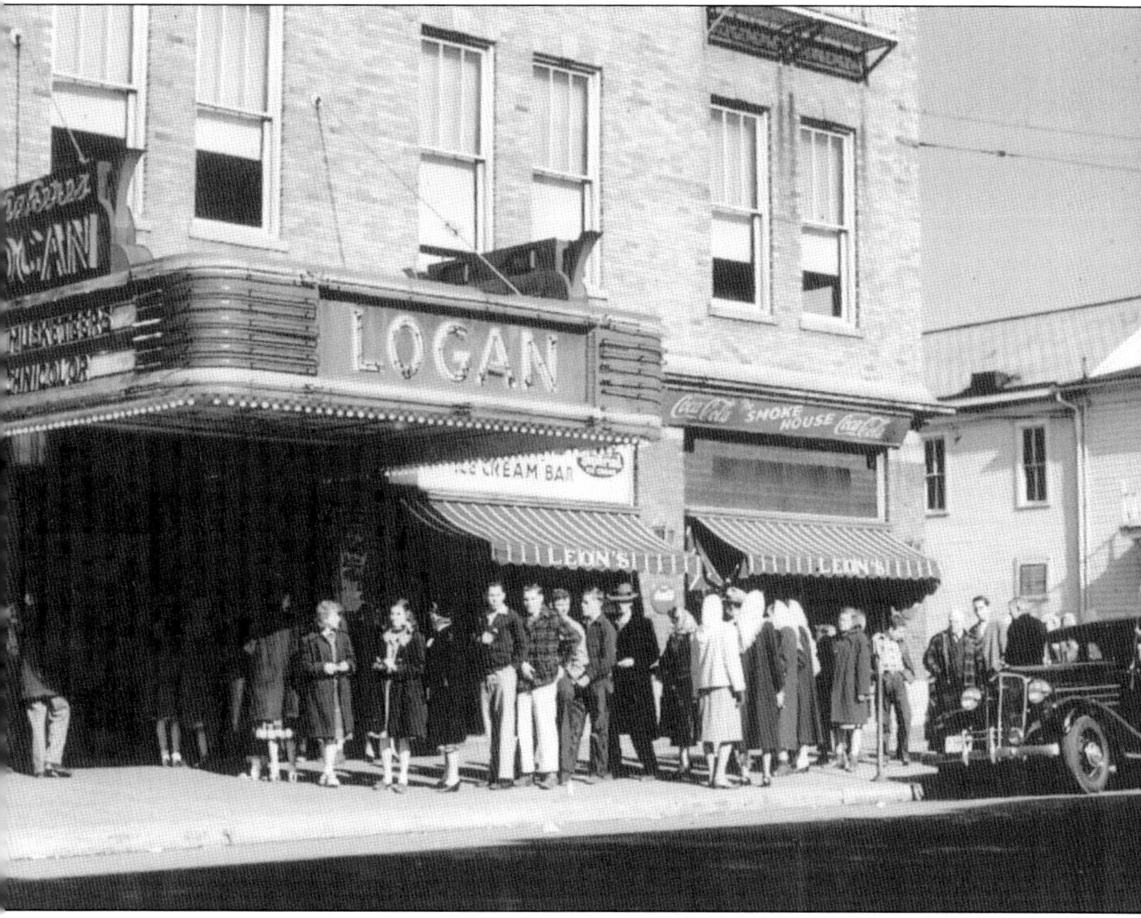

This photograph of the theater is not an unusual scene, as locals were always willing to stand in line to purchase tickets to see a new movie. In this case, the marquee is advertising the 1948 Technicolor movie *The Three Musketeers*, starring Gene Kelly. (Courtesy of GBJ.)

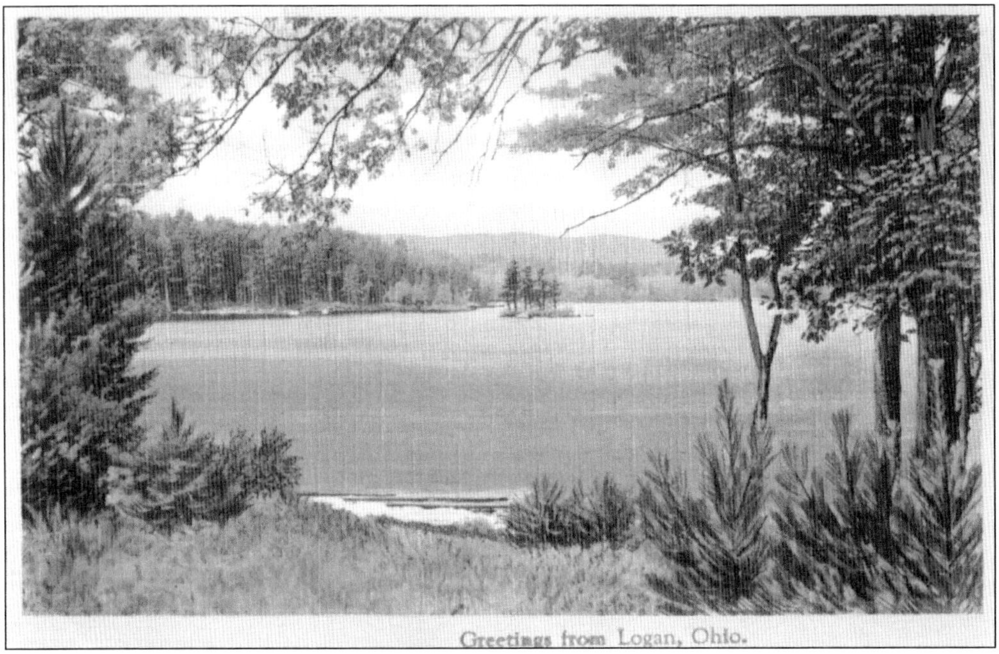

A linen postcard sending greetings from Logan, Ohio, displays another view of the Hocking River. (Courtesy of CCH.)

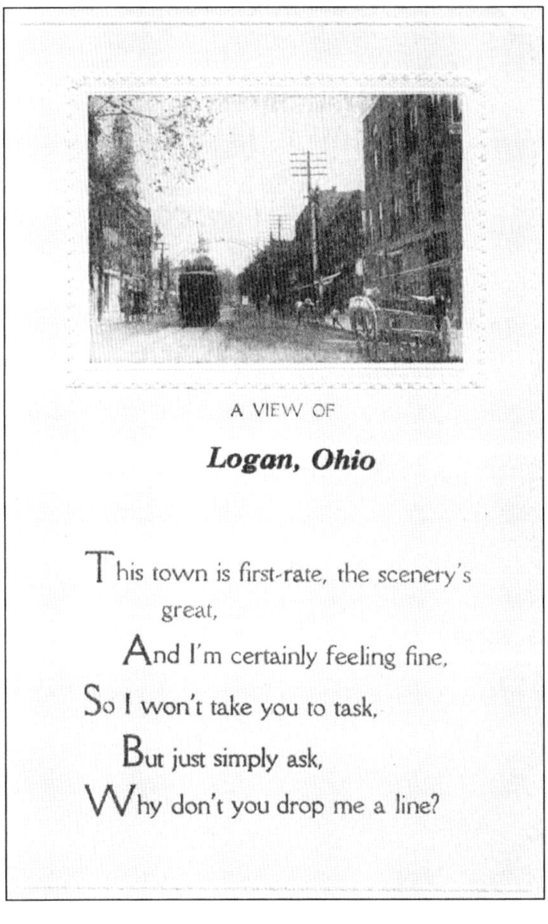

This appears to be a nice poem about the town, but look closely and a trolley car can be seen, which is not part of the area's heritage. Obviously, the postcard maker had another Logan in mind. Logan, West Virginia? Logan, Utah? (Courtesy of JM.)

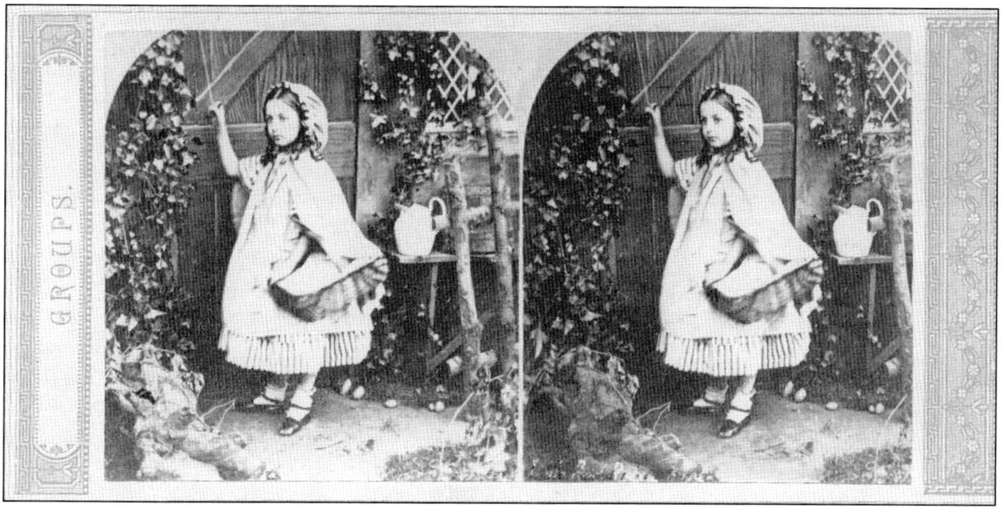

Stereopticon photographs (two exact images) were just as popular as postcards. They were used as parlor entertainment in the United States, beginning about 1862 when Oliver Wendell Holmes and Joseph Bates invented the Holmes Stereopticon. Stereoscope cards pictured famous places, Bible stories, or nursery rhymes. The stories and images helped educate several generations of adults and children about the wonders of the world. This image is depicts the children's story, "Little Red Riding Hood." (Courtesy of HH.)

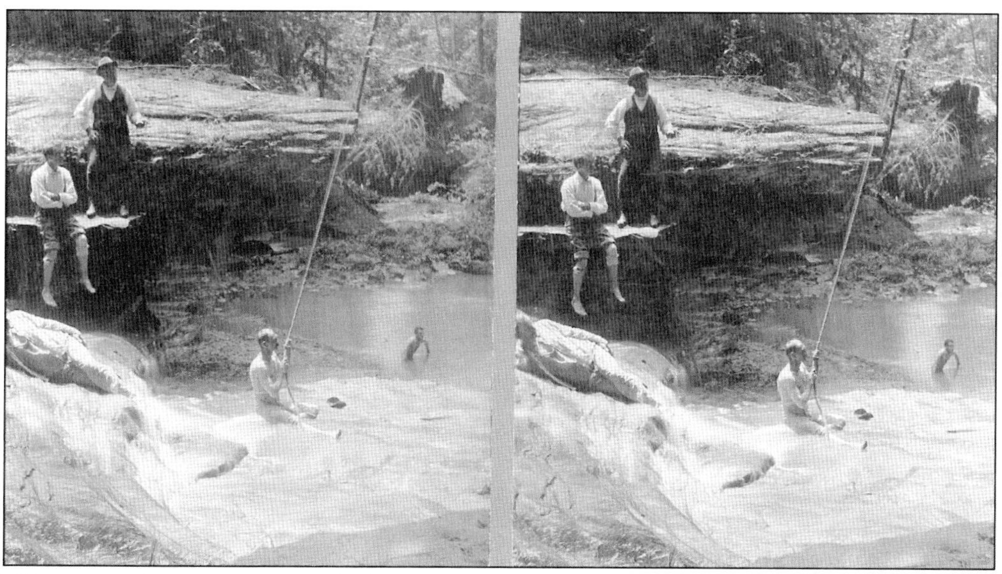

This stereopticon image is marked "Helber's Rocks," a favorite swimming spot for Hocking County residents. These boys are not skinny-dipping, but they are making use of a long rope on which to swing and then drop into the water. Local stereopticon images are somewhat rare and are desired by collectors. (Courtesy of HH.)

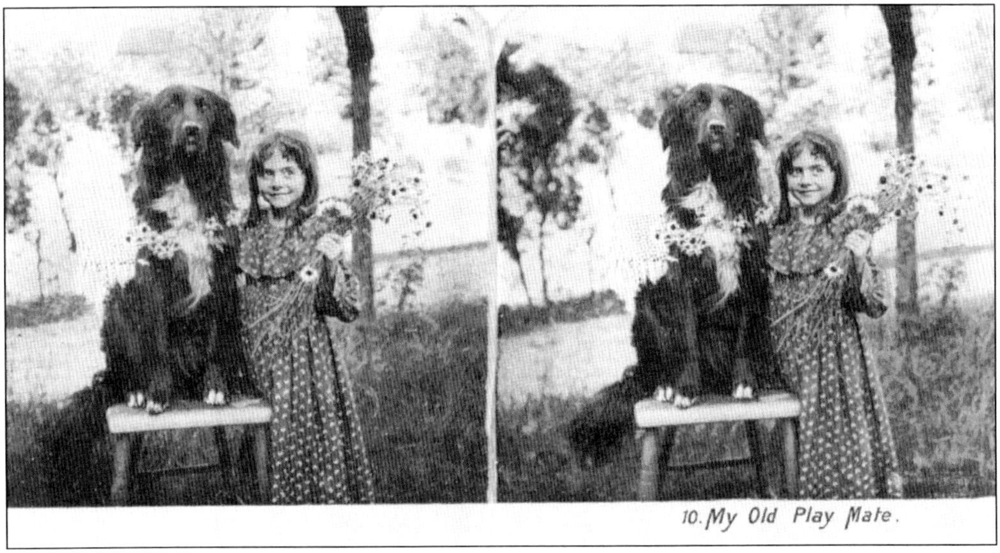

Stereopticon views that featured young children and pets were very popular. "My Old Play Mate" (above) with a girl and her pet dog, and three small children saying their nightly prayers in "Now I Lay Me Down to Sleep" (below) were typical images of the day. (Both courtesy of HH.)

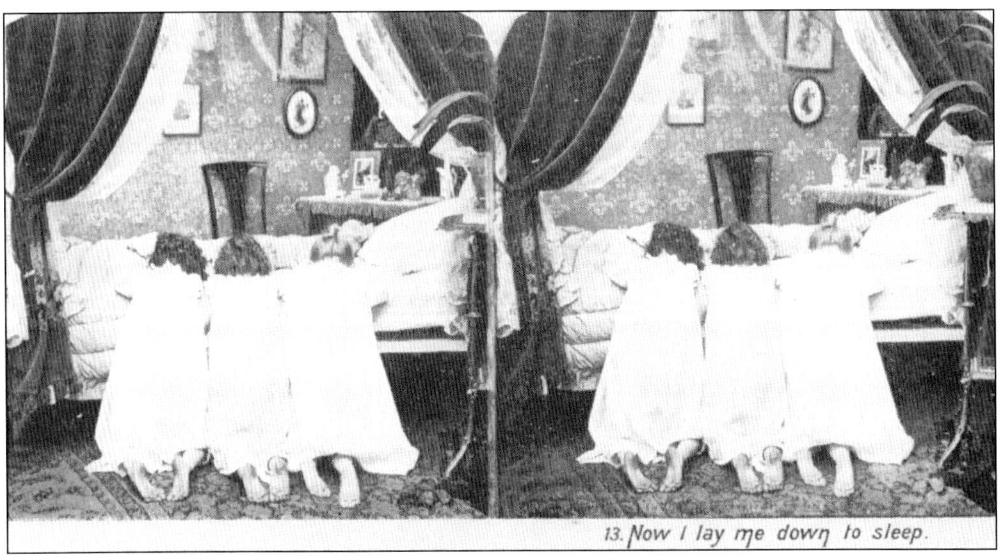

Four

Booming Business

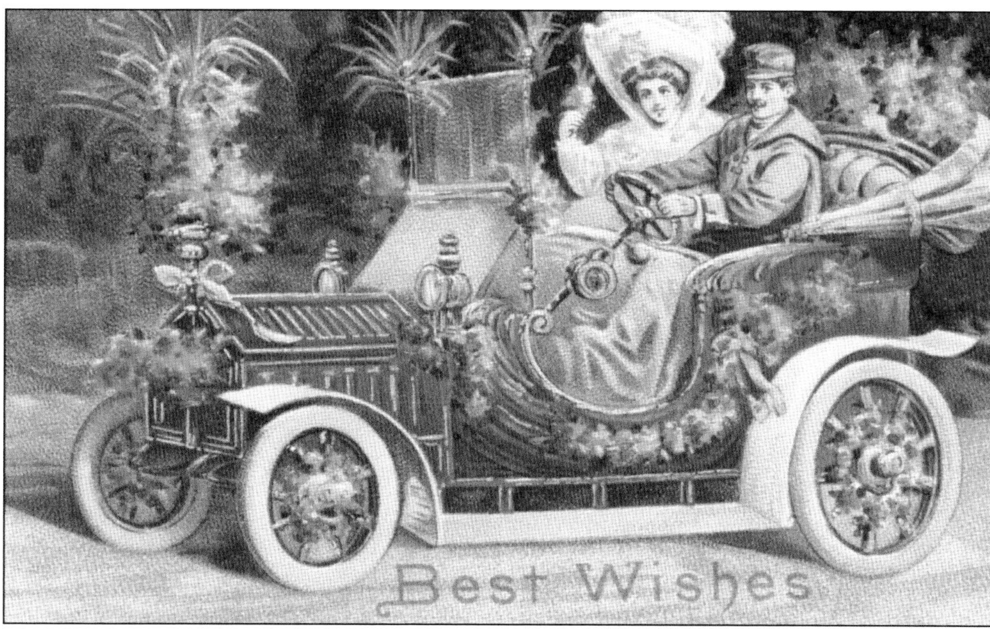

In 1897, Roman Eli Olds of Geneva, Ohio, founded the Olds Motor Vehicle Company and began to manufacture the popular Oldsmobile. This undated postcard matches old photographs of the Oldsmobile as it looked at the turn of the 20th century. (Courtesy of JM.)

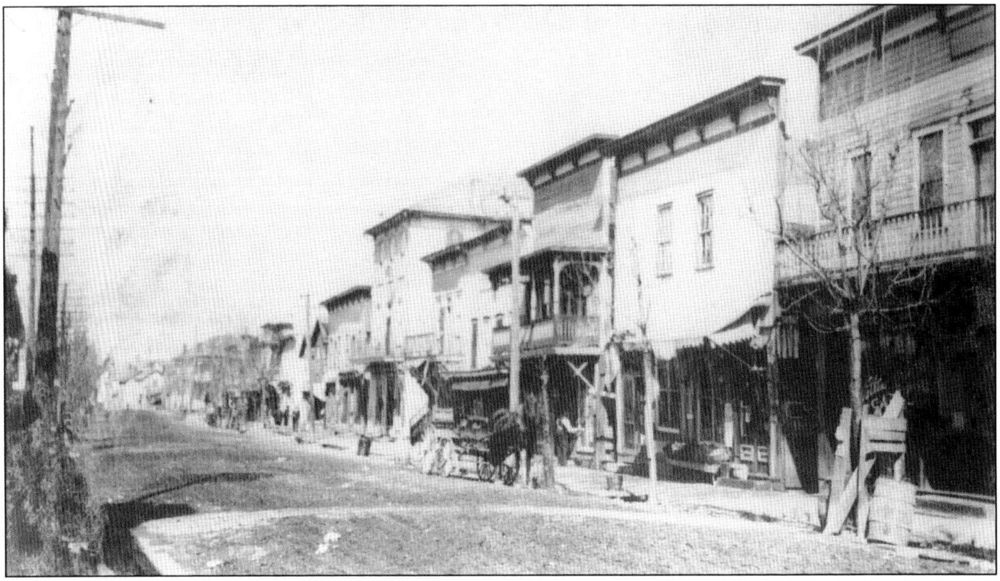

Main Street has had more than its share of photographs taken that recorded the town's progress. Most of the postcards shown were taken looking west. The oldest photograph on file (pictured) was taken prior to 1909 and shows primitive frame business structures. The upper floors could be used as living quarters or other offices. (Courtesy HH.)

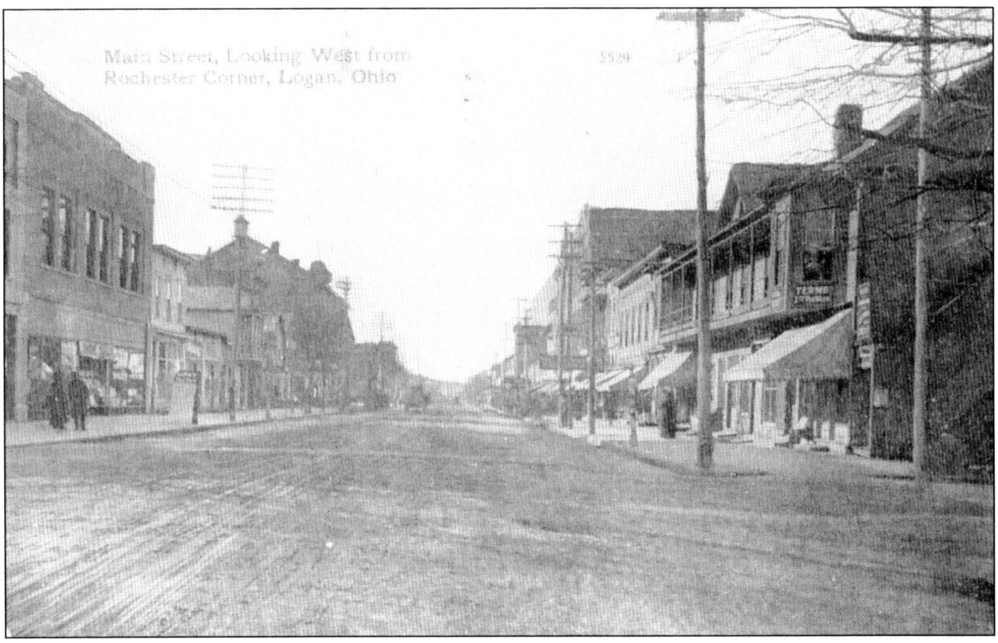

This postcard is of "Main Street, Looking West from Rochester Corner, Logan, Ohio." Dated 1912, the streetscape has been greatly improved. The J. Rochester & Sons store began in the early days of Logan as a general merchandise and trading establishment. Originally called Hatch and Rochester, it anchored the southeastern corner of Main Street for many years. During the Civil War, letters from the county soldiers would be sent to the Rochester store, and the proprietor would distribute them to the proper families. (Courtesy of GRF.)

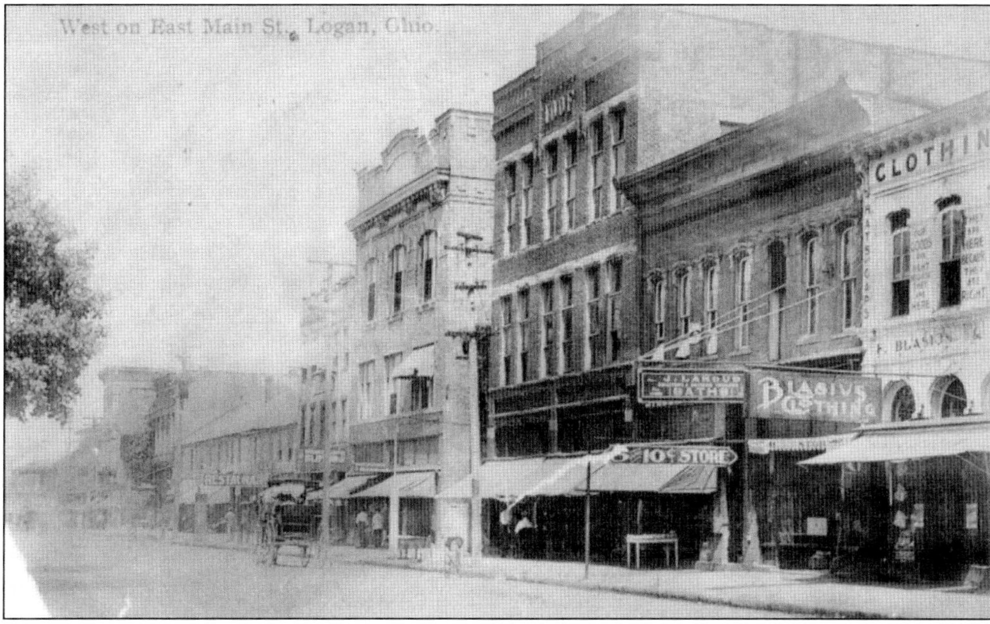

By 1915, the frame buildings had been replaced by ones made of brick. Blasius and Son Clothiers was owned by Frank Blasius, a native of Germany. The store occupied two floors and was a men's tailor shop where suits and coats were made by hand. Fred C. Grove was one of the skillful cutters at the establishment. The *Logan Daily News* was later housed in the building. The three-story building on the right was built by the International Order of Odd Fellows (IOOF). (Courtesy of JWH.)

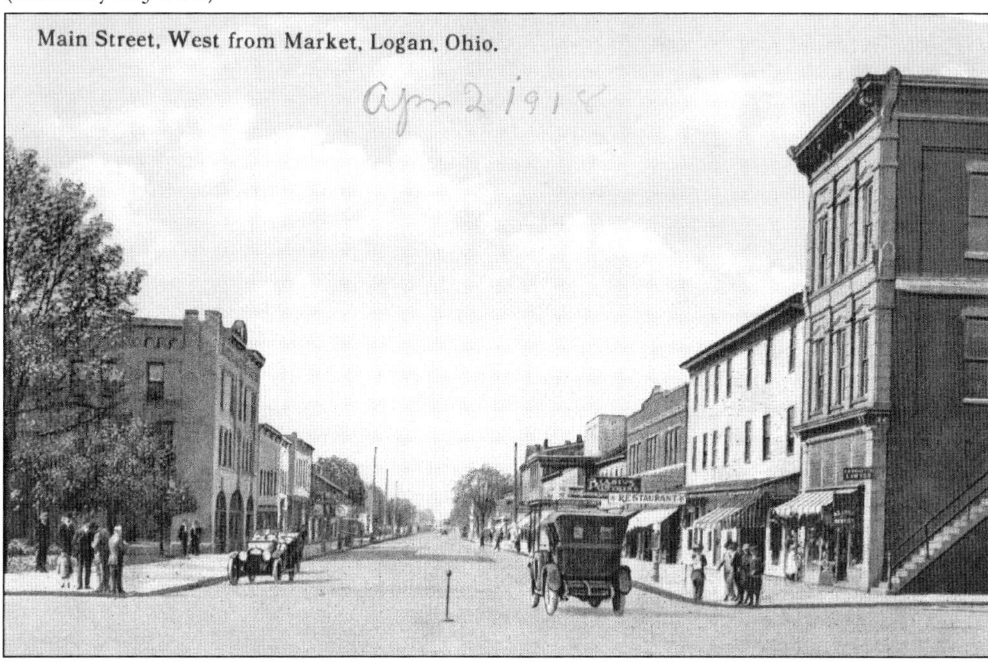

This tinted linen postcard shows the center of town, Main and Market Streets, with Worthington Park to the left. Dated 1918, notice there are no stoplights to guide the automobile traffic. (Courtesy of HH.)

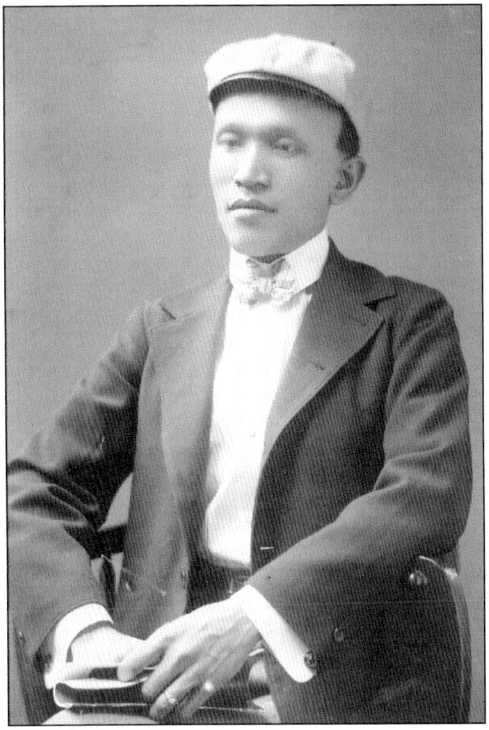

Chan Hop Sing sat for the photograph at left in 1908. He was born in Canton, China, and was the well-respected owner of the Star Laundry, located at 71 West Main Street across from the Opera House. His son Yee Hing Sing worked in the laundry from the age of 12. The younger Sing continued the laundry business after his father returned to China, moving it to a shop next to the Ruble Theater on North Market Street. After World War II, the laundry business slowed. Logan businessmen Earl and Merl Bell gave Sing a job at their Shamrock Café on Main Street and provided a place for him to live. For the next 45 years of his life, Yee Hing Sing was the short-order cook at the Shamrock. He died in 1989. The photograph of Chan Hop Sing belonged to Andrew Inboden, who was the older Sing's close friend. In the postcard below, the man in the derby hat is Inboden. (Both courtesy of JM.)

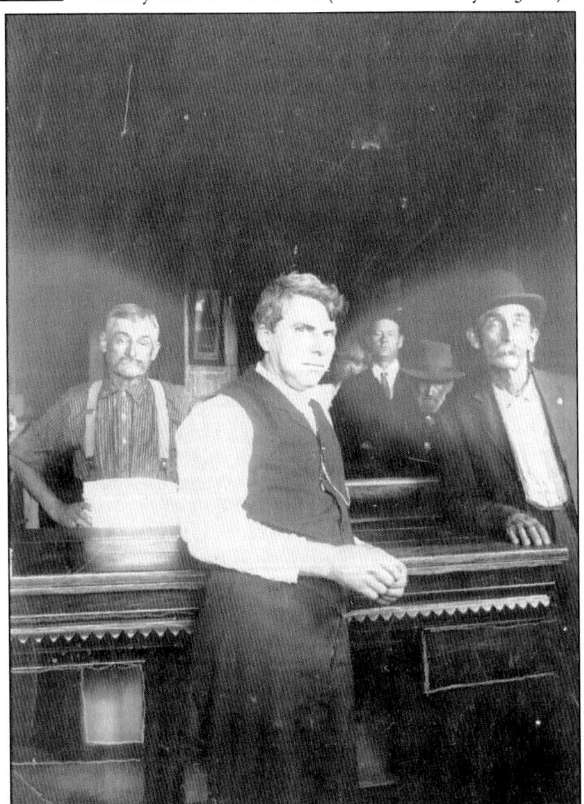

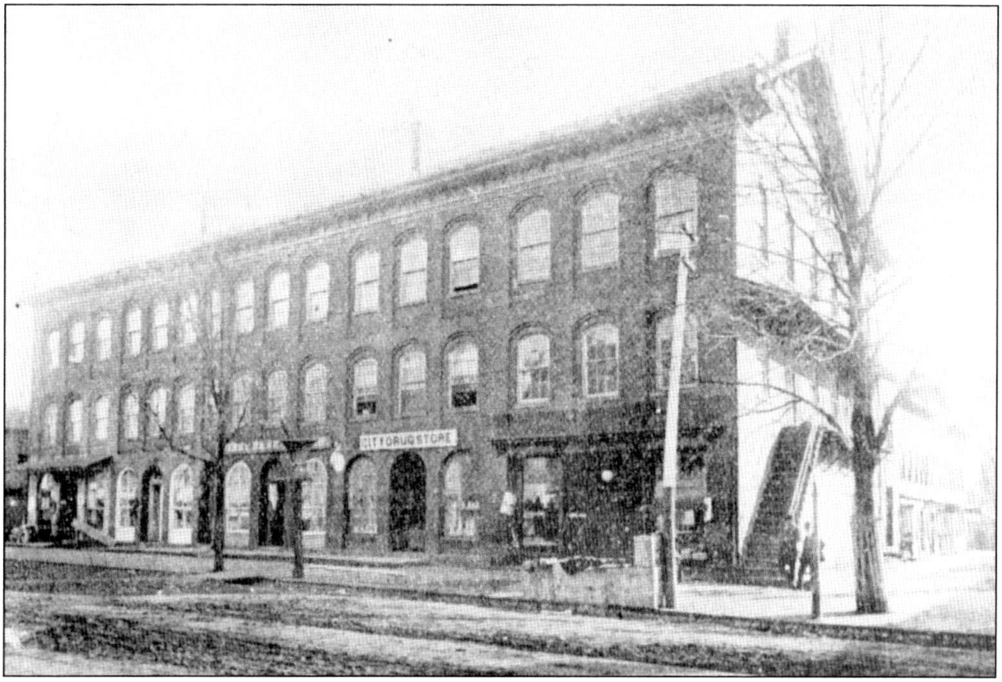

Charles W. James, the first mayor of Logan, constructed the James Building in 1860. The impressive three-story building was situated next to the Hocking County Courthouse, where it housed several businesses at the street level. At one time, the newspaper offices of the *Hocking Sentinel* were on the second floor. Having served the Logan community for over a century, the building was demolished in the 1970s to make way for the courthouse parking lot. (Courtesy of HH.)

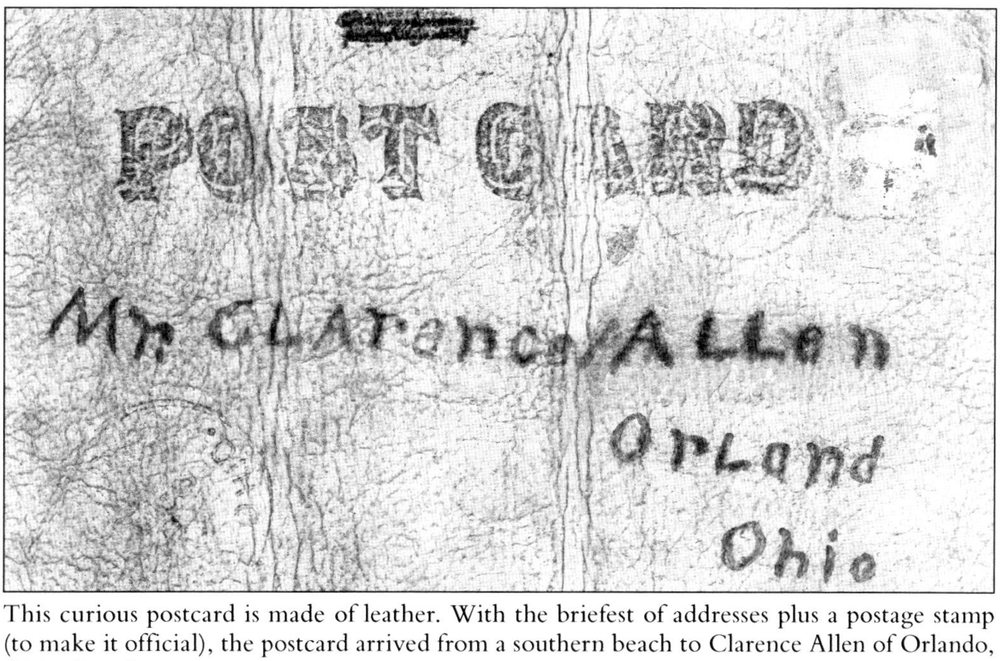

This curious postcard is made of leather. With the briefest of addresses plus a postage stamp (to make it official), the postcard arrived from a southern beach to Clarence Allen of Orlando, Ohio. (HH.)

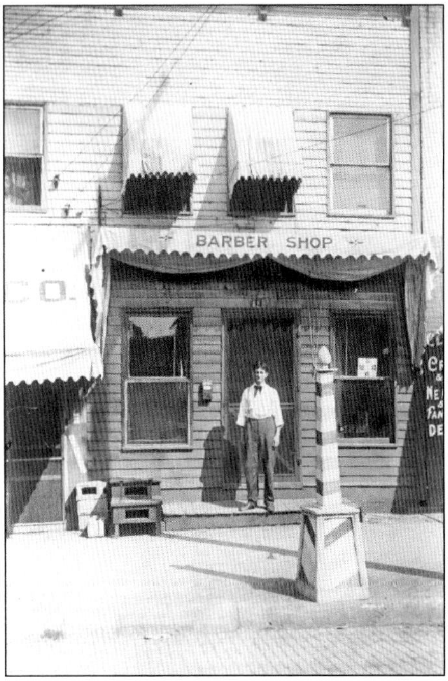

John Schempp's barbershop was located at 62 West Main Street, across from where the Elberfeld Building was later constructed. His son Charles and grandson Clarence continued the business, eventually moving it to a Victorian-style home at 98 North Culver Street. Clarence and his wife, Gertrude, operated a combination barbershop and beauty salon in the house for many years. The "Schempp House" is now a part of the Hocking County Historical Society campus and is open to the public for tours. (Courtesy of HH.)

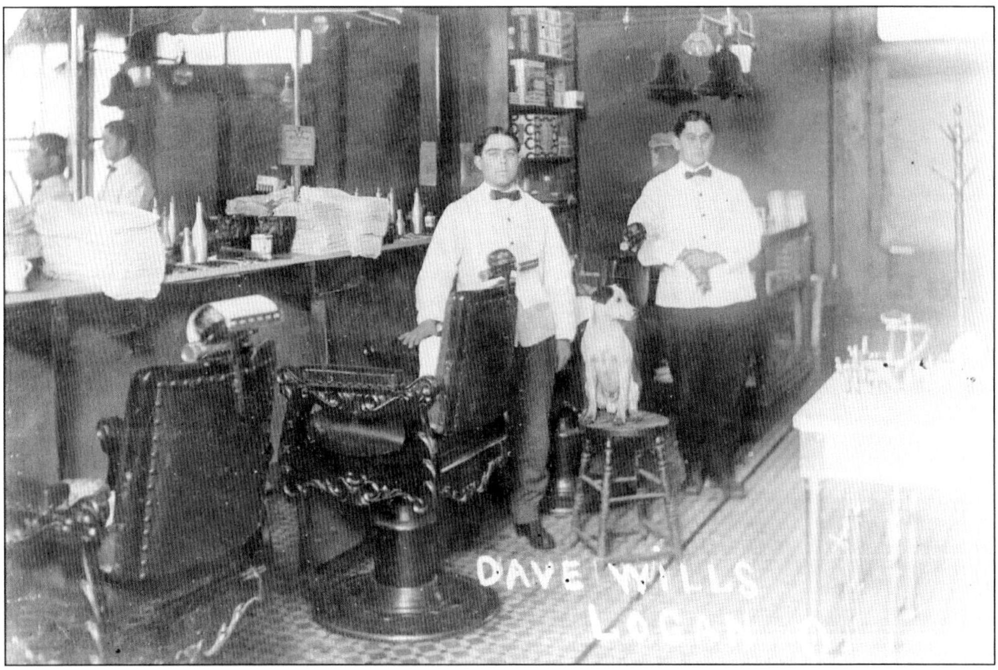

Back in the day, a well-appointed tonsorial parlor was sure to attract customers. Oliver Wills was a barber and owner of Wills Barber Shop, located "on the avenue." The phrase referred to the Gallagher Avenue Business District, and old-timers may still refer to it as such. This postcard shows two men, believed to be Oliver and his brother David C. Wills, who was also a barber. Their shop, at 380 Gallagher Avenue, stood across the street from the present Home Tavern. Unfortunately for Oliver, the printer of the postcard erred and only mentioned David. Oliver Wills died in Logan at the age of 70, and his pallbearers were all barbers. (Courtesy of WD.)

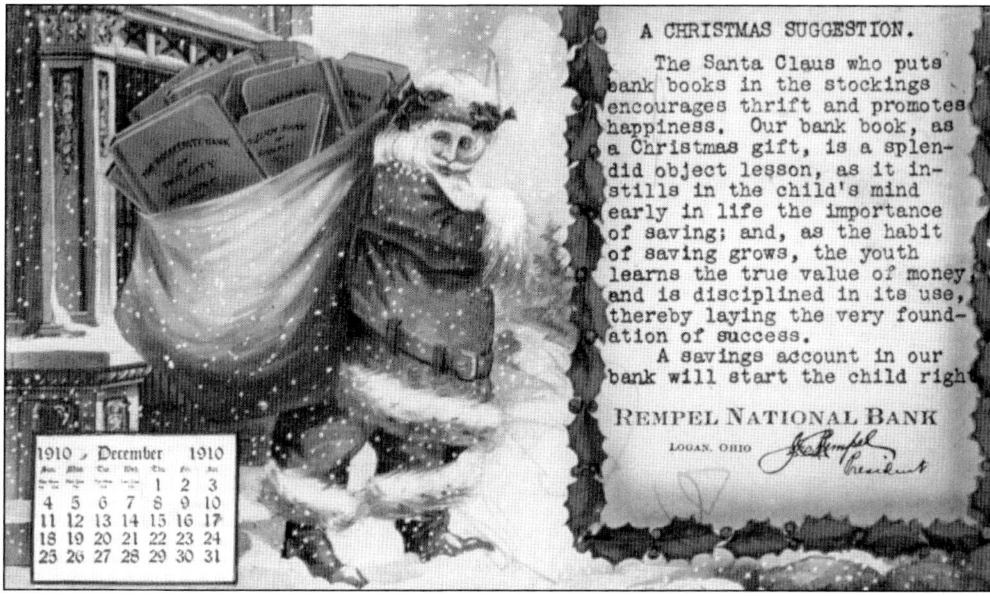

In 1895, Col. F.F. Rempel, one of the wealthiest men in the county (according to the "1916 Logan Centennial Souvenir Booklet"), opened the Rempel National Bank with assets of $220,000. He placed F.F. "Ferdie" Rempel Jr. in charge, with John R. Rempel as cashier and D.C. Bright and George C. Hengst as tellers. Colonel Rempel died suddenly in 1901. In 1911, the bank was reorganized with Howard E. White as president. The yearly calendar postcards were sent to patrons of the bank, urging for their continued support. The Rempel Building at the corner of Main and Market Streets, across from the courthouse, has since been home to Farmers and Merchants Bank, Keith's Men's Shop, and the Computer Store. (Courtesy of HH.)

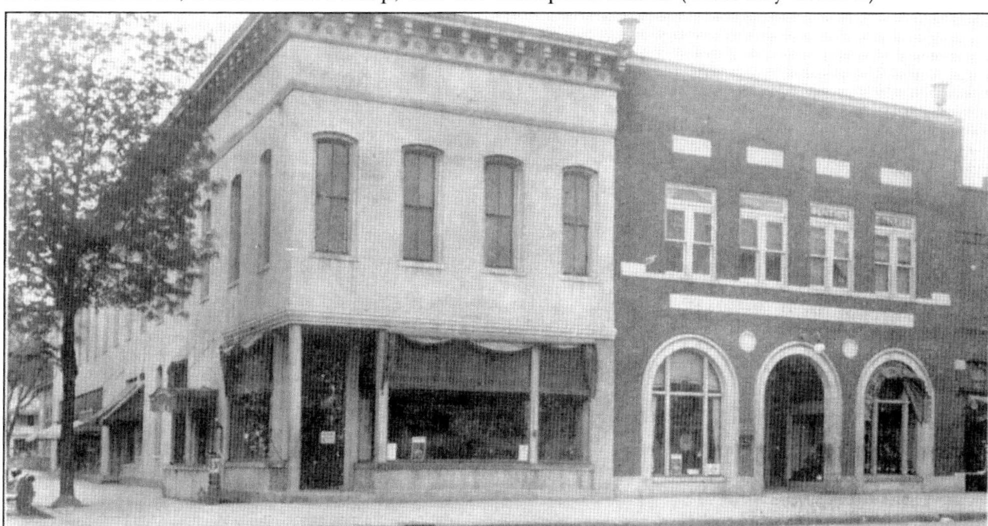

The White Arcade (with arches) was built in 1922, the brainchild of Howard White, president of the Rempel National Bank (at left). According to an August 28, 1937, article in the *Logan Daily News*, the arcade had an infinite variety of business enterprises, including a drug store, a confectionery, a haberdashery, the Arcade Shoe Store, and Poling's Barber Shop, among others. It remained an arcade until 1930, when the passageway was closed for more space. (Courtesy of HH.)

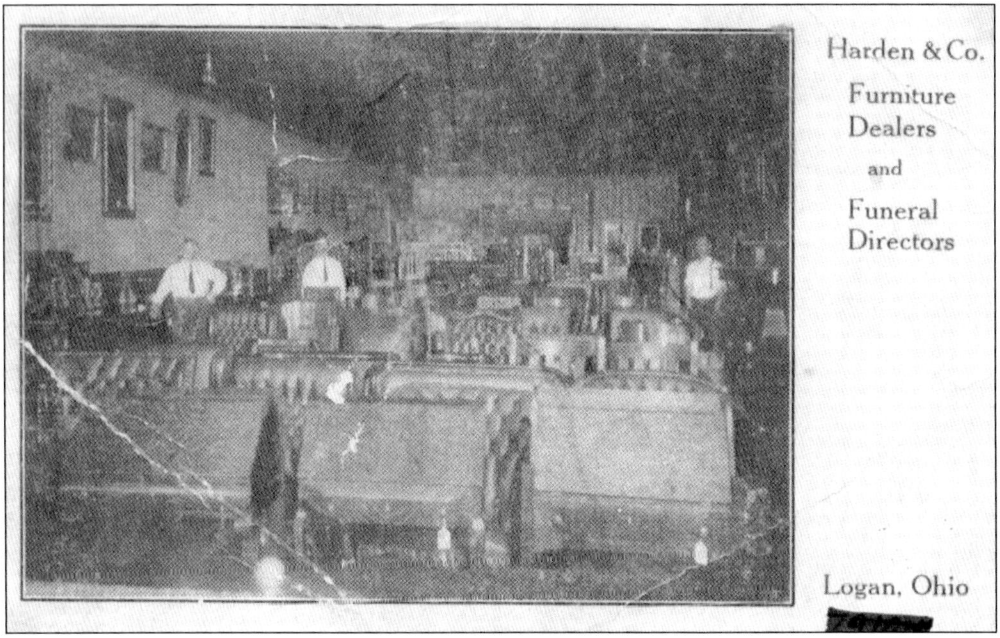

The Harden Company, Furniture Dealers and Funeral Directors, was founded in 1893 by Jasper F. Harden. Harden was an embalmer and funeral director, and R.E. Stevenson of Lancaster was his partner. The firm was located at the corner of East Main and Walnut Streets. When Harden died in 1915, Stevenson was named president. E.A. Gutliph purchased Harden's interest and was named both secretary and treasurer. Paul K. Foster was employed as an embalmer and funeral director, and Floyd Duffy was a salesman for the business. (Courtesy of HH.)

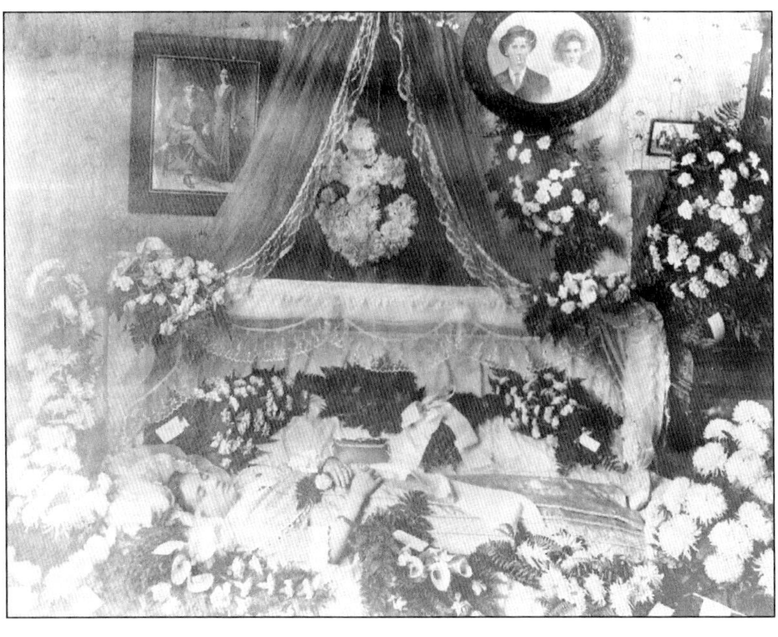

A postcard of the deceased was not an unusual sight. Mourning is a part of life, and the tradition of flowers and photographs to embellish the casket are still common today. Many years ago, the deceased would have been taken to the family home for viewing and visitation. (Courtesy of DB.)

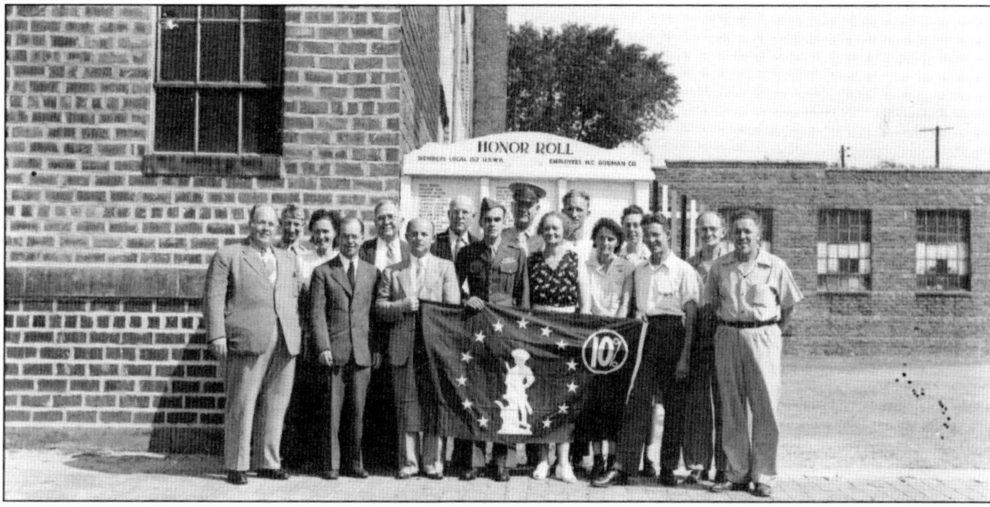

In May 1934, the H.C. Godman Shoe Company opened its doors in Logan with 300 new employees. Members of the CIO-WSWA Union Local 153 are pictured in this 1943 postcard. The Shoeworkers Union was being congratulated by local organizers of the Hocking County Unit of the US Saving Bond drive. Pictured here from left to right are (front row) Jimmy Young, Bertha Dearing, Earl Elberfeld (drive chairman), unidentified, Fred Shively, Rose Miller, unidentified, Marvin Kuhn, and John Belhorn; (second row) Fred Miller, two unidentified persons, Chuck Dalton, Teresa Kaiser, Harry Casto, and Rex Keller. Godman Shoe was located on Gallagher Avenue, and the building still stands today as a part of the Columbus Washboard Factory. (Courtesy of JM.)

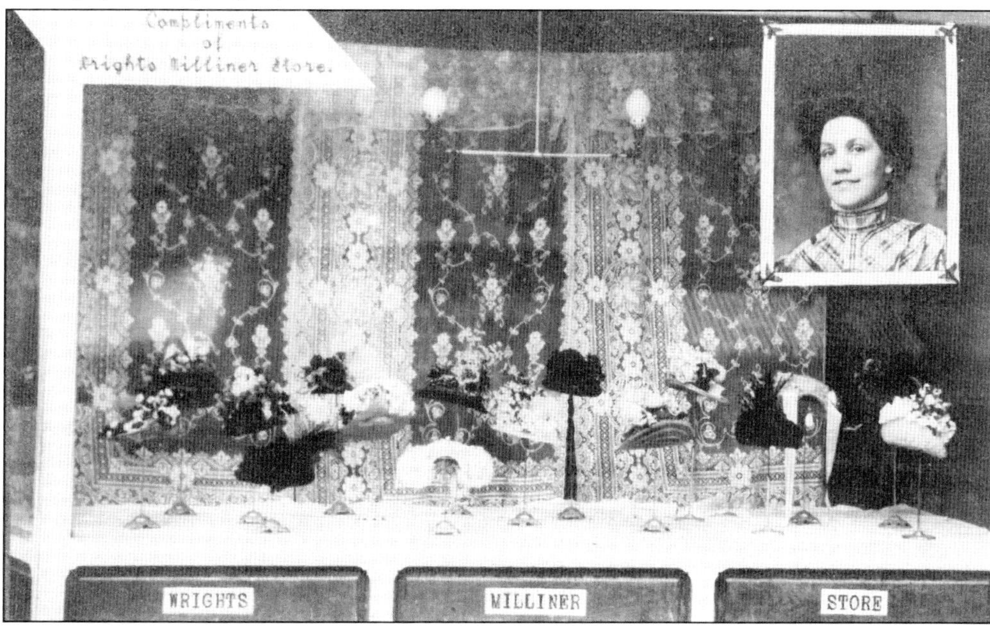

Postcards were a popular way to advertise a business, new or established. Millinery (hat making) was a popular career that was pursued by many women at the turn of the century. On March 15, 1907, future customers were invited to the grand opening of the Wright Milliner Store. It was located in the James Building on Main Street. Lulia P. Wright, owner, is pictured in the inset. Mary Goss was mentioned as the trimmer. (Courtesy of HH.)

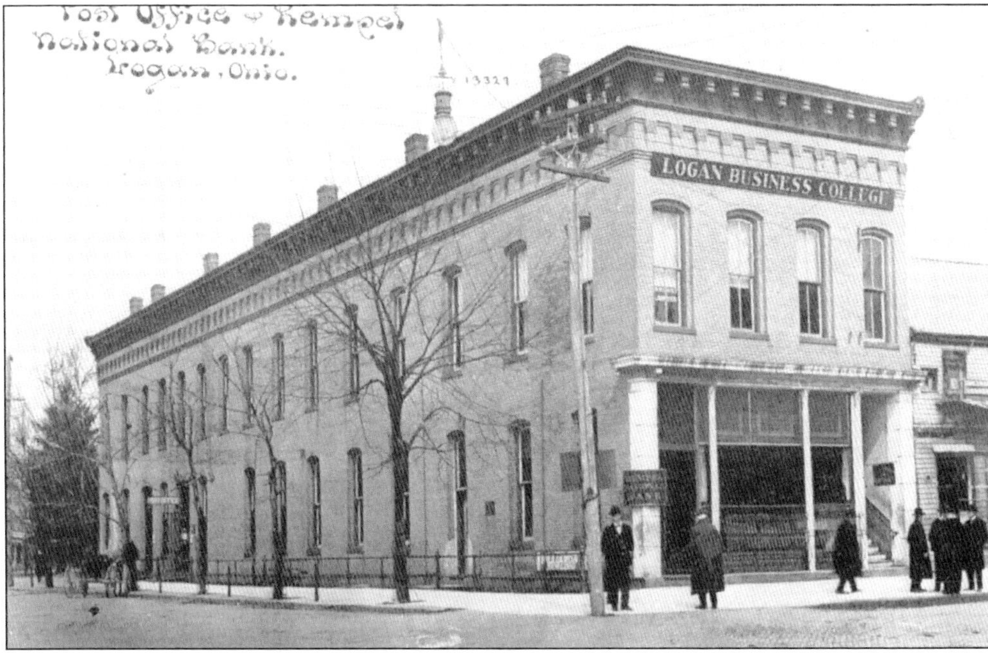

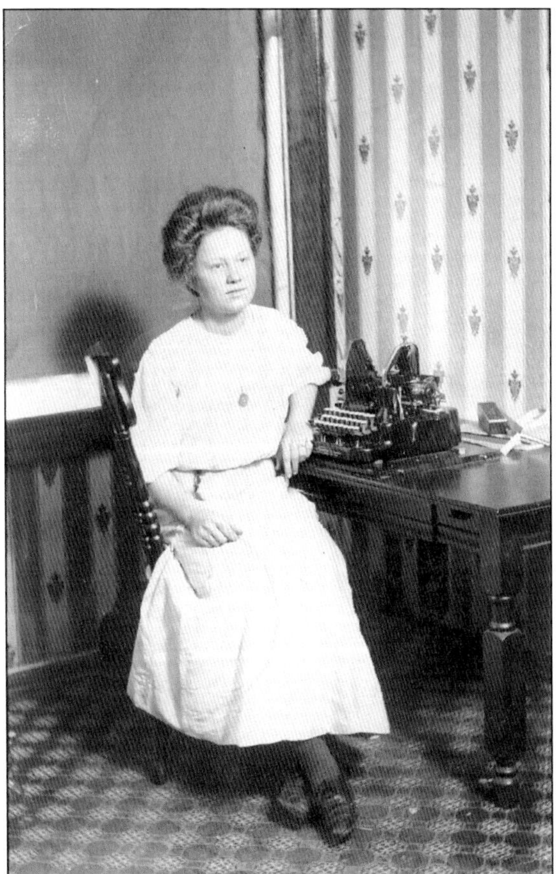

Logan Business College was founded by Prof. Arthur Kindler, several years prior to World War I. The school, located on the second floor of the Rempel National Bank Building, was popular but short-lived. In 1917, Kindler relocated his school to Lancaster, but it was closed when he entered the military. Notice the post office sign on the Market Street side of the building and the billiards sign referring to the lower-level entrance. (Courtesy of JM.)

This postcard is dated 1908 and was mailed from Nelsonville in Athens County, Ohio. Signed "Garnett," it shows an early typewriter, the Oliver Typewriter No. 3, which was distinguished by the U-shaped typebars that hover over the platen (large rubber roll). Garnett noted the photograph was taken at her place of employment, but the typist did not name the firm. (Courtesy of JM.)

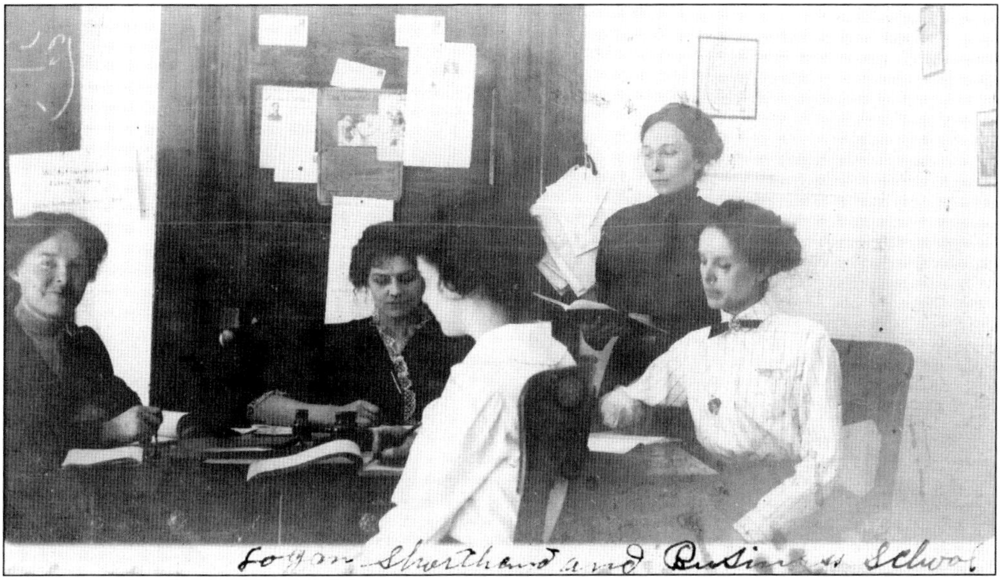

A rare postcard shows several young women studying what appears to be shorthand at Logan Business College. Nannie Young Winters was listed as a shorthand teacher in the "1910 Logan City Directory." The classes also taught the students typewriting and general office curriculum, educating women and enabling them to pursue a popular career. (Courtesy of HM.)

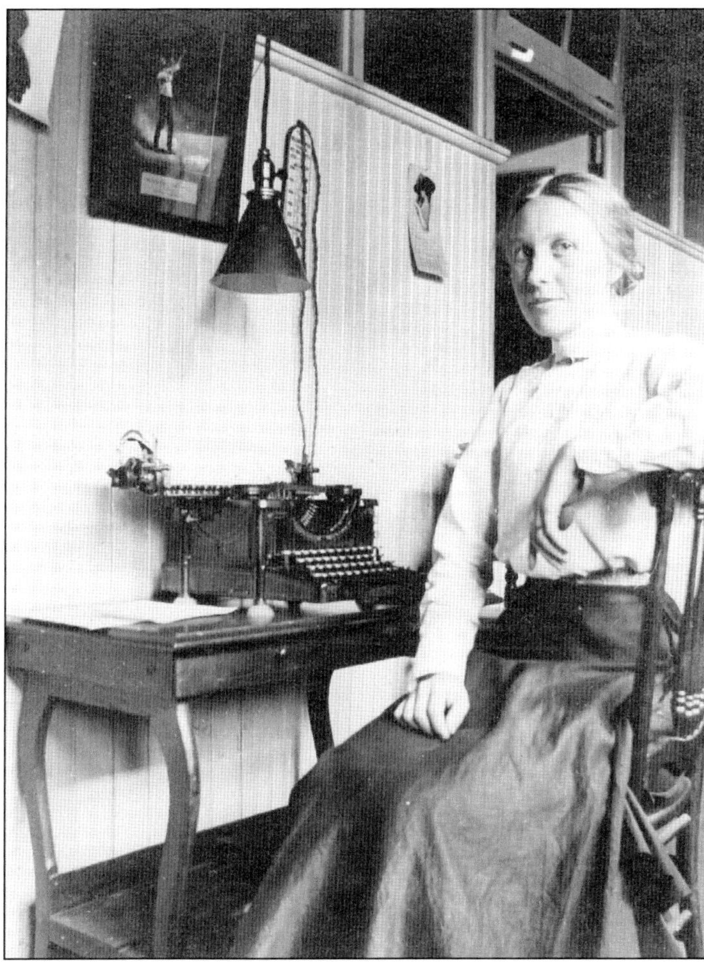

This 1913 image depicts a typical secretary's workstation. Although not spacious, it was her domain, earned by her ability and organization. It took physical effort to use the old typing machines. (Courtesy of HH.)

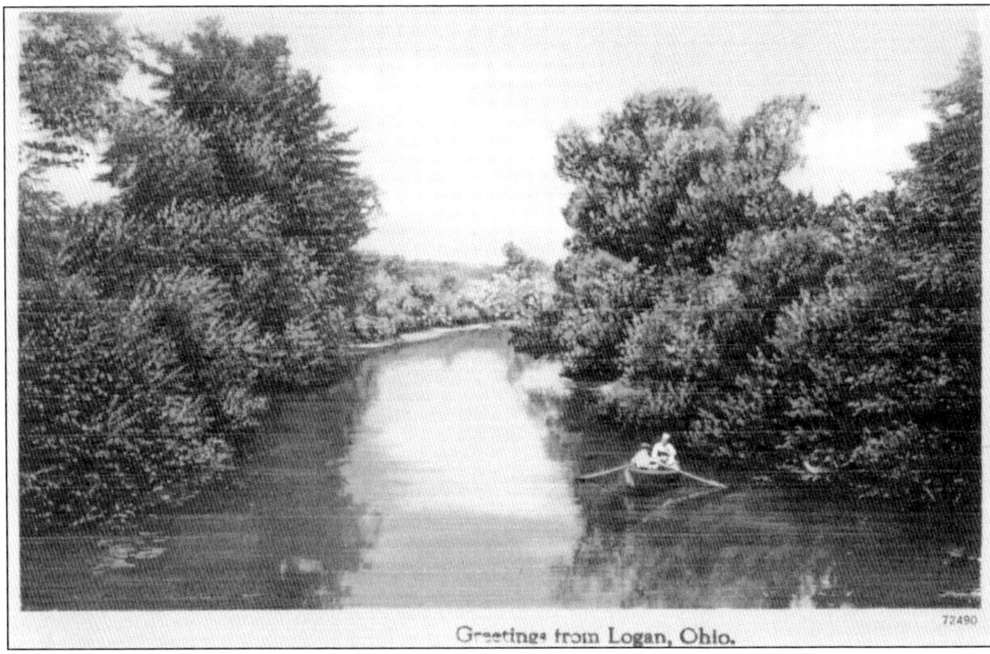

A couple is seen rowing down the peaceful Hocking River (above) in a 1944 greeting postcard from Logan, Ohio. A calm Hocking River scene (below) was captured "below Falls Mill." *Hockhocking* was the Native American word for "neck," which described the river at its beginning, near Lancaster. The settlers shortened the name to Hocking. (Both courtesy of CCH.)

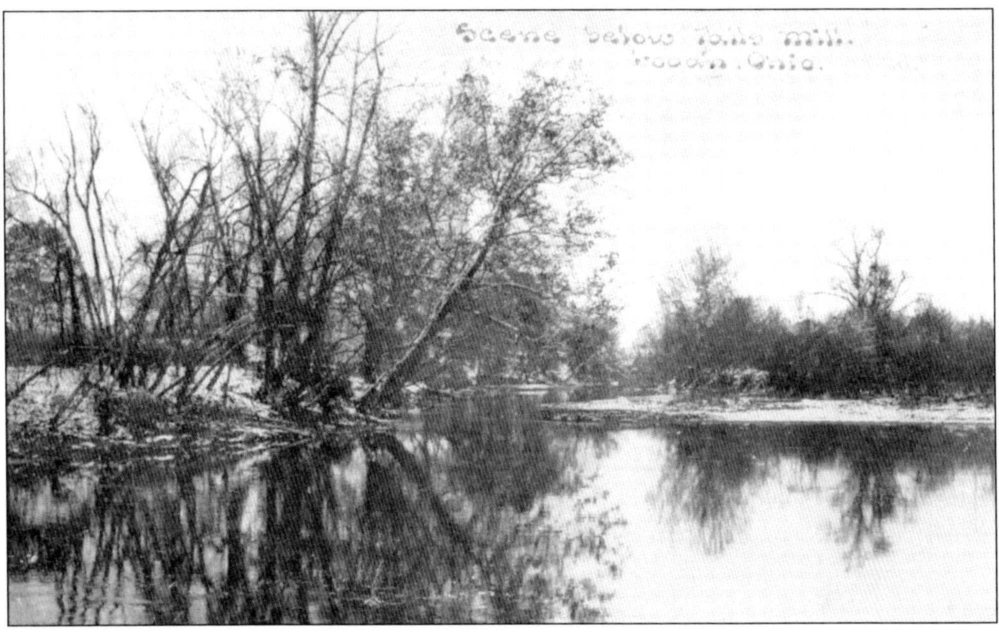

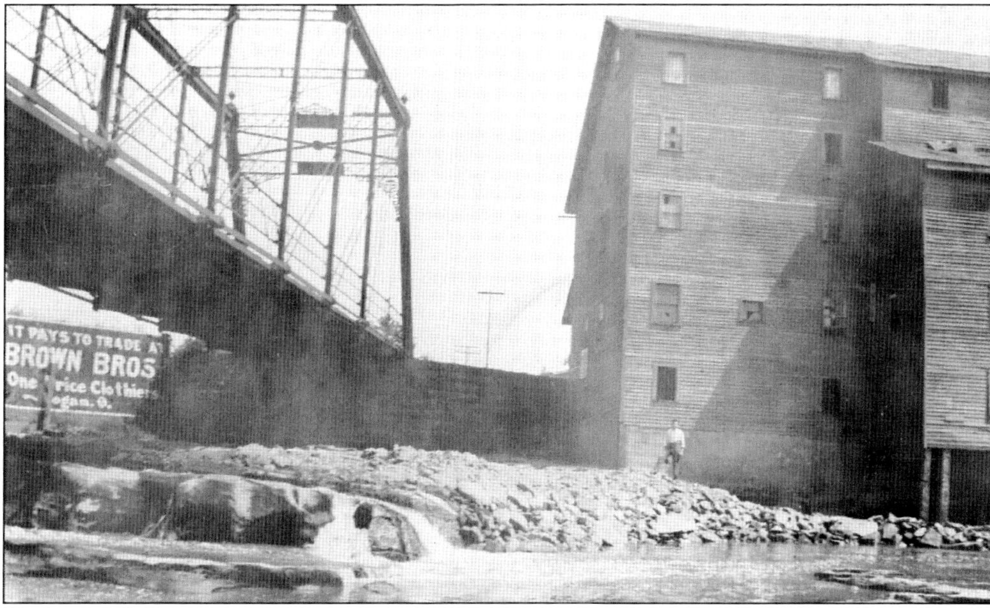

This scene from the Hocking River, showing the three-story Falls Mill and bridge, gives a glimpse of an early advertising billboard for Brown Brothers Clothing. The brothers—Daniel, Frank, and Rudolph—were merchant tailors. In the "1909 Logan City Directory," the Browns advertised that the clothing store was selling men's suits and overcoats from $10 to $20. Brown Brothers was located on East Main Street. (Courtesy of HH.)

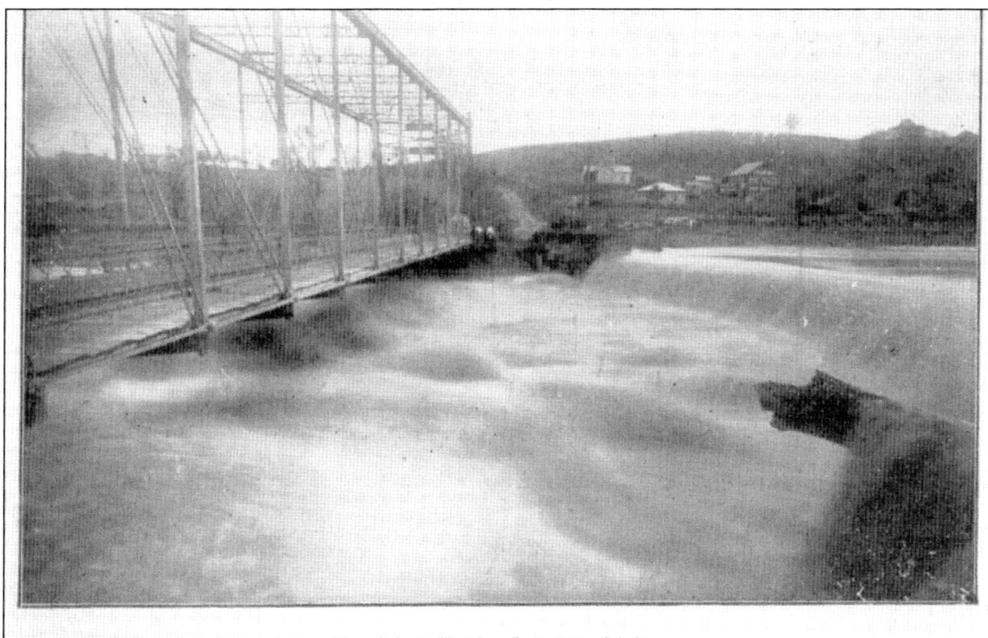

The Falls of the Hocking were the reason Thomas Worthington, the sixth governor of Ohio, chose the location for his mill. The waterpower needed to turn the mill wheel was ideal. Worthington owned many mills, but in 1816 he laid out a town and named it Logan, after the famous Native American of the Mingo tribe. (Courtesy of HH.)

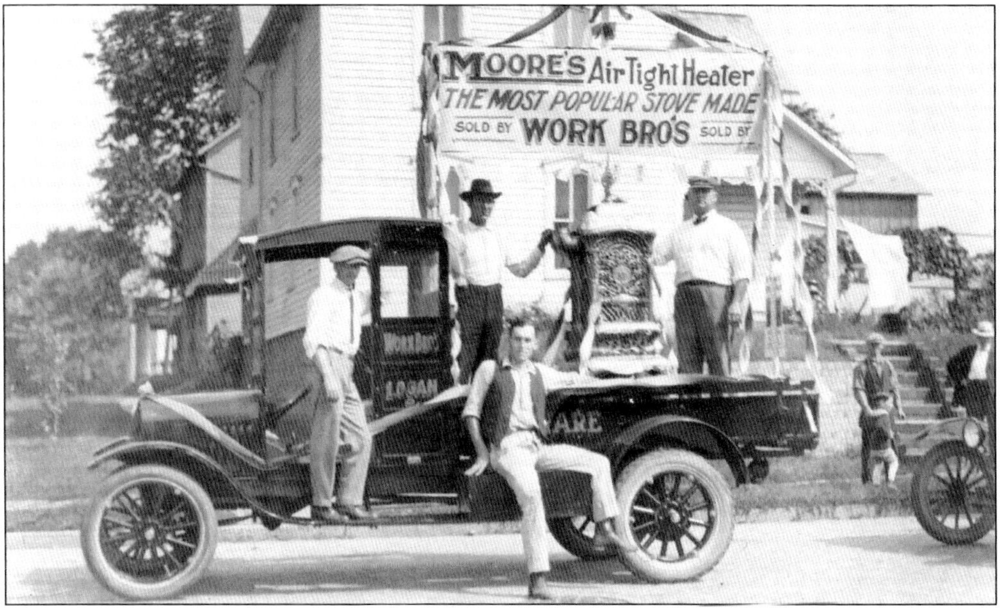

Another parade offered another chance to advertise. Work Brothers Hardware at 125 East Main Street was opened in 1890 by Robert R. Work and son Charles, who managed the business. Two of the men on the truck are identified as Merve Martin and Fred Kleinschmidt. According to old advertisements, the Works were "dealers in hardware, stoves, and ranges." J. Walter Saving purchased the business in the 1930s. Saving's sons John and Walter F. successfully operated the business for 50 years, and now, 65 years later, several grandsons continue the operation. Saving Hardware is a Main Street landmark. (Courtesy of HH.)

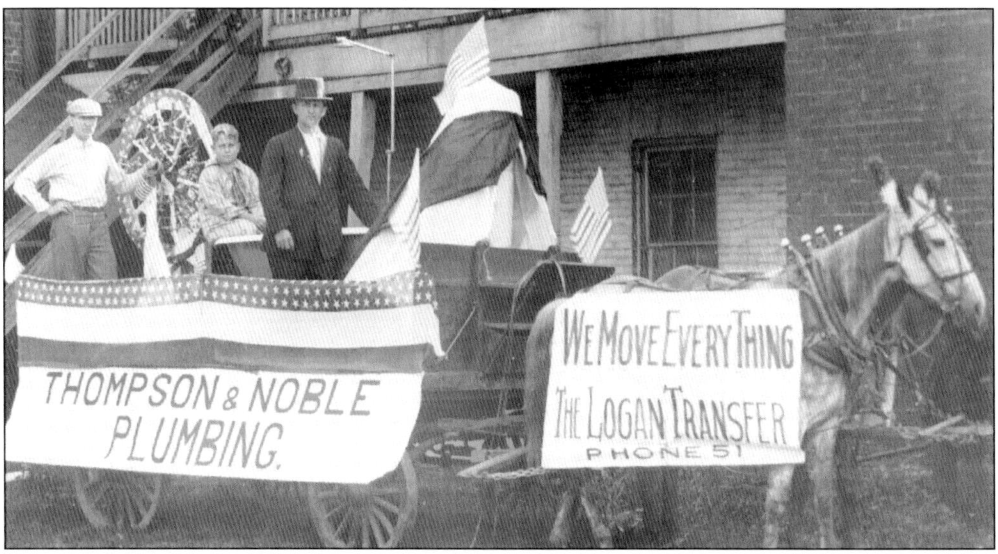

The banner for the Logan Transfer and Storage Company reads, "We Move Everything," and to prove a point, they used a horse to pull a fully loaded wagon. Note the young boy sitting on the edge of the tub on the wagon. Lewis Price, proprietor of Logan Transfer, had a building at 47 East Hunter Street that was used for furniture storage. In later years, Price's sons Carl, Ernest, and Kenneth continued the transfer business until the 1970s. The Thompson and Noble Plumbing Company was in business on Orchard Street. (Courtesy of TP.)

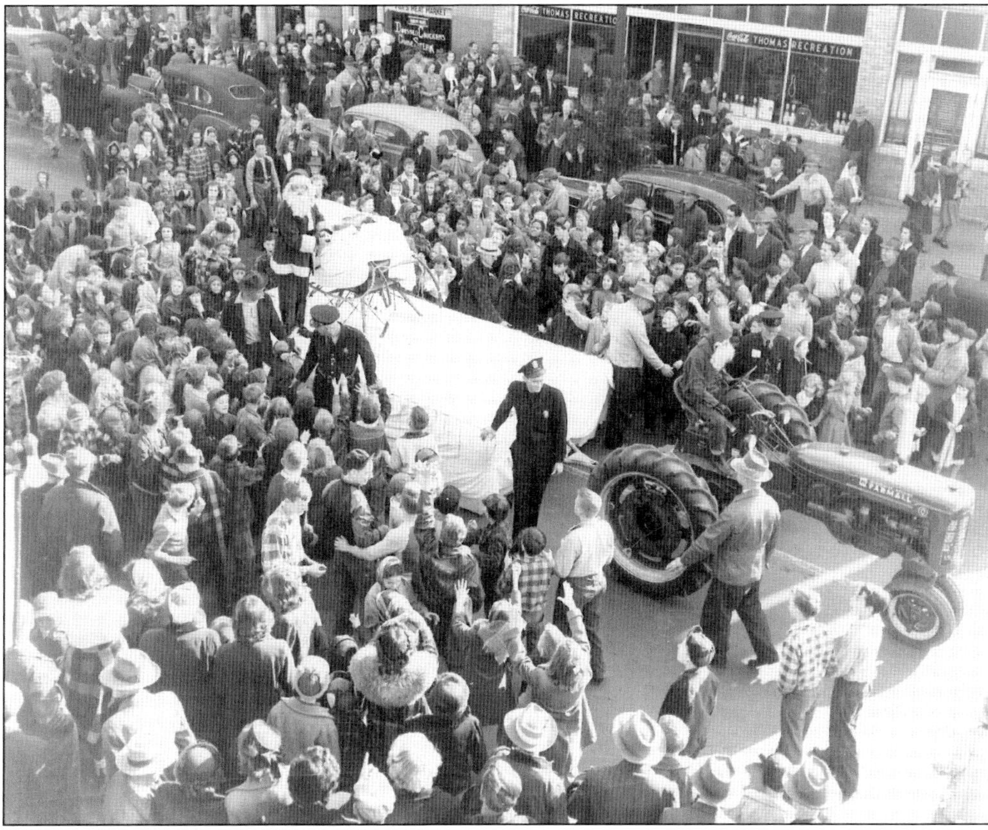

Logan has always been a parade town, and Main Street is a perfect setting for any event. A Santa Claus parade about 1948 shows the throngs of young people anxious to see Santa and his elves. As Hocking County is farm country, a tractor served as Santa's sleigh. (Courtesy of HH.)

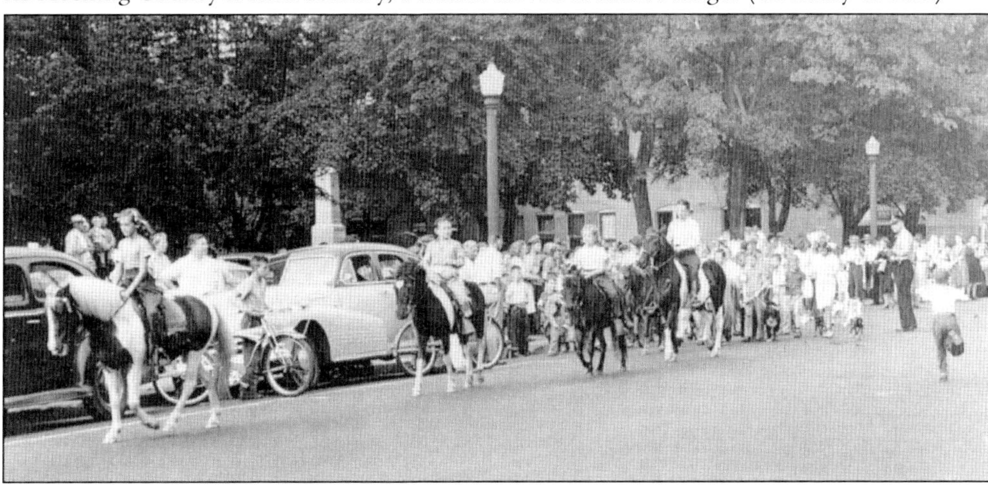

For several years, a pet parade was held in conjunction with the Hocking County Fair. The competitors would line up at Worthington Park and parade down Main Street to the judging at the fairgrounds. In this photograph, two people are identified: the girl leading the parade is Kay Cannon, on her pony Lady; and Janie Risch, third from the left, is riding Teddy, her Shetland pony. Children with assorted pets bring up the rear. (Courtesy of HH.)

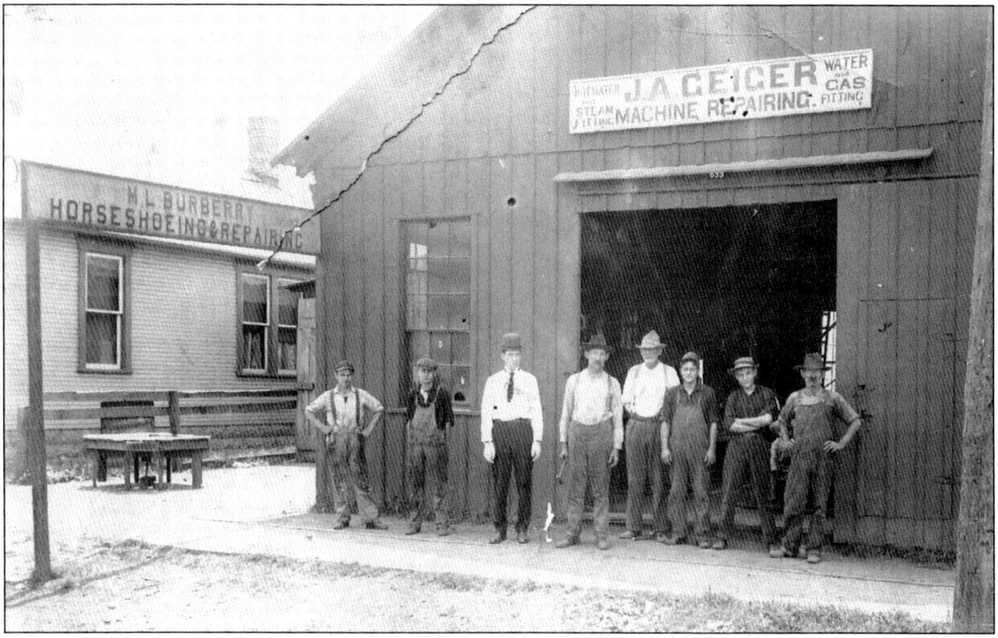

John A. Geiger, a machinist by trade, opened a shop in Logan about 1880. As the business prospered and the years progressed, it became J.A. Geiger and Sons. This postcard shows the shop when the business was located at 538 West Front Street, near the alley where Bob's Pizza is located today. J.A. is the gentleman fourth from the left, and the boy second from the right is one of his sons, Jacob Geiger. After World War I, Geiger's sons Bernard and John rejoined their father in the plumbing business. (Courtesy of PNG.)

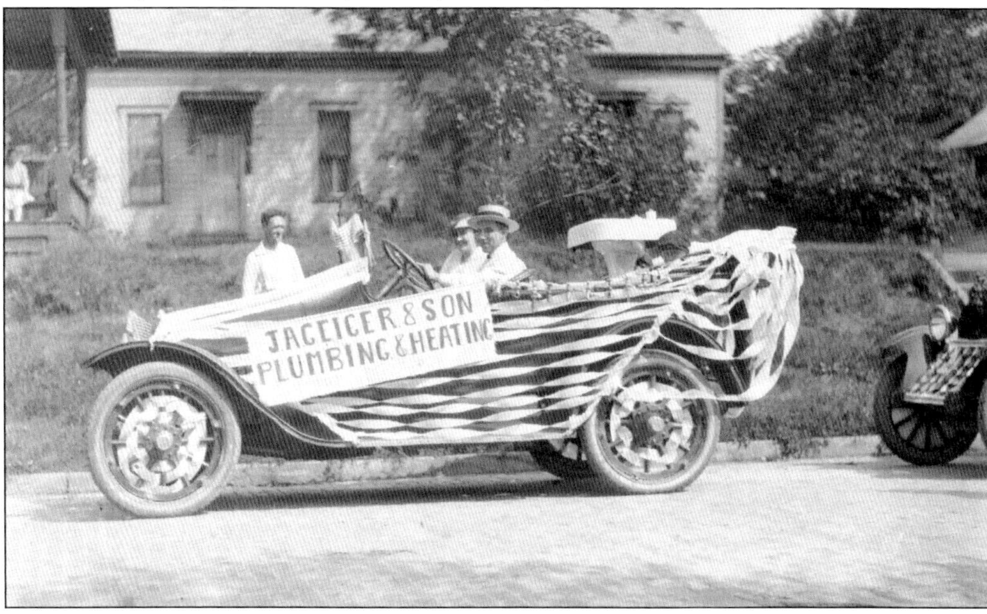

This postcard shows a parade car advertising J.A. Geiger and Sons Plumbing. At the wheel is Bernard Geiger, and by his side is his wife, Leota. Notice the sink in the back seat. Geiger Brothers continued operation with extended family members and remained an important business in the area until the company was sold in the late 1950s. (Courtesy of PNG.)

A fairly new idea known as a carryout business was begun in Logan in 1948. Nick Maniskas Sr. opened his shop at 609 West Hunter Street and built a loyal following of customers for the next 30 years. His clever slogan, "Pick Nick's for Pic-Nic supplies," was used in advertising for years. In the 1970s, the business was moved to larger quarters and featured food takeout as well. Maniskas retired in 1975, and his son Nick Jr. managed the business. (Courtesy of TP.)

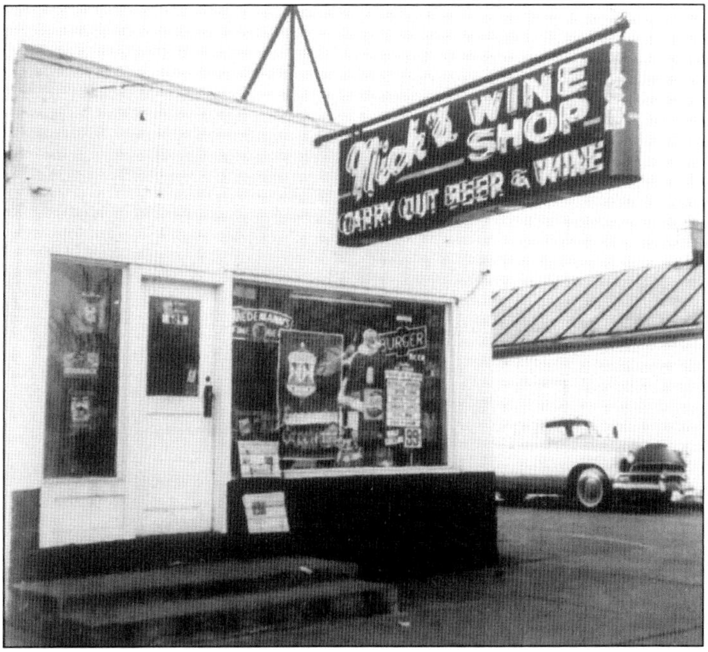

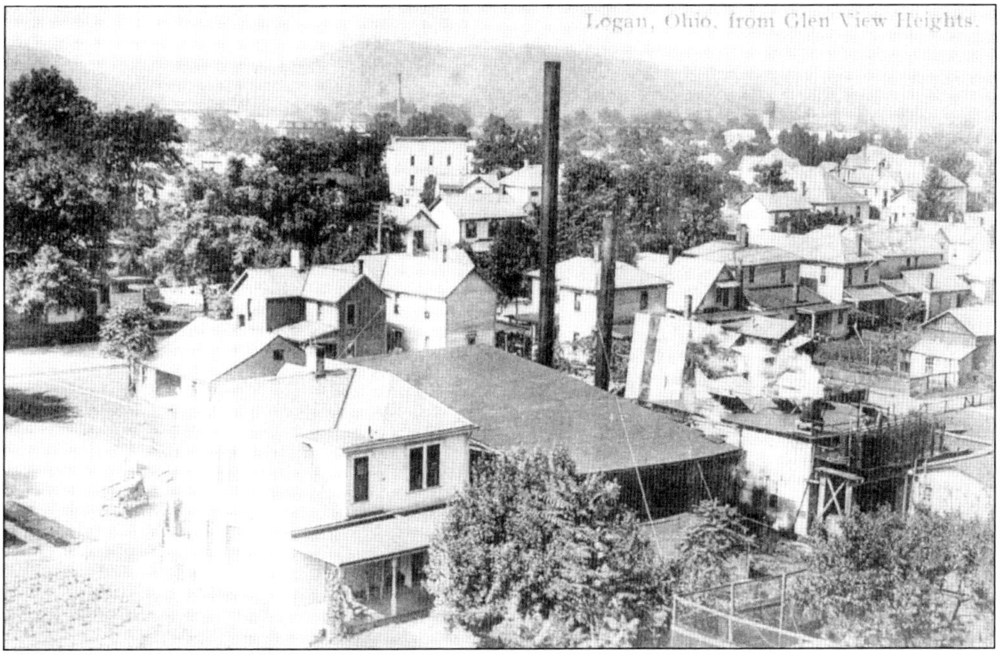

In 1930, an unusual view of Logan was taken from Glenview Heights, as noted on the postcard. The building with the tall stacks is the Hocking Ice and Storage Company, listed at 150 North High Street. The president and owner was Linden Showalter, and his son Robert managed the business. Ice was manufactured in blocks, broken into smaller chunks, and hand-delivered to homes and businesses. In 1937, the company was selling "modern ice refrigerators for the home." (Courtesy of MT.)

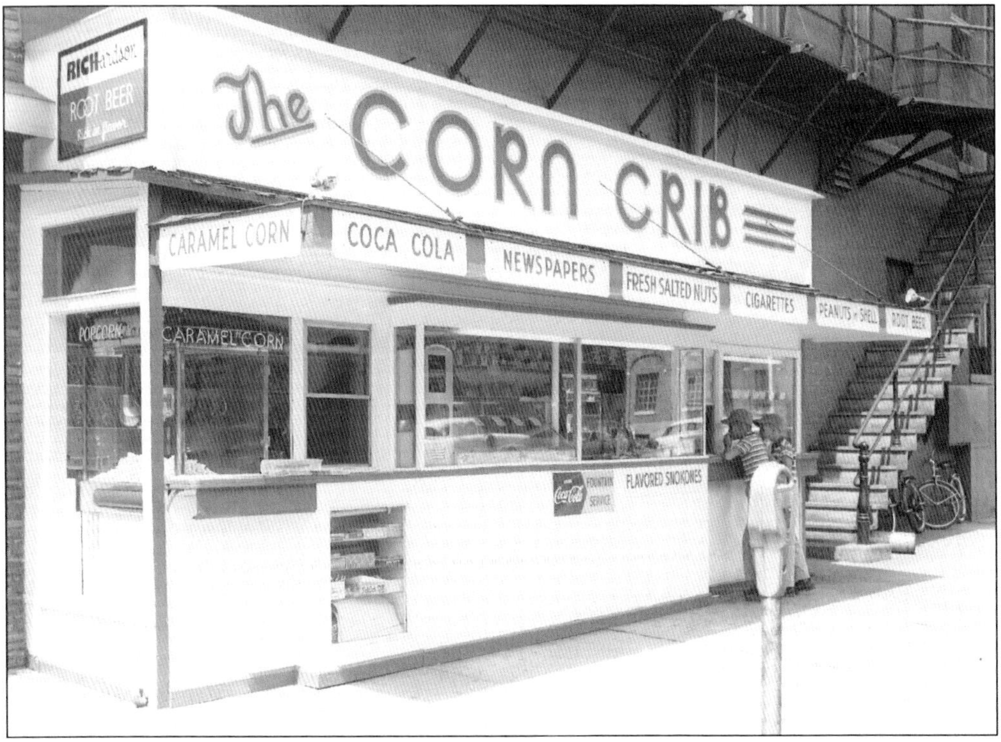

On June 16, 1938, a small notice appeared in the *Logan Daily News* announcing the opening of The Corn Crib, a new business. The proprietor of the galley-like structure on the Market Street side of the McCarthy-Blosser Building was Lyle Hall. Logan native Ned Gabriel purchased the popular spot in 1948. The Gabriel family, including teenage daughters Bonnie G. St. Clair and Sandra G. Wells, helped run the store. Others known to have been employed there over the years include Bea Lash Stallsmith, Louise Lash Van Fossen, Donna Kuhn, Dorothy VanVooris, and Linda Brenick. Gabriel sold the business in 1963, and it has since been razed. (Courtesy of HH.)

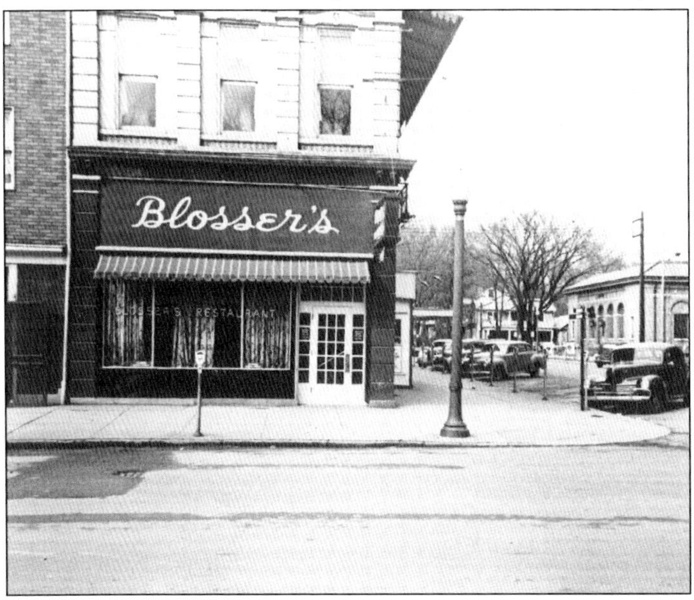

In April 1934, Clarence Blosser opened a fine dining restaurant on the northwest corner of Main and Market Streets. Blosser's Restaurant was a popular establishment in the area, with several local clubs meeting regularly in the banquet room. Many travelers to the Hocking Hills made the restaurant part of their destination. Blosser and his wife, Mary Keller Blosser, continued operation of the business until their retirement in 1966. (Courtesy of HH.)

The Shake Shoppe was a success from its opening day in 1950. Owned by Kenneth Conaway, it specialized in soft-serve ice cream. The Shoppe was located at 1205 West Hunter Street, which Conaway enlarged many times over the years and added an eat-in restaurant. Conaway's son Dwight and granddaughter Kathy Conaway Hartman were the second owners and added a catering service. In 1998, just 10 days after a major remodeling of the interior, the Shake Shoppe burned to the ground. The property was sold to Burger King. (Courtesy of MT.)

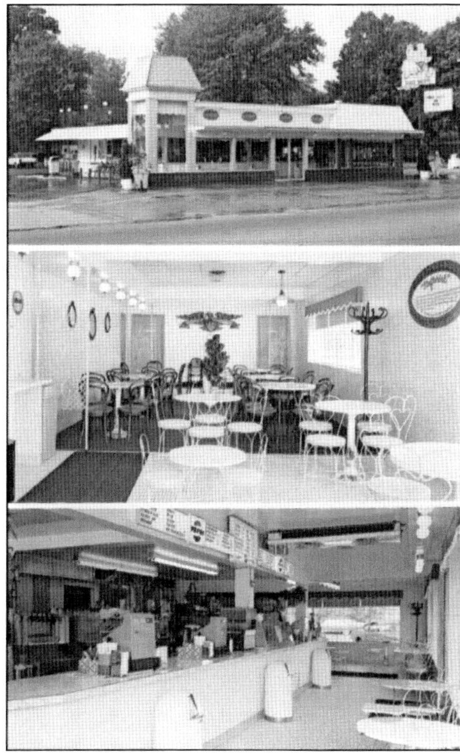

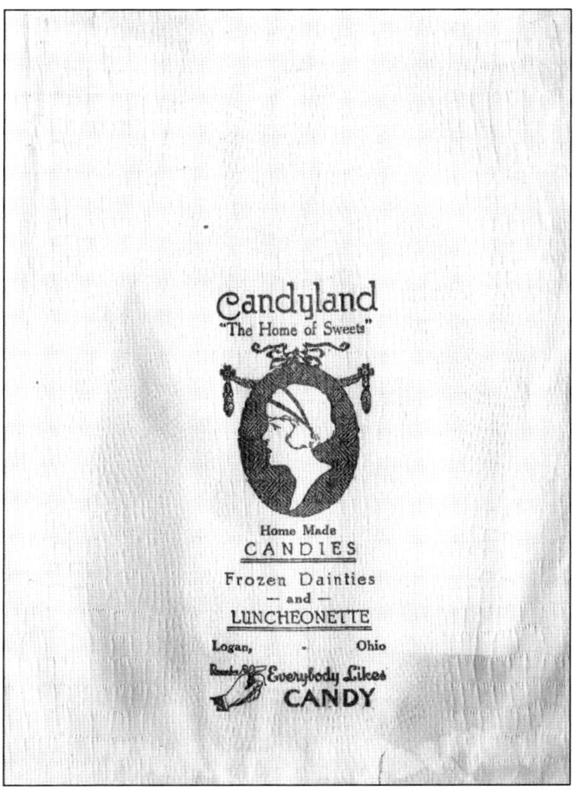

Candyland, "The Home of Sweets," was located at 28 West Main Street, opposite the Ambrose Hotel. Hays R. and Elizabeth Pritchard's homemade candy business thrived, and later a fountain and luncheonette were added to the shop. Eventually, the name was changed to Pritchard's Restaurant, and it operated well into the 1940s. This image is of a candy bag that has survived the years. The building is currently occupied by M&M Diner. (Courtesy of JM.)

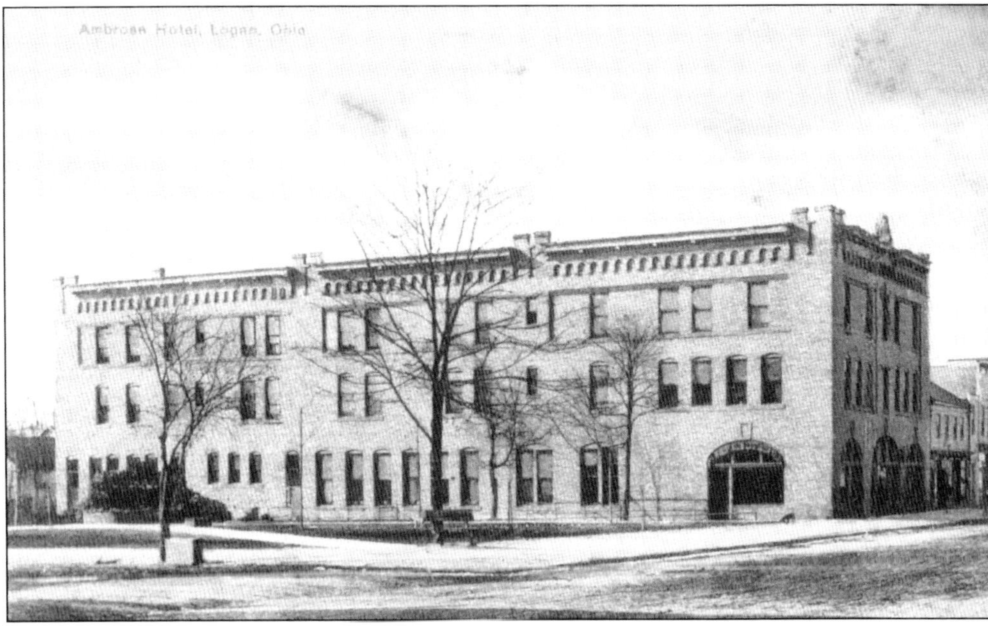

The Ambrose Hotel (above) was built in 1907 by H.F. "Hod" Ambrose, a hotelier from Lancaster. It was an oasis for travelers due to its fine dining and spacious sleeping rooms. A later view of the Ambrose (below) includes a scene of Worthington Park. (Both courtesy of JM.)

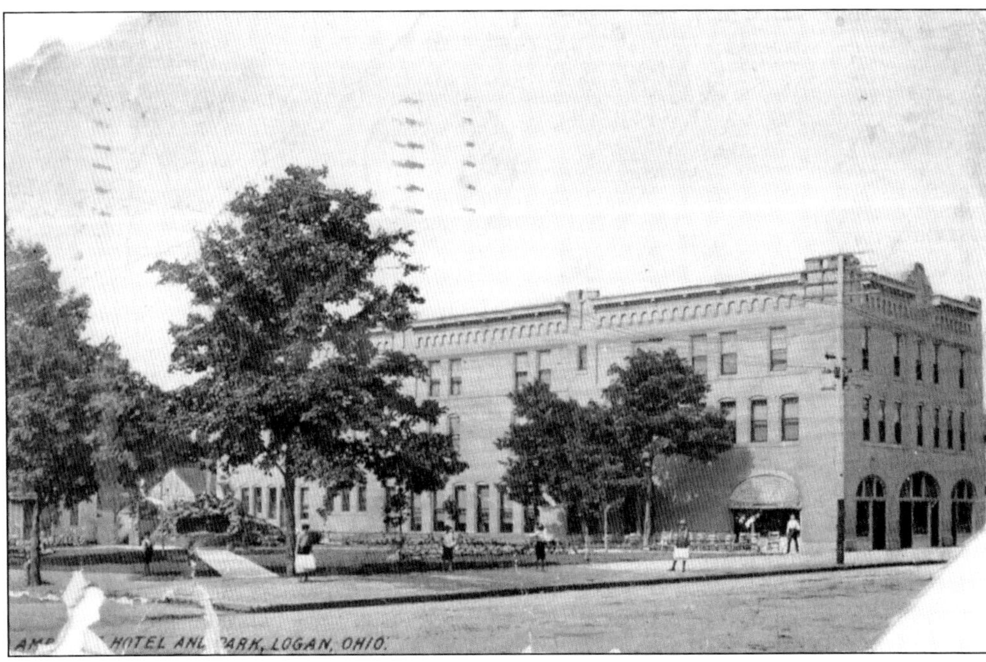

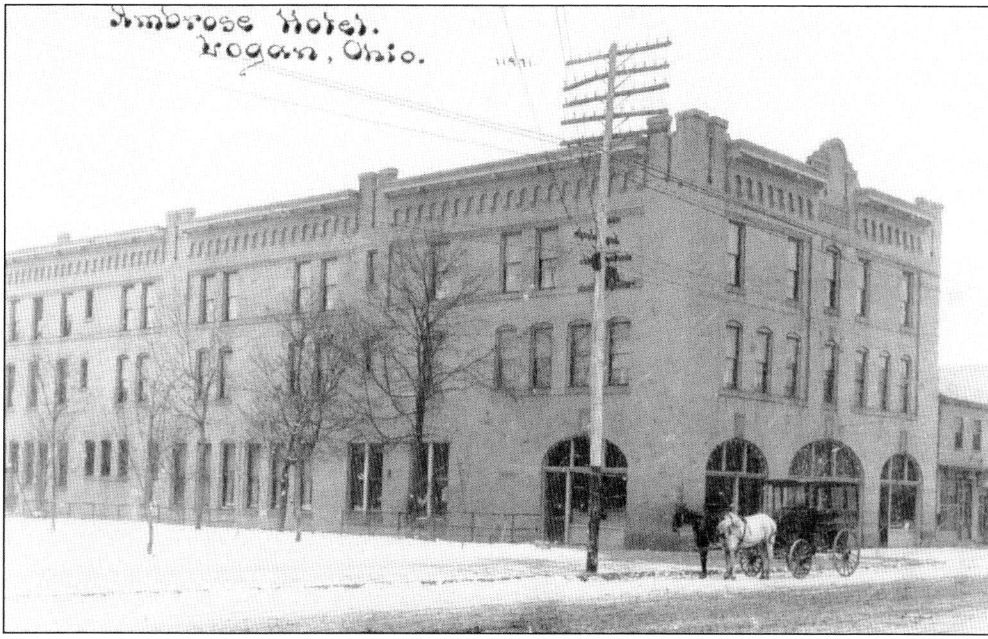

The Ambrose Hotel (above) is shown in a winter postcard. The year is about 1909, as Logan's streets were not paved until that time. The horse and buggy were the main mode of transportation, but time marches on, and the linen postcard (below) shows the paved street and automobiles. In 1921, the park fountain was replaced with the statue, *The Boys in Blue*, honoring Civil War veterans. (Both courtesy of JM.)

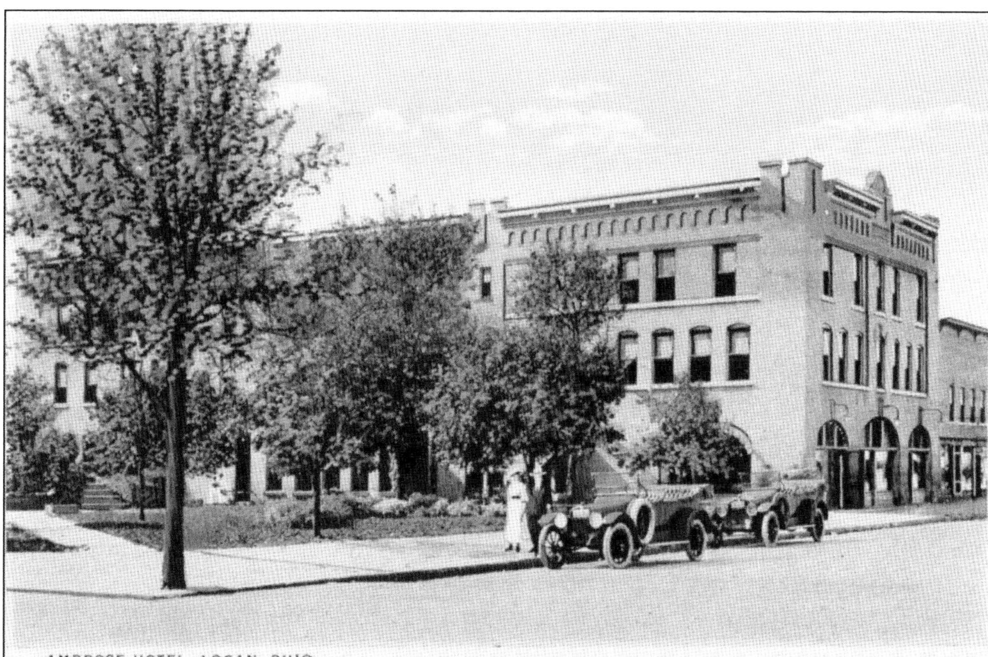

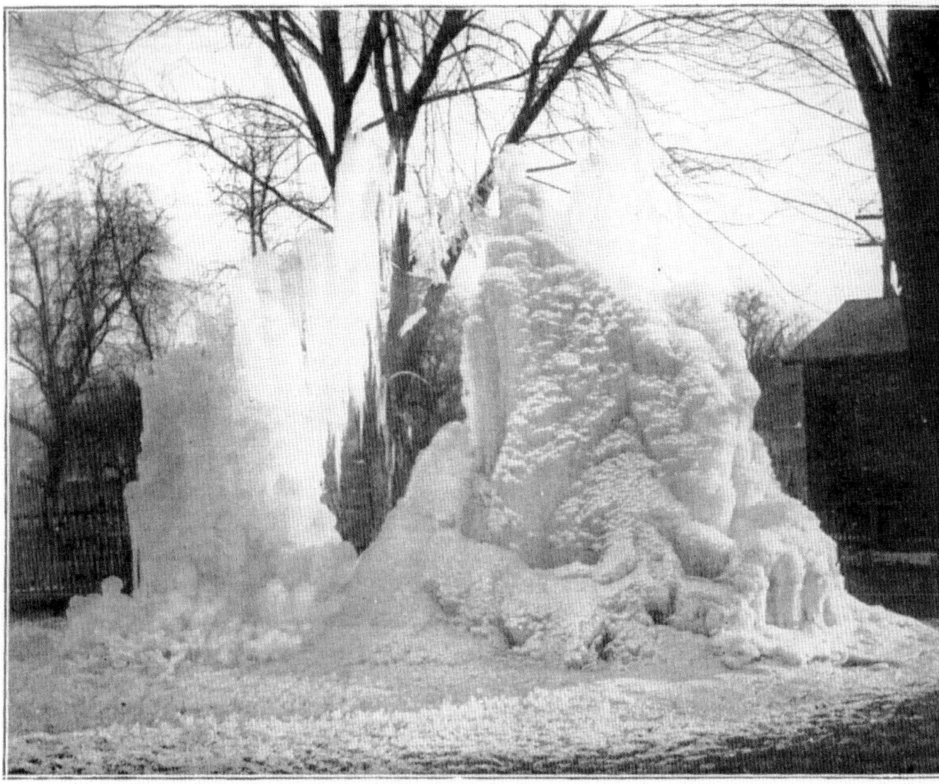

Depot Hotel Fountain in Winter, Logan, Ohio

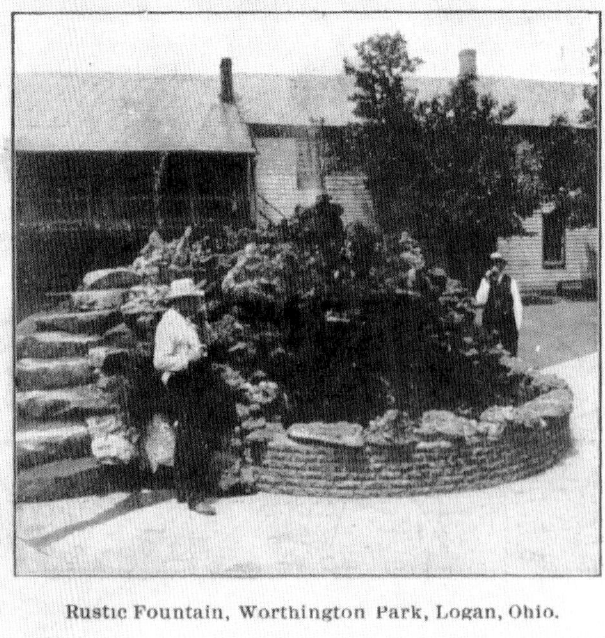

Rustic Fountain, Worthington Park, Logan, Ohio.

The Depot Hotel at the railway station (above) had an impressive decorative fountain to welcome travelers to town. This is a postcard showing the fountain's ice formation in winter. In its early days, the city park lot was unkempt until the editor of the newspaper implored the women of Logan to organize a cleanup and plant trees and flowers in the square. (Both courtesy of JM.)

American Fence was sold at Edgar Pleukharp's hardware store in Logan. This card, dated 1911, was sent out to Pleukharp's customers as a reminder that "now is the time to buy fence." The business also sold stoves, implements, paint, and hardware. The store was located on East Main Street at Hunter Street. (Courtesy of HH.)

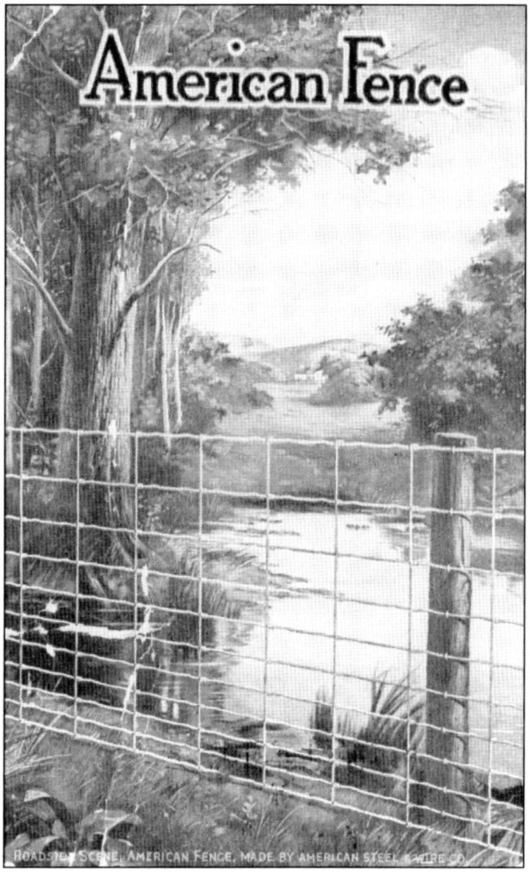

Gen. Lewis "Lew" Wallace was a lawyer and Civil War general, best remembered as the author of the 1880 epic novel, *Ben-Hur: A Tale of the Christ*. A memorial edition of the book was offered by Sears, Roebuck and Company, but the year is unknown. The postcard depicts the chariot race scene from the book jacket. Originally, the book sold for $1.56, but Sears, Roebuck offered it for 48¢. If shipped by mail, postage would be an additional 12¢. (Courtesy of HH.)

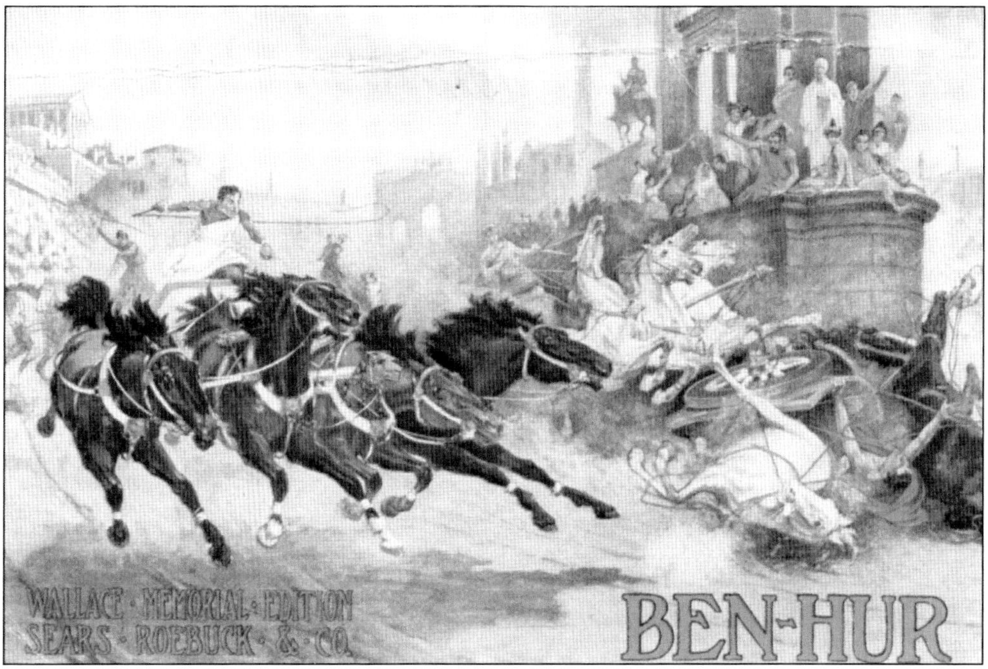

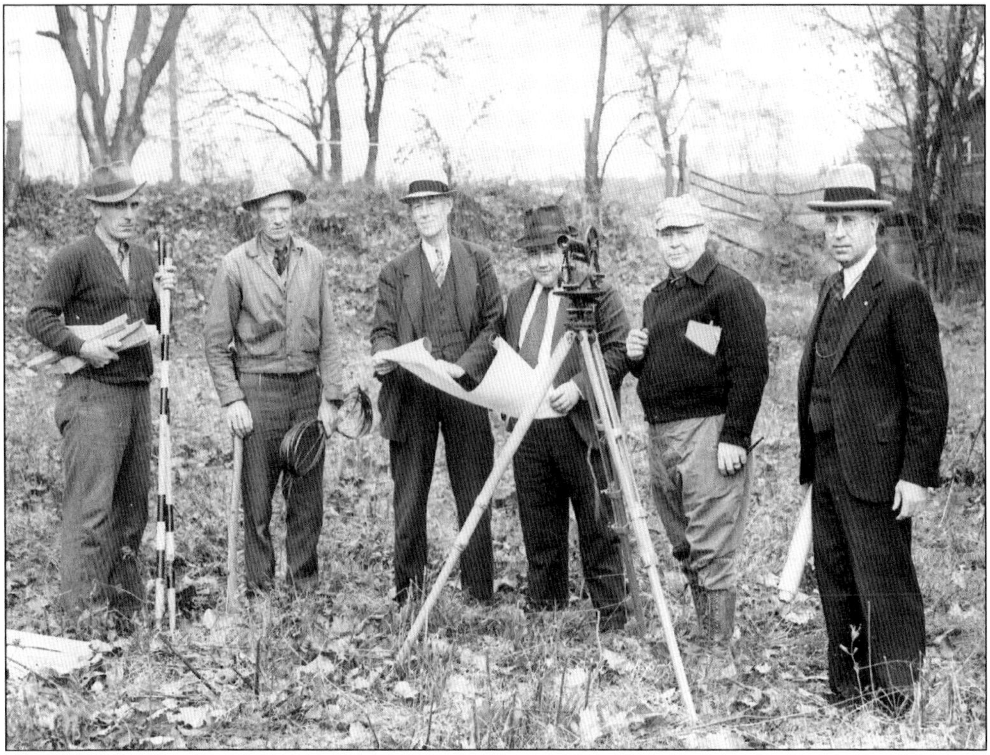

This photograph was taken about 1936. From left to right are Sol Stoughton, Anthony Cook, Ed Colvin, Ernie Schaal, Albert Seabright (Hocking County engineer), and George E. Carr (superintendent of schools). The men were surveying land for the Works Progress Administration (WPA) in Ohio. Logan was one of 65 towns chosen to have stadiums built for high school athletics. Local unemployed men were put back to work for this project. (Courtesy of HH.)

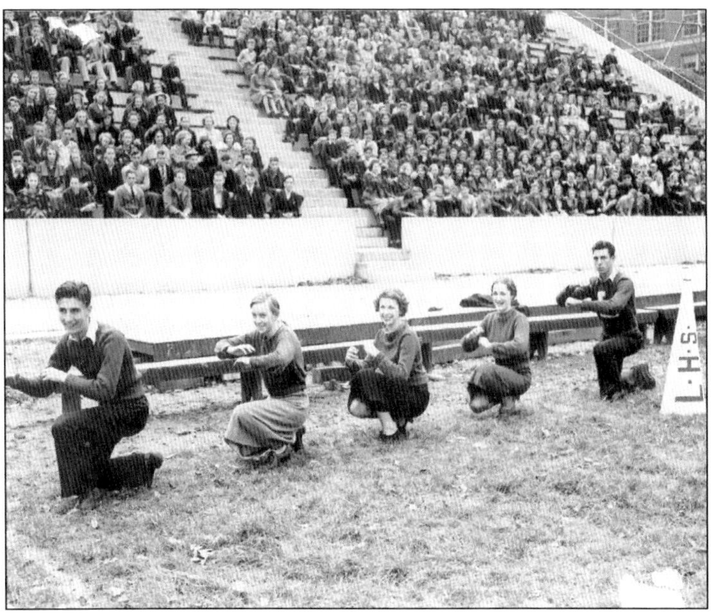

Logan High School cheerleaders rally the crowd at the first football game in the new stadium. Pictured here are, from left to right, James Huffman, Dorothy Krumlauf, Phyllis Leonard, Shirley Mooney, and Edward Richards. The football coach was T.E. Bender. The stadium seated 1,560 fans and cost $7,170 to build in 1936. It served the school until 2010, when the current LHS campus was built. (Courtesy of HH.)

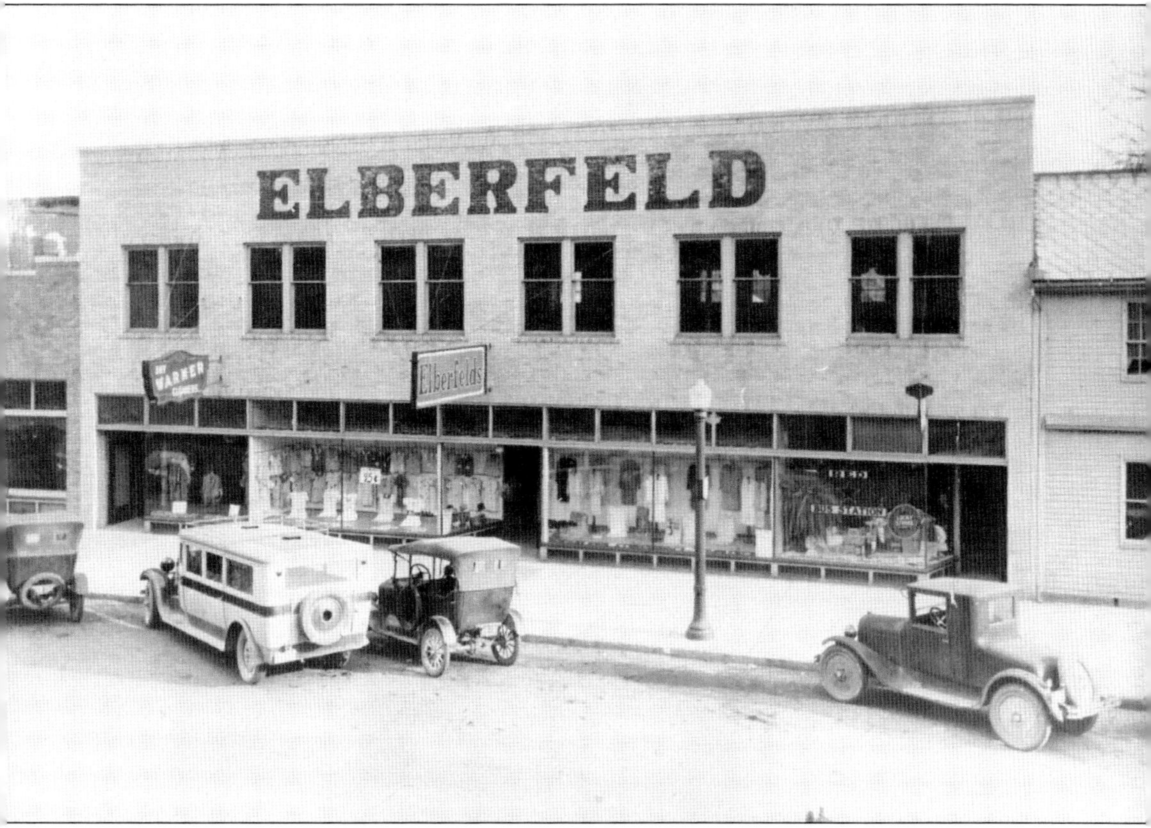

Entrepreneur Earl H. Elberfeld purchased land in downtown Logan, replacing a row of cottage-type businesses. In 1926, he built a large general merchandise store that stood on the south side of West Main Street. Elberfeld owned and operated the store and offered clothing, furniture, carpet, and appliances. An addition was constructed in 1953, and the original building still stands. The civic-minded Elberfeld died at age 93 in 1996. (Courtesy of HH.)

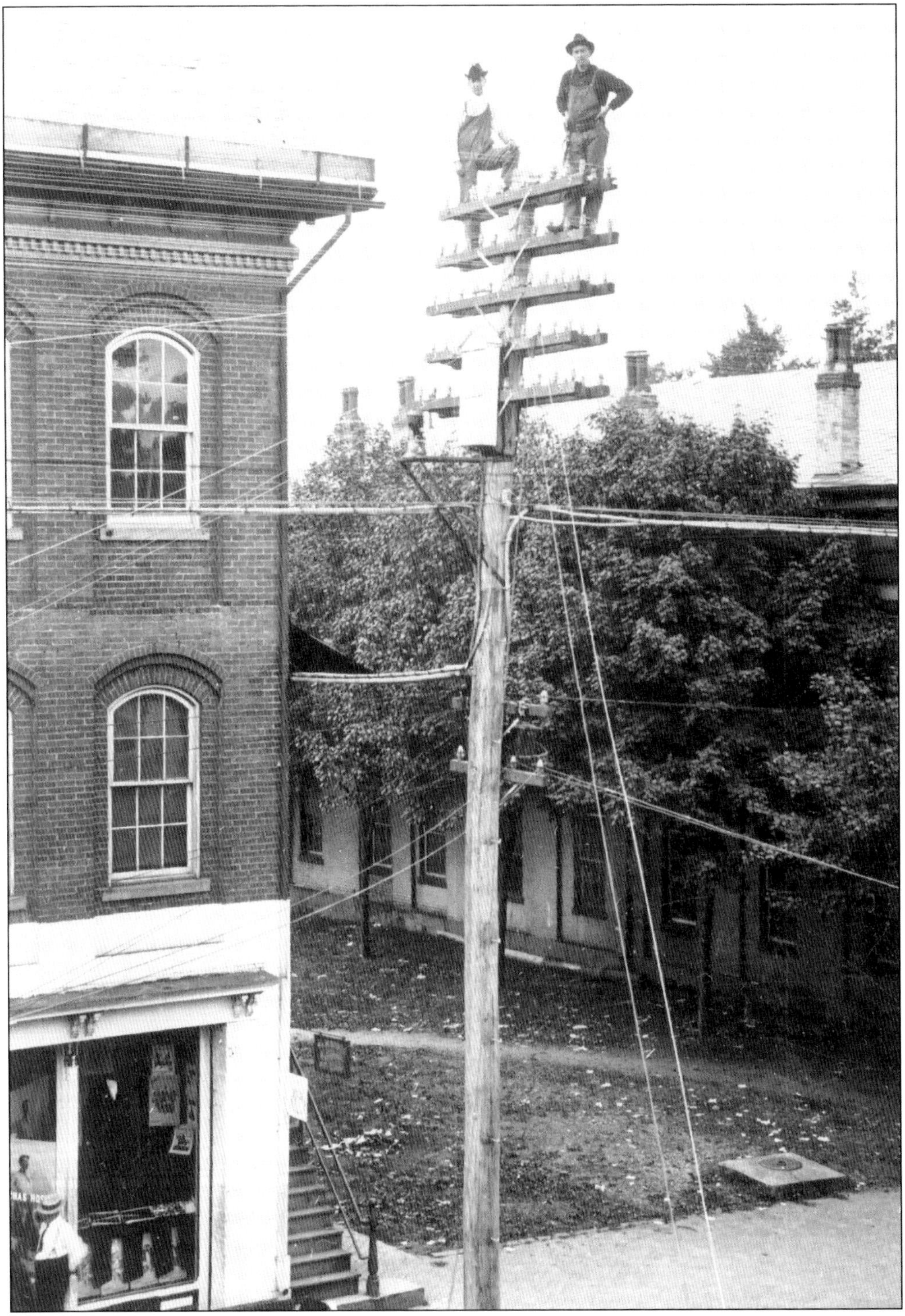

Clyde Van Gordon (left) and Henry Krospeter are perched high atop a telephone office terminal pole around 1903. To the left is the Charles Rose Clothing store on the ground floor of the James Building. (Courtesy of HH.)

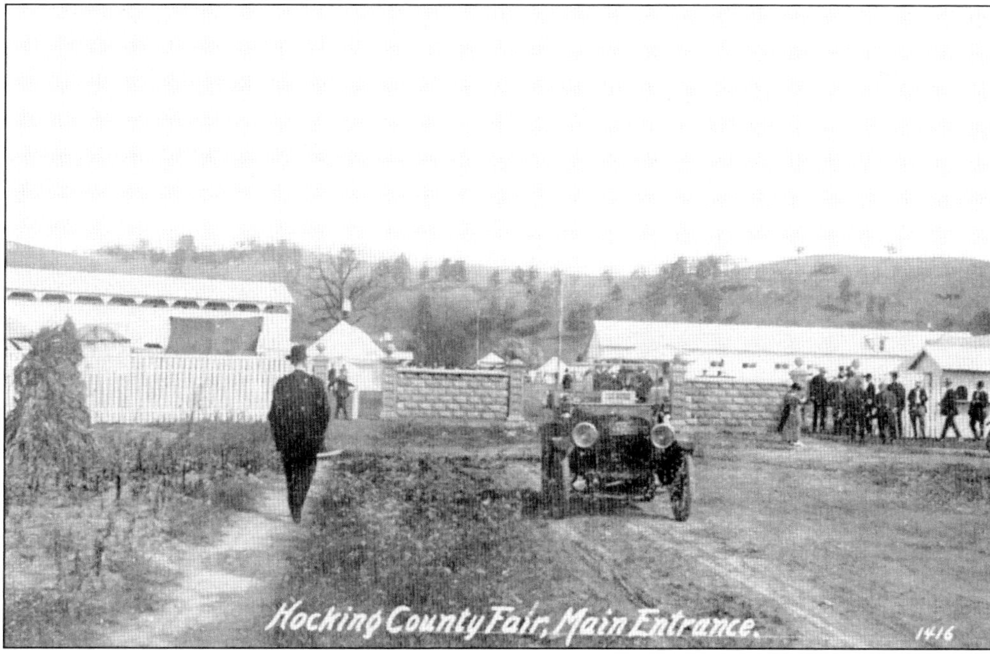

This postcard, dated 1915, shows the main entrance to the Hocking County Fairgrounds at the east end of Logan. The fair has moved several times since 1853, when the Hocking County Agriculture Society was organized. (Courtesy of HH.)

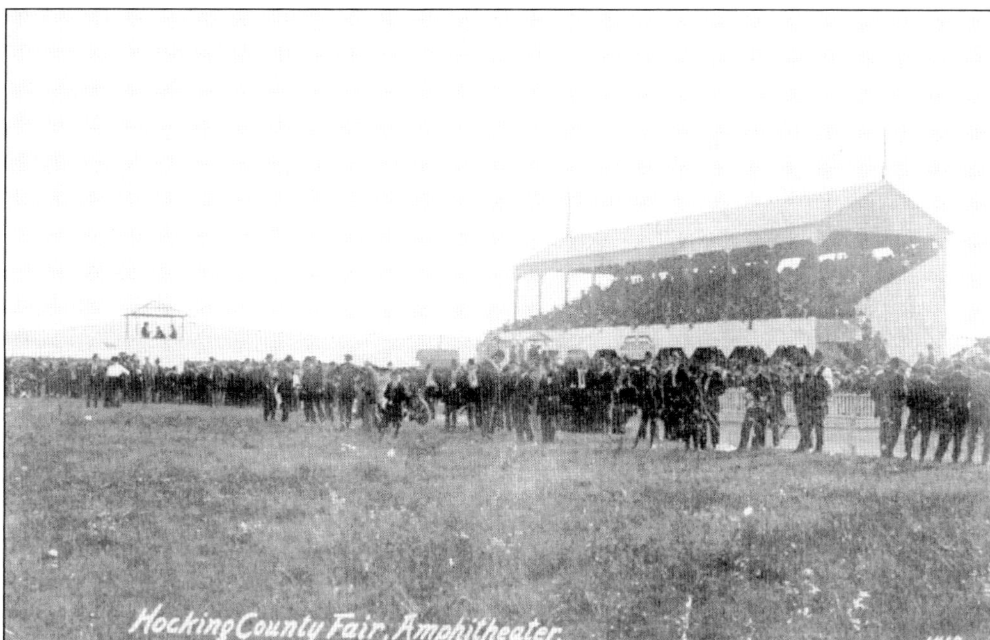

The original wooden grand stand, dated 1915, was a fine addition to the fair. It appears the stands are filled, and the perimeter of the horse-racing track is lined with fairgoers. Today, the frame stand has been replaced with one made of concrete. (Courtesy of HH.)

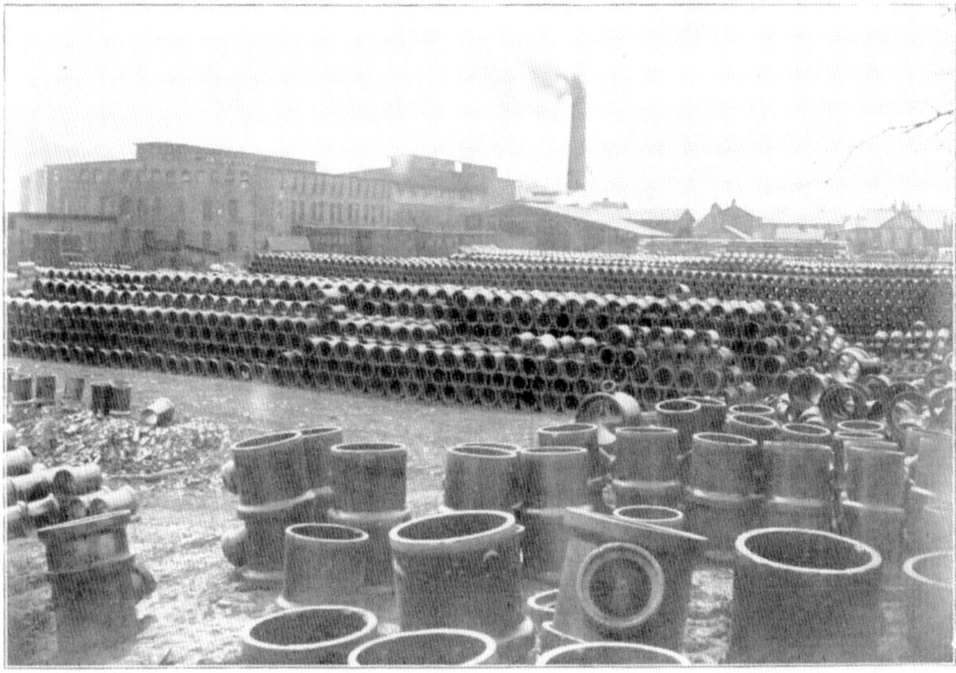

Logan Clay Product Company's Works, Logan, Ohio.

The Hocking Valley is all about clay. Two of the factories that were successful in the clay industry were Logan Clay Products (above) and Logan Pottery (below). Logan Clay mainly manufactures sewer pipes and is still in business today. The Logan Pottery made farm and household items, but the popularity of less expensive, foreign-made plastic items reduced its sales, and the company closed in the mid-1960s. (Both courtesy of HH.)

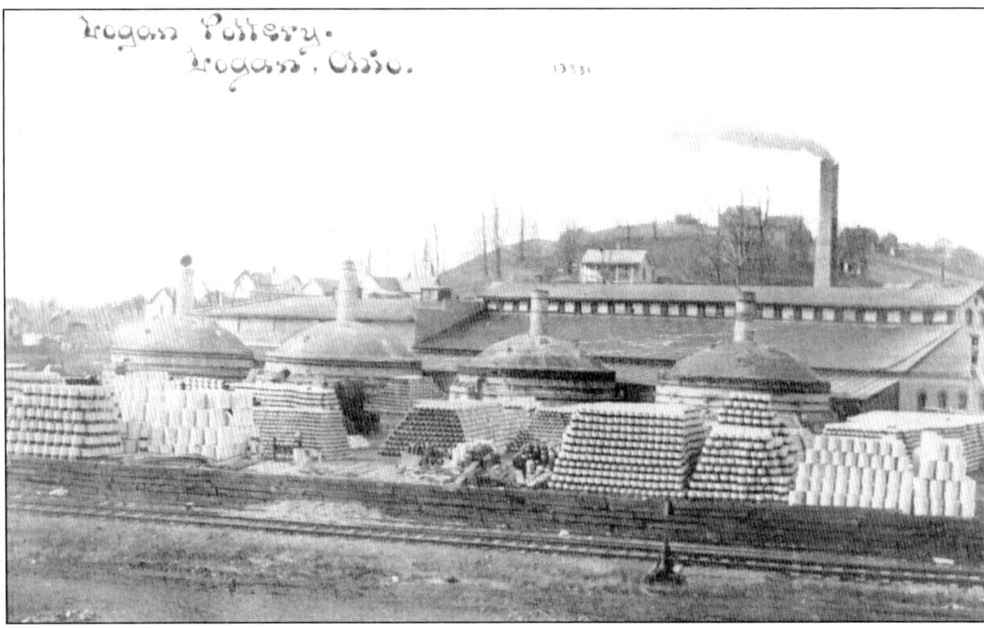

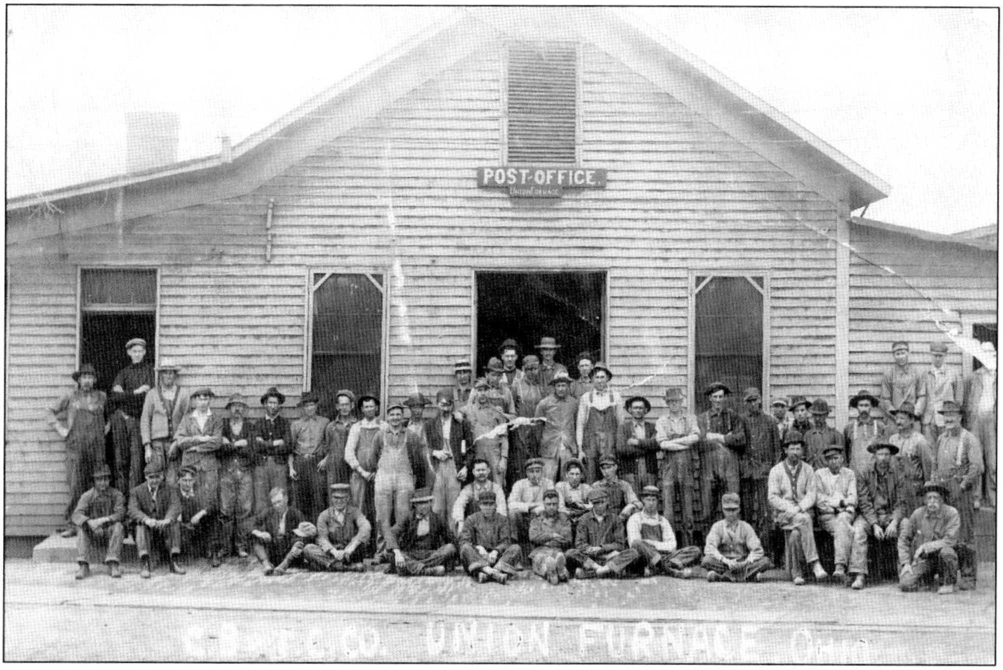

Union Furnace, formerly called New Cadiz, is located just five miles below Logan in Starr Township. This postcard shows employees of the Columbus Brick and Terra Cotta Company that was in business from 1890 to 1916. According to the late historian David V. Stivison, 197 men were employed with wages from 15¢ to 25¢ an hour. Average rent for a cottage in the company town was from $4 to $8 per month. (Courtesy of HH.)

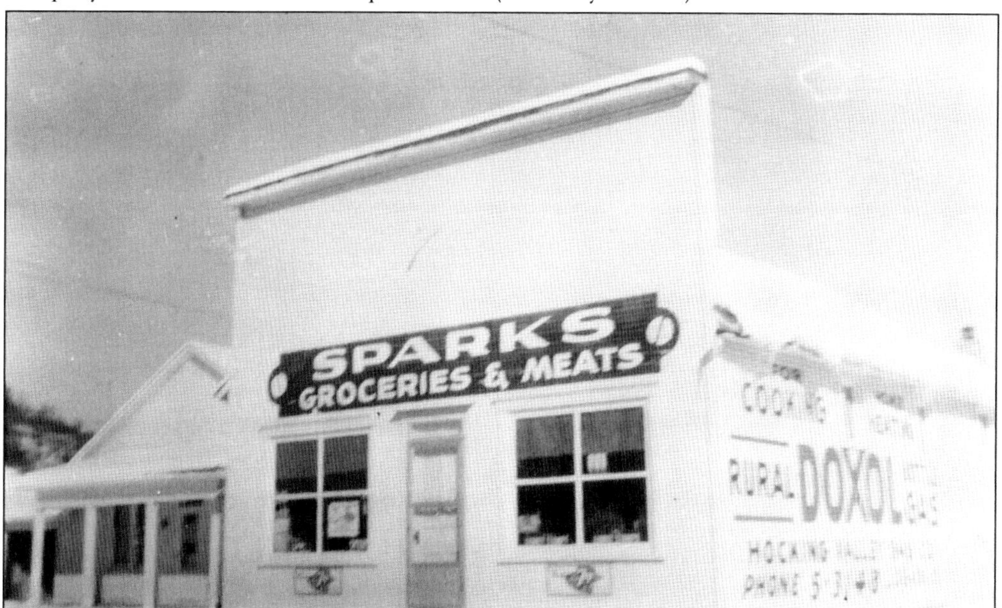

This photograph shows Spark's grocery store in Haydenville, which served the small village. The store was owned by Albert "Red" and Gertrude Sparks. In the 1920s, it was owned by Jesse Francis and later operated by his son Clark Francis. (Courtesy of NV.)

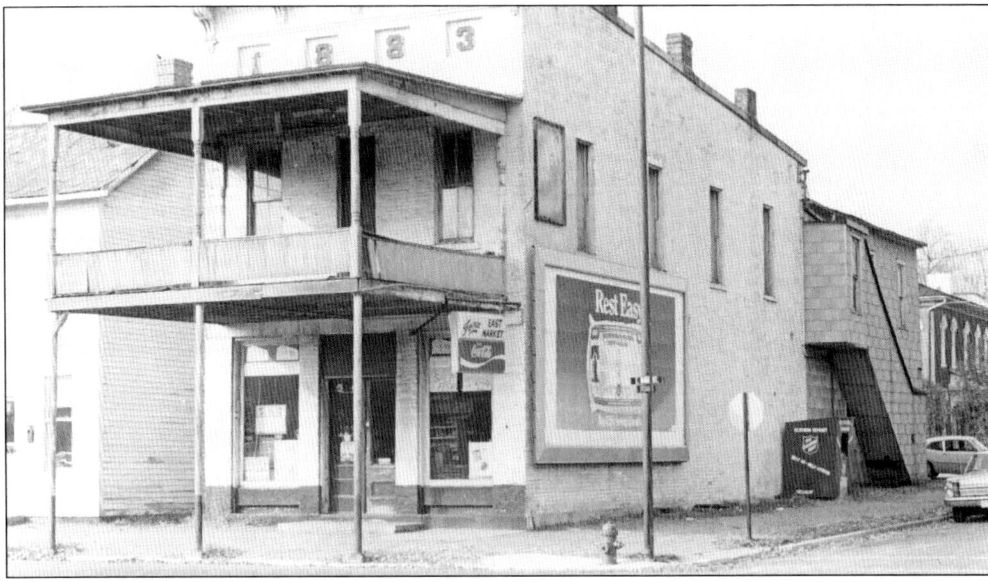

This building, at the corner of Orchard and East Main Streets, was a long-standing grocery store. George Hartman constructed this frame building in 1883. A.C. Tipton, the owner of a large, wholesale apple orchard in the area (thus the name Orchard Street), operated a grocery here. Carl Judy owned the store for many years until 1943, when he sold it to Leo and Evelyn Haley Fox, who operated the store for almost 30 years. In 1972, Ralph and Donna Fick purchased the business. The building was razed in 1985, and Tansky Motors now owns the lot. (Courtesy of HH.)

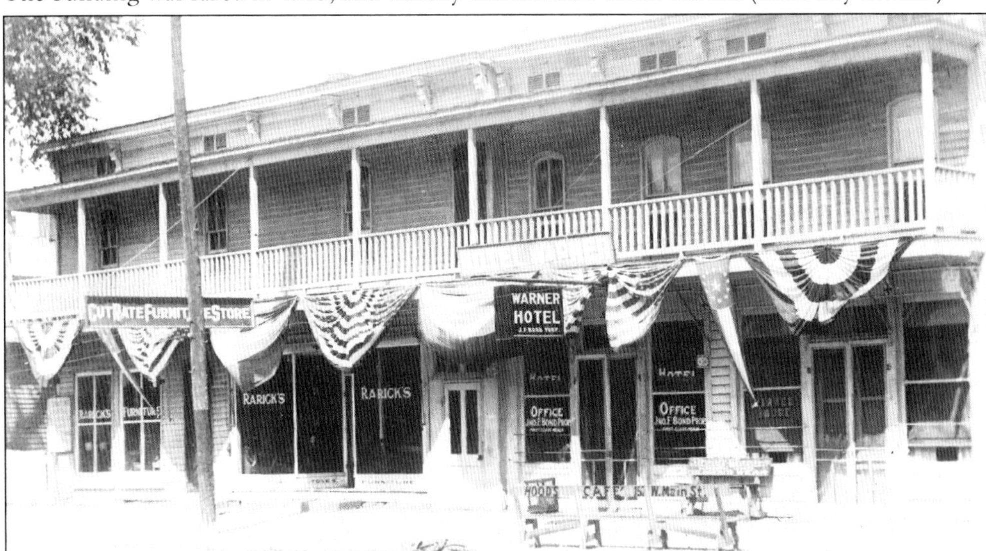

The Warner Hotel had been a landmark on West Main Street for many years when it was razed in 1931 to make way for a new Standard Oil Company service station. John F. Bond was manager of the hotel until his death in 1931, and Dr. J.B. Lyons and his son Dr. Claude Lyons, both optometrists, had offices upstairs. N.J. "Nick" Rarick and his son had a furniture store at the west end of the building, and Warner's Dry Cleaning completed the occupants. The Sohio station was on the corner of Spring and West Main Streets well into the 1960s. A bank is now located at that site. (Courtesy of HH.)

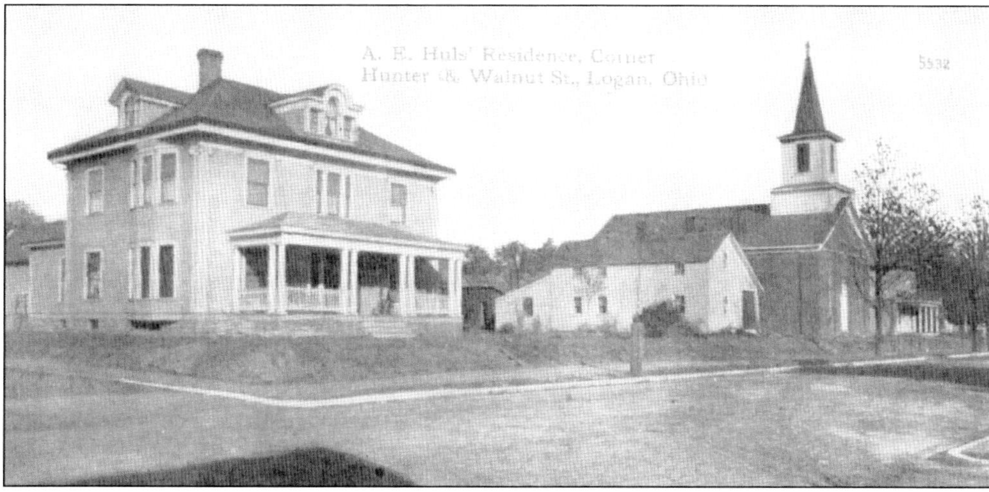

This postcard shows the impressive home of Alpheus E. Huls at the corner of Walnut and East Hunter Streets. Huls was the editor of the *Logan Republican*, owner of Huls Printing Company, served as mayor from 1912 to 1916, and was Logan postmaster from 1931 to 1934. Huls and his wife, Anna, were both fatally injured in an auto accident in July 1934. The Huls home is now a day-care center, and St. Matthew Lutheran Church is pictured at right. (Courtesy of DB.)

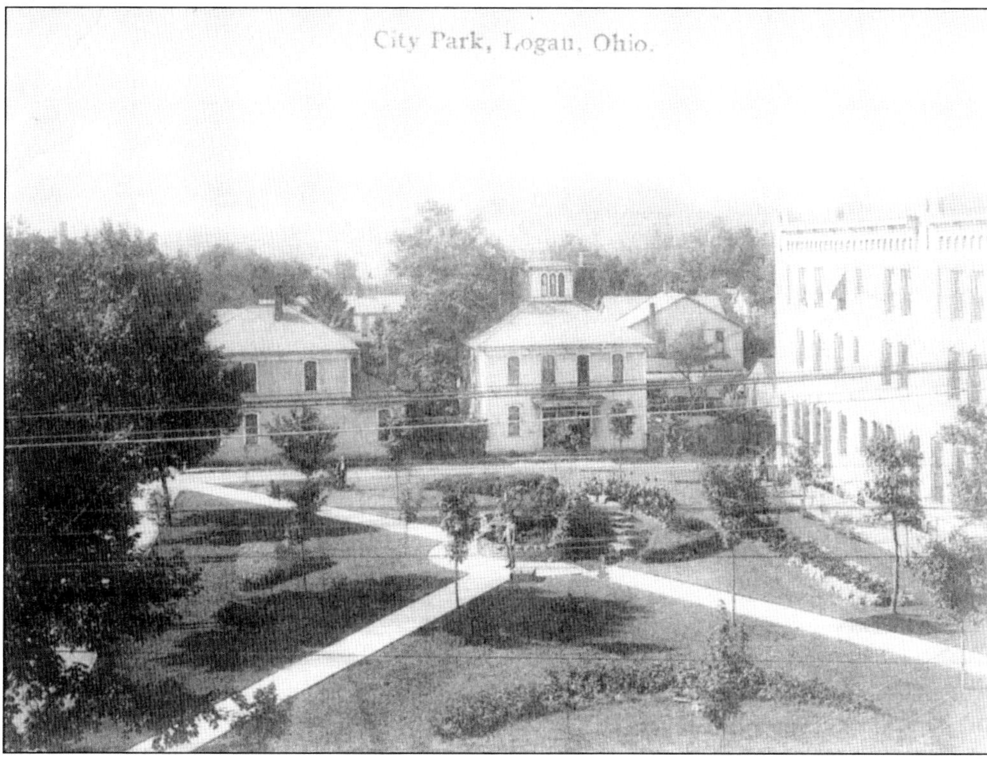

This unusual postcard view of Worthington Park is thought to have been captured around 1915. It appears to have been taken from atop of the former McCarthy-Blosser Building. To the right is the east side of the Ambrose Hotel, and the park with its familiar sidewalks is on the left. The house in the center of the photograph is no longer standing. The city park was laid out for use as a farmers' market by founder Thomas Worthington in 1816. (Courtesy of DB.)

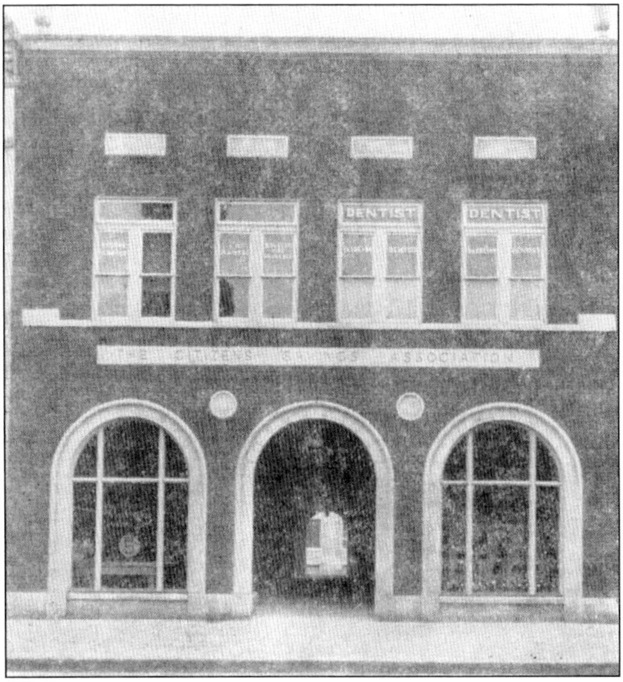

In 1937, the White Arcade building was purchased by Charles Bell. The Morris Company 5-10¢ to $1 Store occupied the street-level space. Arthur Gasser was the store manager, and opening day was May 20, 1938. The first 21 salespeople hired were Dorothy Marks, Nancy Smith, Margaret Harbarger, Martha Eberst, Anna Oancea, Virginia Canter, Helen Bright, Ruth Griffith, Margee Tschappat, Bertha Schubert, Lola Hockman, Ruth Lance, Margaret Knapp, Bernice Knox, Retha Green, Mable Blosser, Juanita Wolfe, Doris Hammon, Florence Rectenwald, Madge Dawley, and Margaret Wolfe. (Courtesy of HH.)

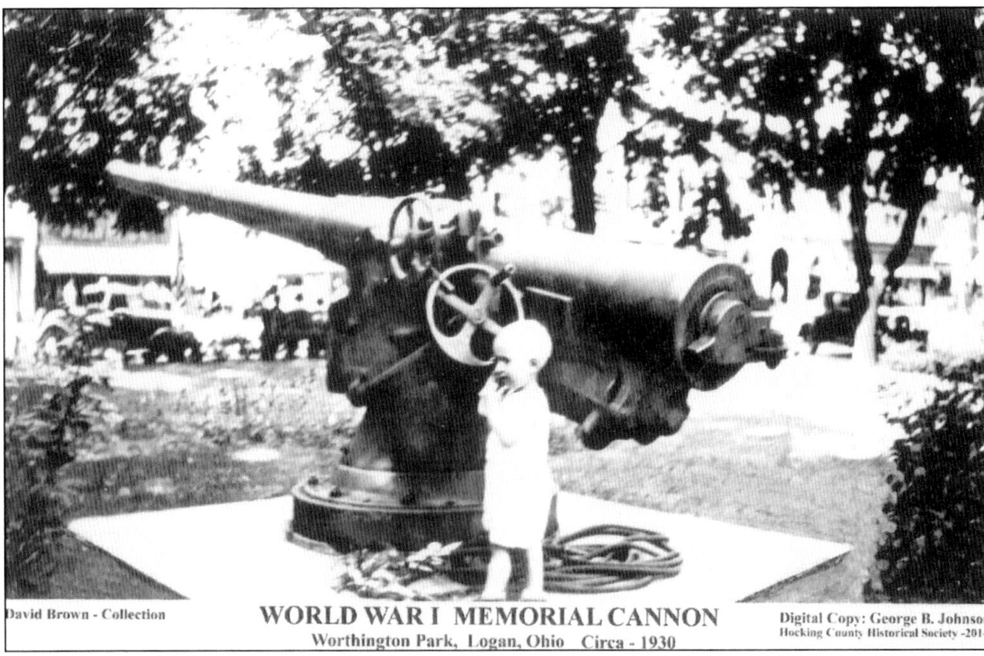

This World War I five-inch naval cannon was placed in the city park when it was brought to Logan about 1920. Edwin Ricketts, the 11th District congressman, made the arrangements, and the local service veterans' clubs paid for the cannon's transport. In 1942, Mayor W. Denzil Weltner received notice that the Army Ordnance Department was seeking old World War I cannons to be used to make modern guns. It was decided by city council that the cannon would be returned to the government to assist in the current defense effort. The young boy in this 1930s image is unidentified. (Digital image GBJ, courtesy DB.)

This photograph shows housewives gathered for a 9:00 a.m. store opening to take advantage of a sale at Carpenter's Hardware store, located in the James Building. The sale on aluminum cookware took place in June 1924, and the store reportedly sold $500 worth of goods in the first hour. (Courtesy of HH.)

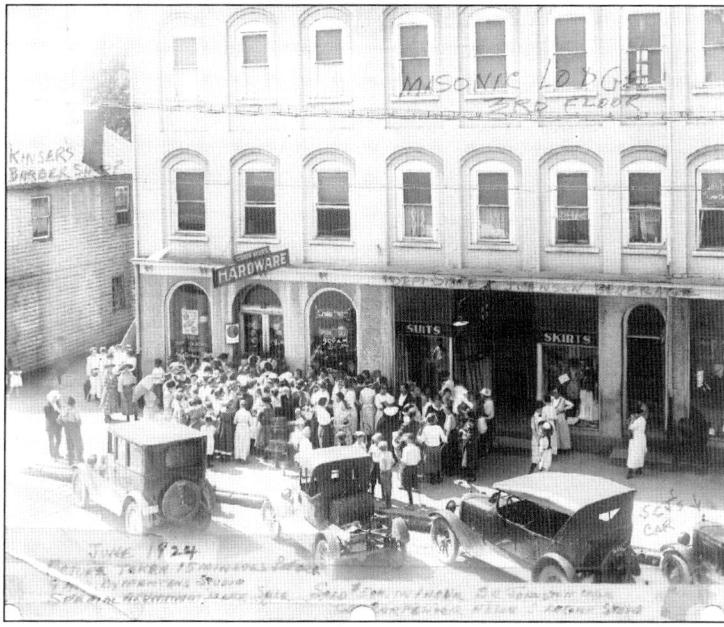

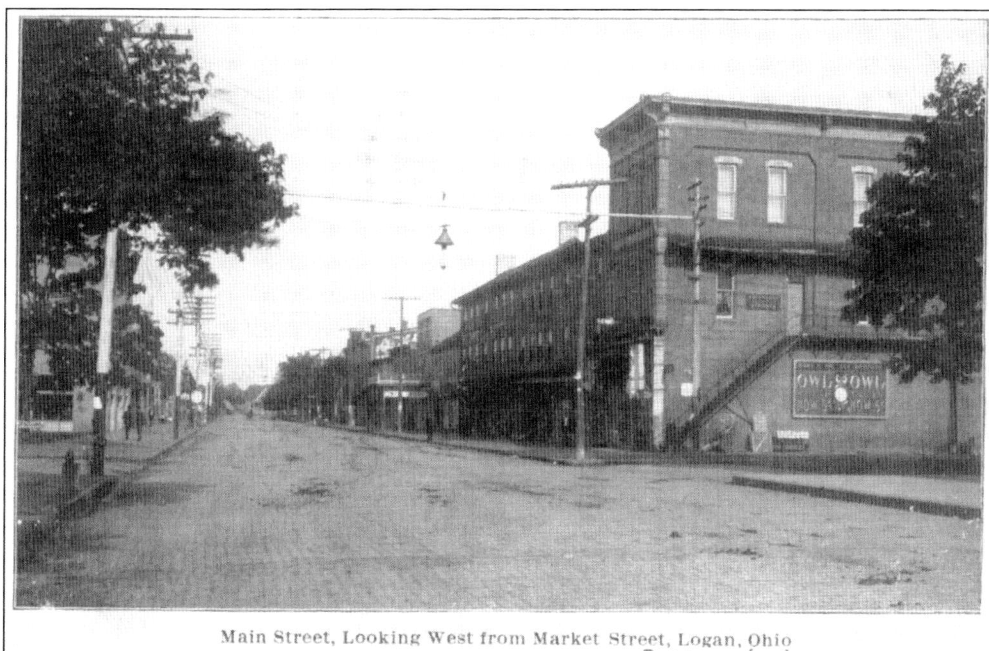

This is another view of Main Street looking west from Market Street. The building on the far right with the stairway is where the Corn Crib was built many years later. (Courtesy GM.)

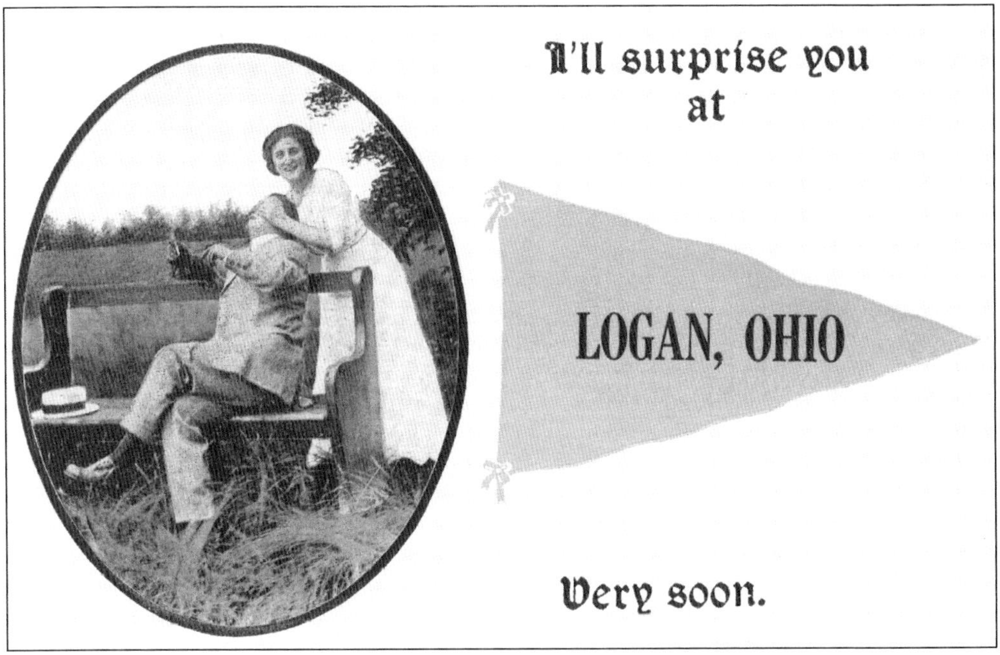

An alert is being given to the recipient of this postcard suggesting a visit. When? Where? (Courtesy of JM.)

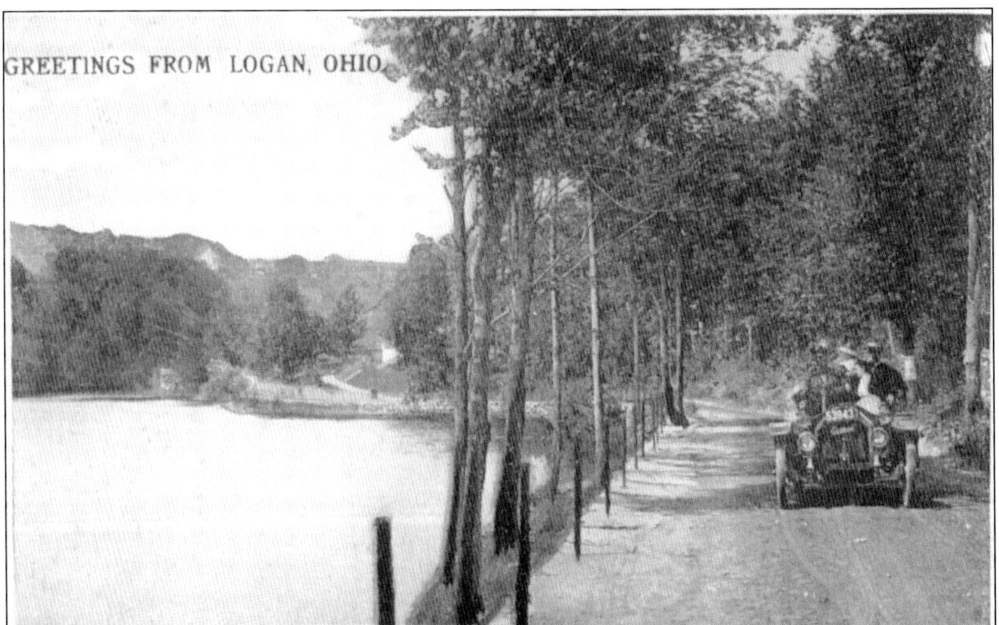

Linen postcards were known to enhance any scene, and here is a jolly group taking a drive by Lake Logan; however, this could not have been possible, as Lake Logan was not created until the 1950s. This view must be another of the beautiful scenery along the Hocking River. (Courtesy of CCH.)

Five

Friends and Neighbors

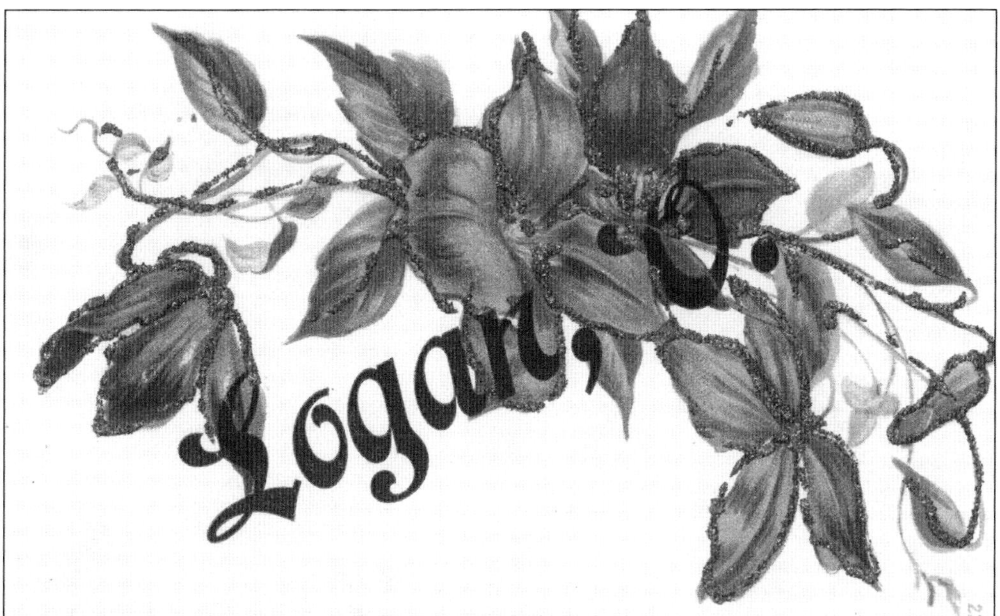

A very attractive Logan postcard is tinted in shades of purple and white. Glitter is sprinkled on the paint for an extra touch. It is surprising that it survived the mail services intact. (Courtesy of JM.)

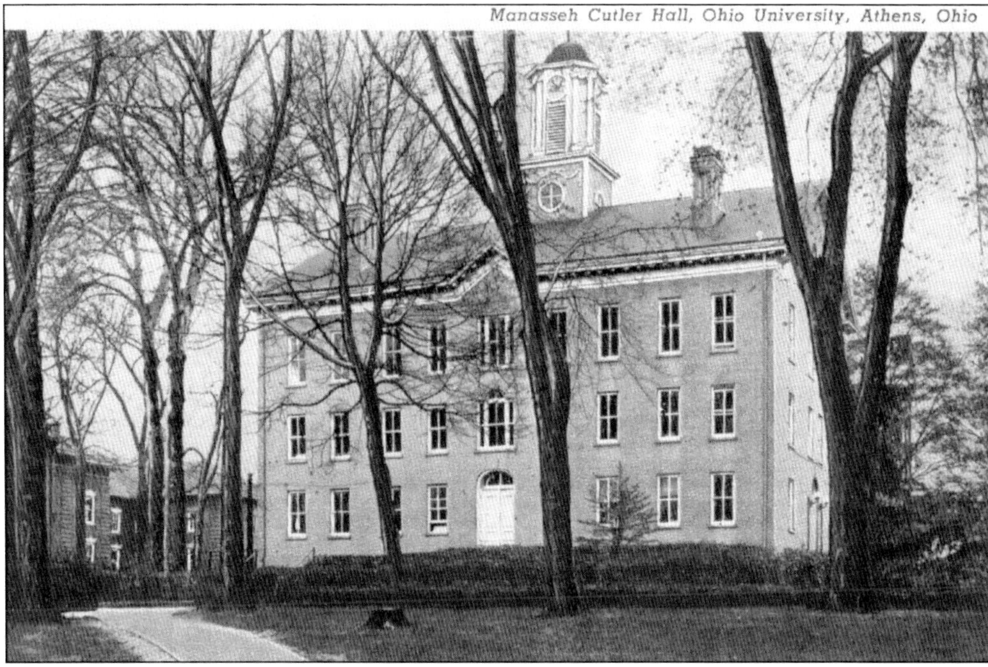

Athens, in Athens County, Ohio, is home to Ohio University, the first college in the Northwest Territory, established in 1804. This postcard shows Manasseh Cutler Hall, which was built in 1817. Cutler was one of the founders of the Ohio Company of Associates. (Courtesy of JM.)

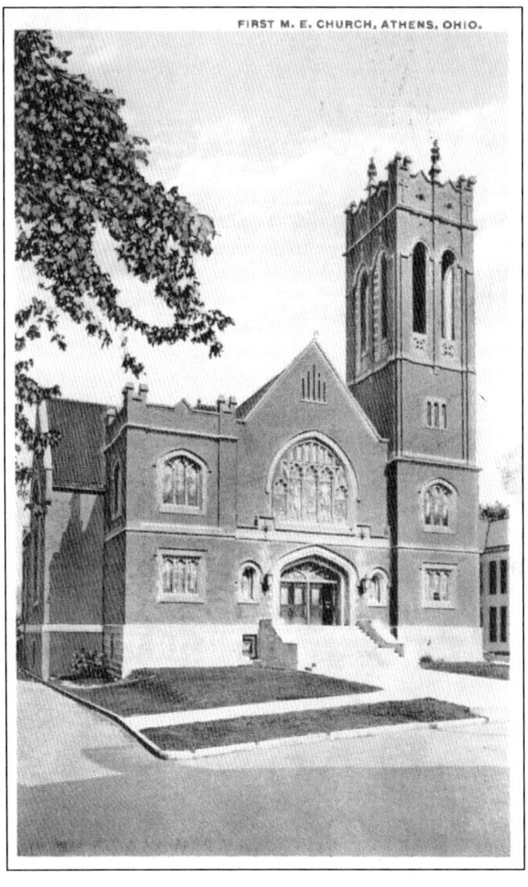

The First Methodist Episcopal Church in Athens, Ohio, is featured on this linen postcard dated 1918. Badgley and Nicklas of Cleveland were the architects. (Courtesy of JM.)

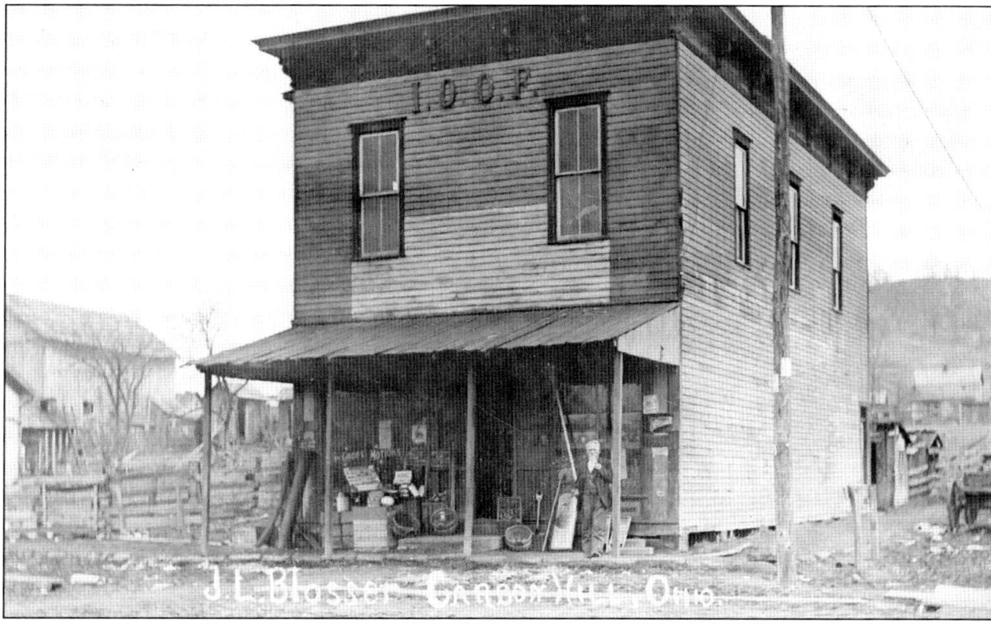

Carbon Hill, in Hocking County, was laid out by Thomas Ewing, son of the famous statesman, in 1873. The image above is of J.L. Blosser's Store, dated 1910. The postcard below is of Carbon Hill School around 1910. George W. Ross was appointed postmaster in 1907, but in 1909 the Sand Run Post Office was closed and added to the Carbon Hill routes. (Both courtesy of DB.)

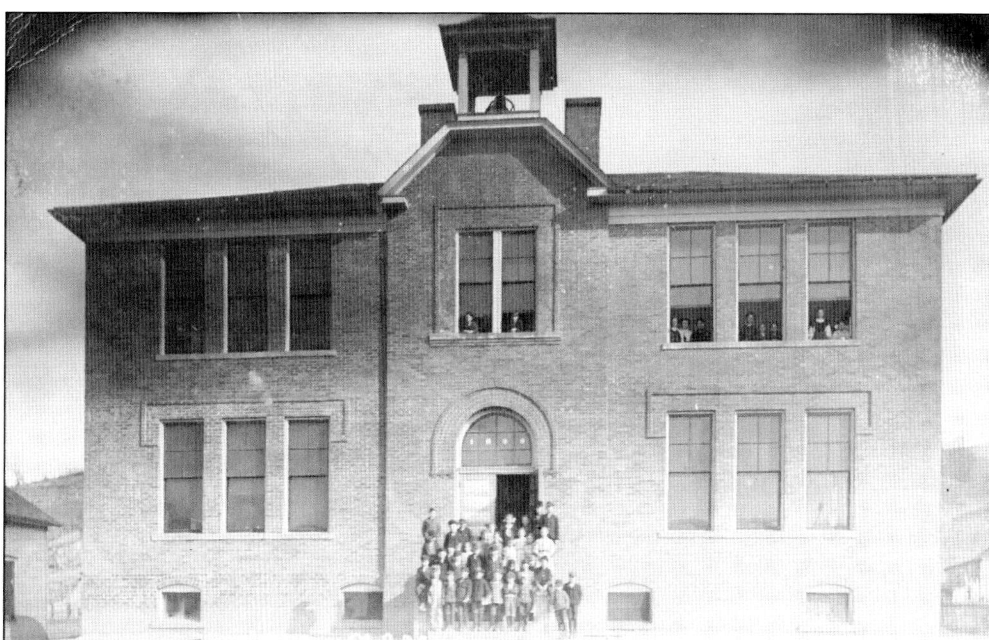

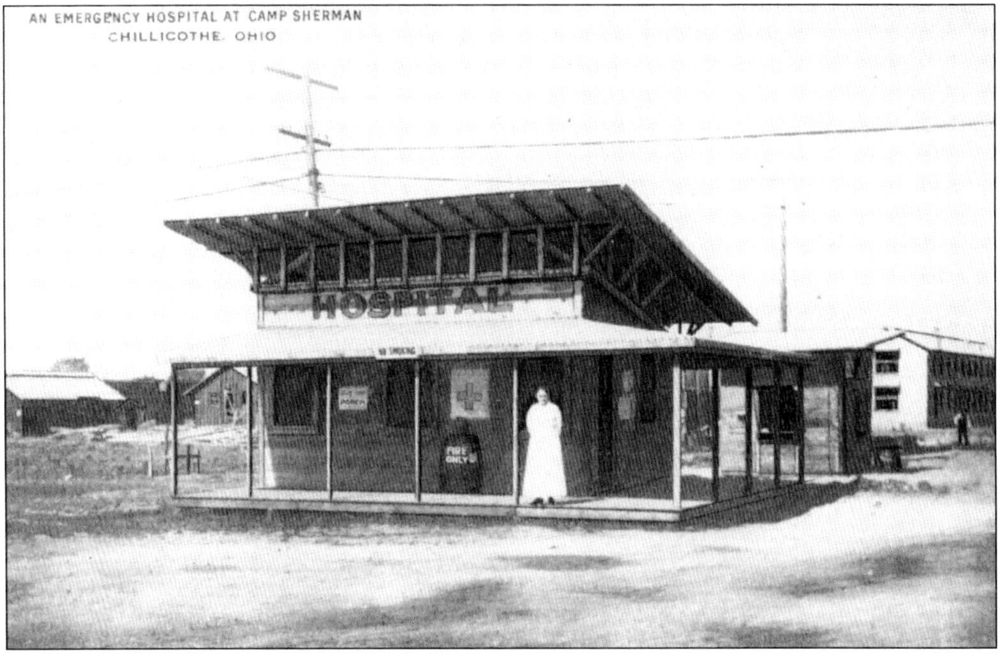

Chillicothe, in Ross County, was the first capital of Ohio. When the United States entered World War I, the country was ill equipped to train the necessary soldiers. Camp Sherman, named after William Tecumseh Sherman, was the first camp in the country to accommodate new recruits. This postcard, dated 1918, is a view of the base hospital. (Courtesy of JM.)

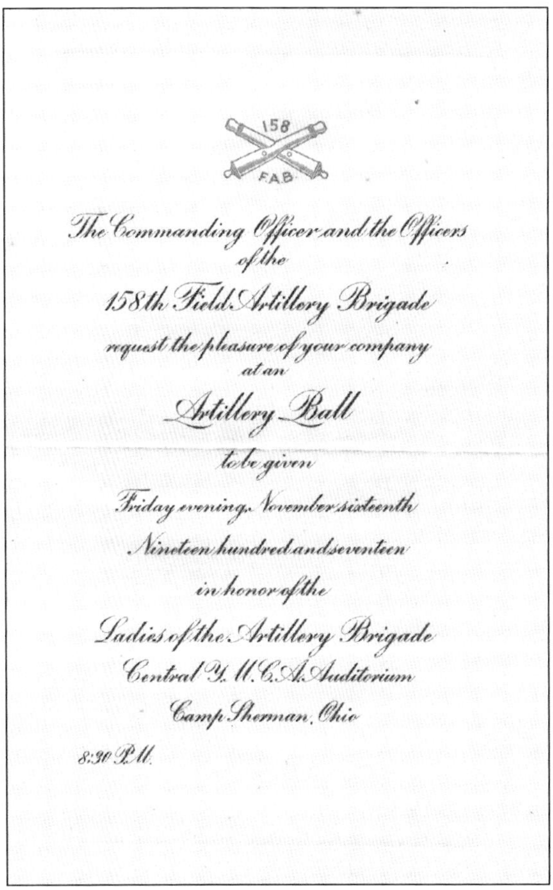
158
F.A.B.

The Commanding Officer and the Officers
of the
158th Field Artillery Brigade
request the pleasure of your company
at an
Artillery Ball
to be given
Friday evening, November sixteenth
Nineteen hundred and seventeen
in honor of the
Ladies of the Artillery Brigade
Central Y. M. C. A. Auditorium
Camp Sherman, Ohio

8:30 P.M.

This engraved invitation is to the elegant 1916 Artillery Ball. The 158th Field Artillery Brigade gave the ball in honor of the Ladies of the Artillery Brigade. (Courtesy of HH.)

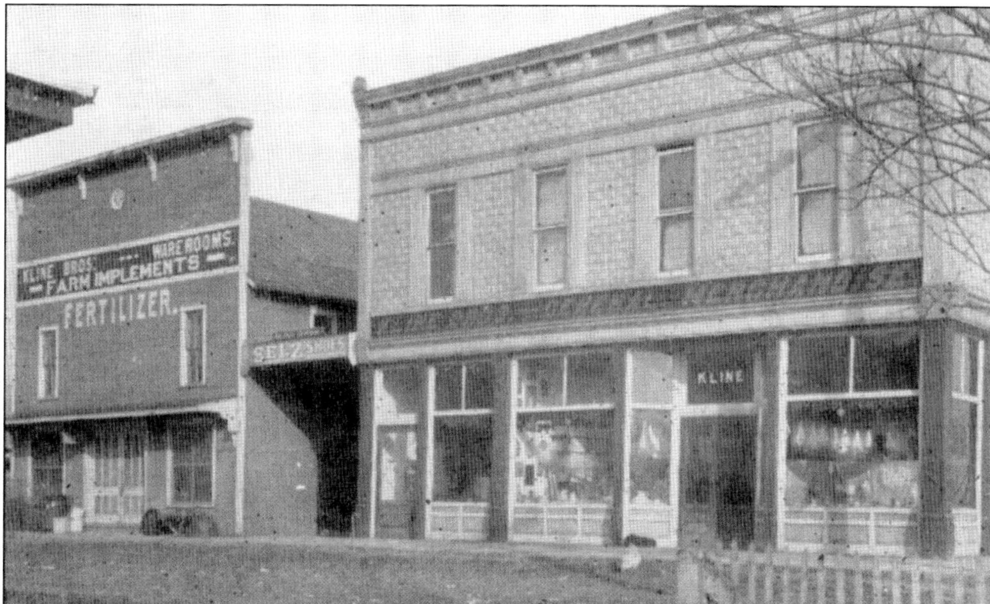

The New Kline Store, Enterprise, Ohio. Josef F. Brashares, Prop.

Enterprise, formerly Stiversonville, is a small community just north of Logan in Hocking County. The postcard above shows a building owned by Josef F. Brashares, part of the small business district. Below is a scene thought to be looking west from Main Street towards Route 33. (Both courtesy of DB.)

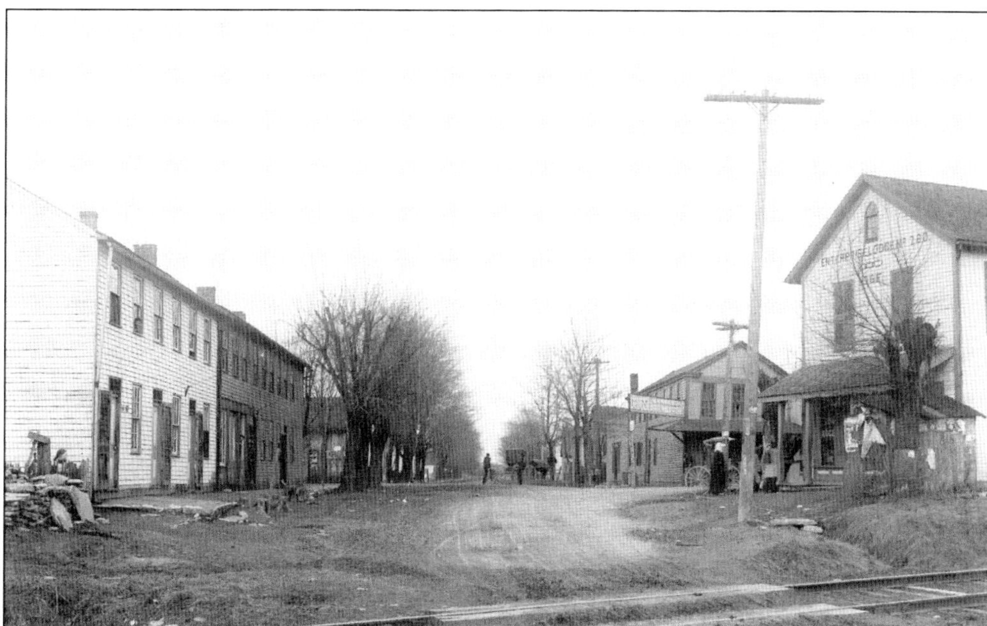

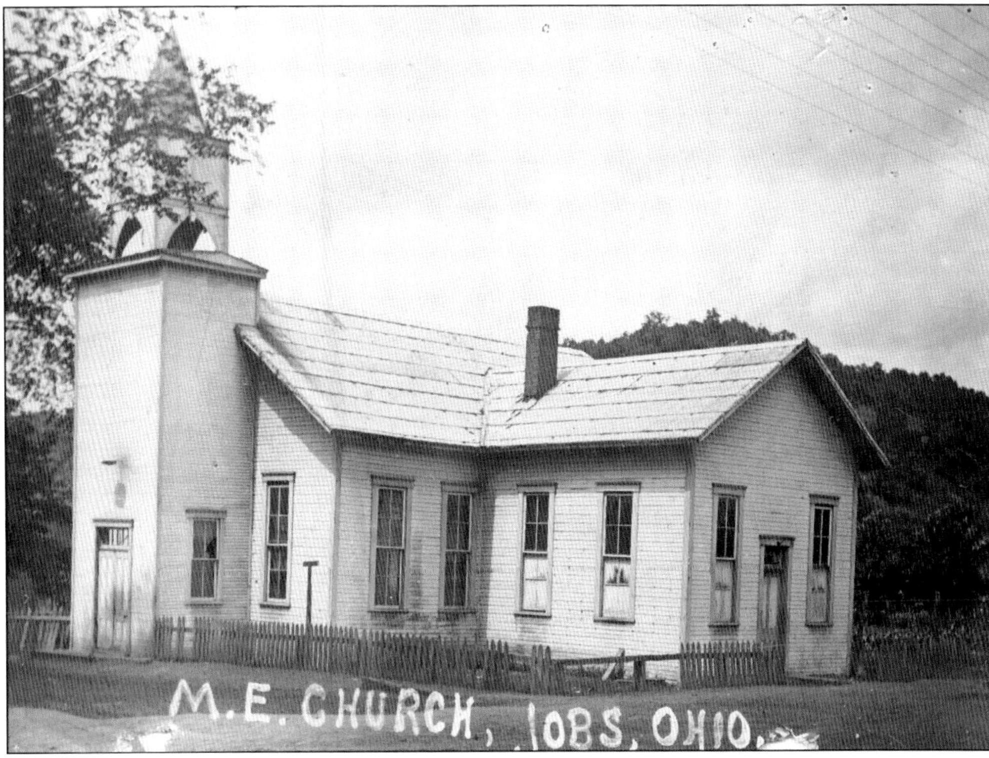

Postcards of the past allow people to see actual parts of the county that no longer exist. Such is the case of Jobs (pronounced with a long *O*). It flourished briefly during the coal mine boom and then disappeared. Above is a postcard of the Methodist Episcopal Church, and below is a bird's-eye view of Jobs. (Above, courtesy of DB; below, GBJ.)

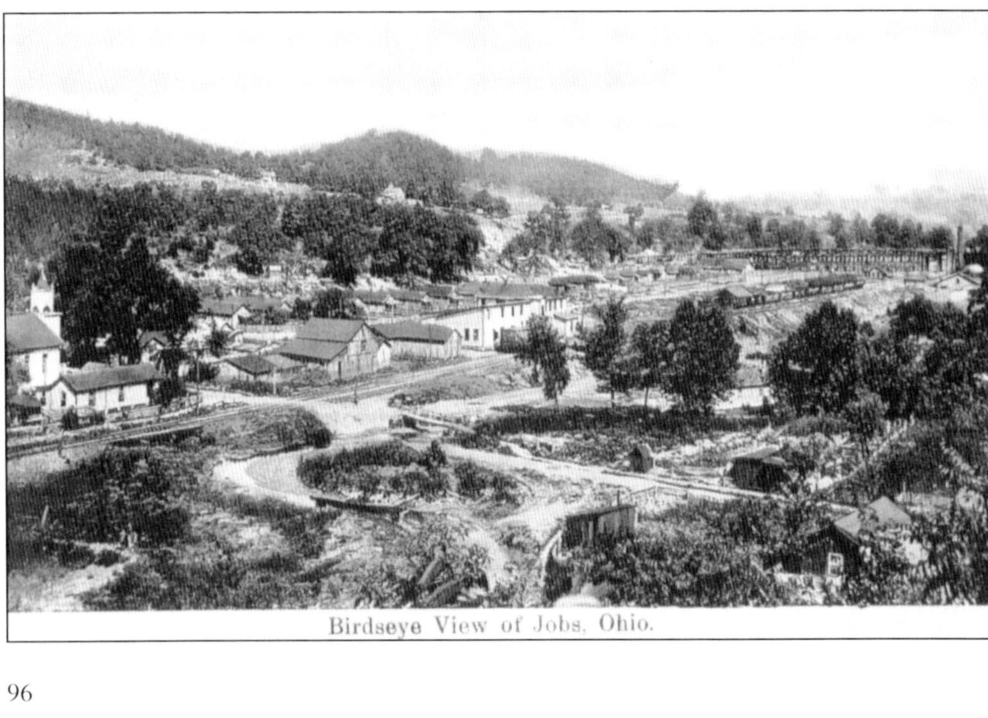

Birdseye View of Jobs, Ohio.

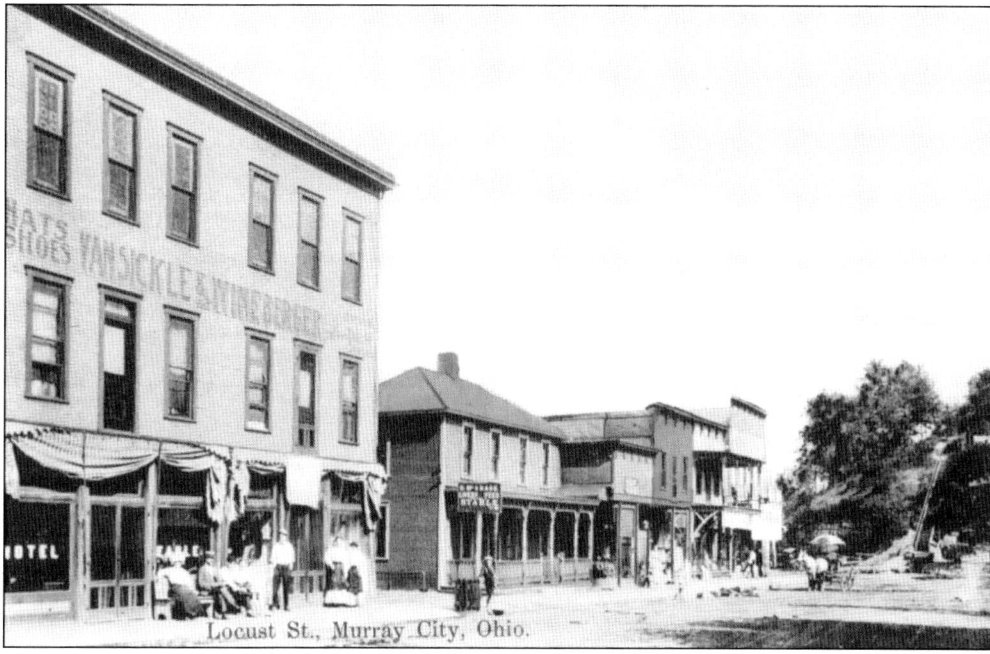

The postcard above shows the old hotel (building on left) in Murray City, a thriving coal town in western Hocking County. By the year 1883, Murray City had about 300 inhabitants. The postcard below is dated 1912 and shows a view of the church and a section of the growing town. (Both courtesy of DB.)

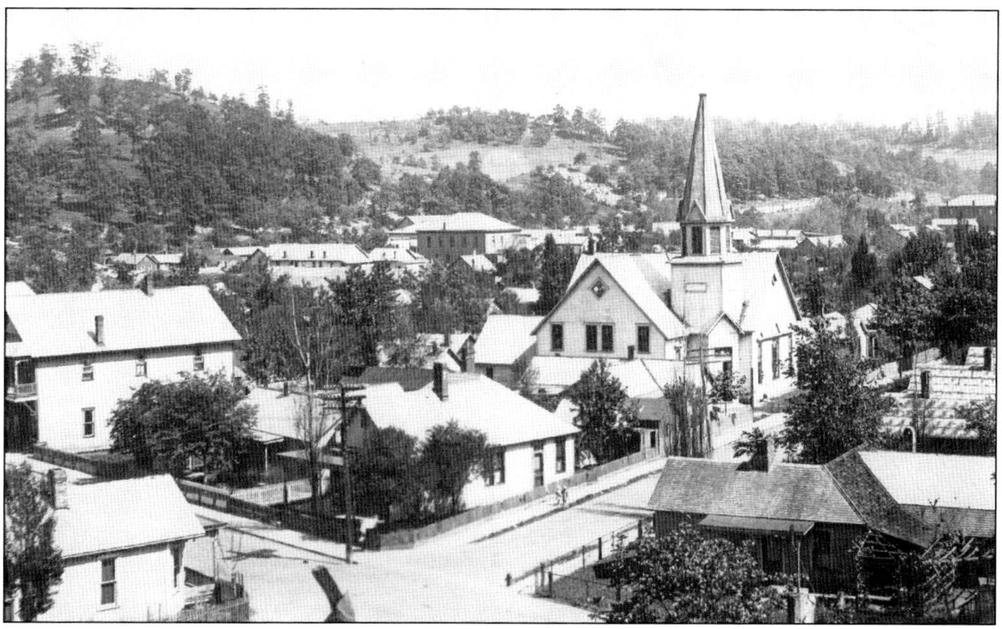

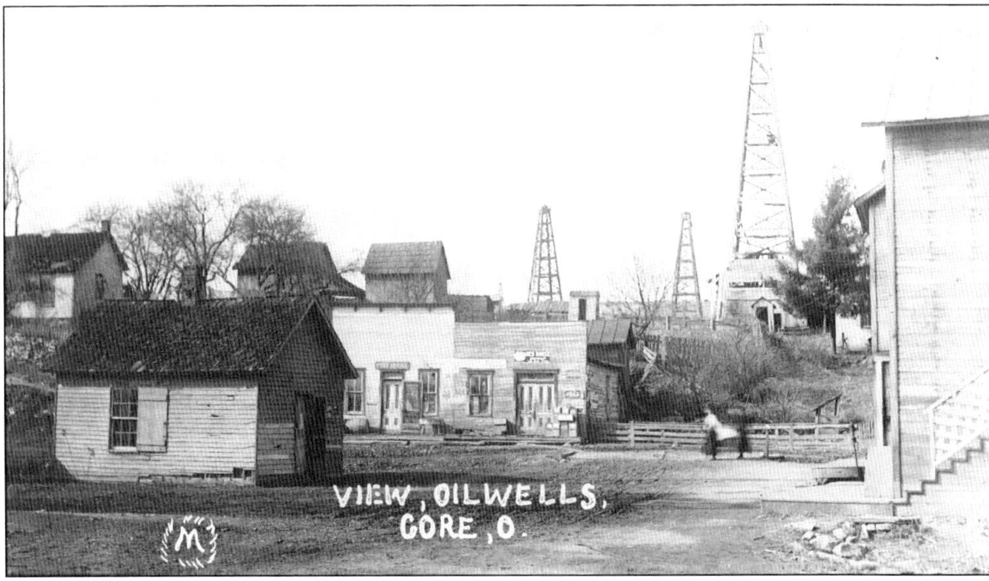

Gore, in Hocking County, was settled in 1852 by Cromwell B. Culver. At one time, there was a large iron furnace that employed 300 men. Gore developed a reputation during the "furnace days," and the belief was that the town was so named because of the bloody encounters between residents. Other authorities suggest looking at the Hocking County map to see that Falls-Gore Township is actually "gored" (a sewing term) into Perry County. (Courtesy of DB.)

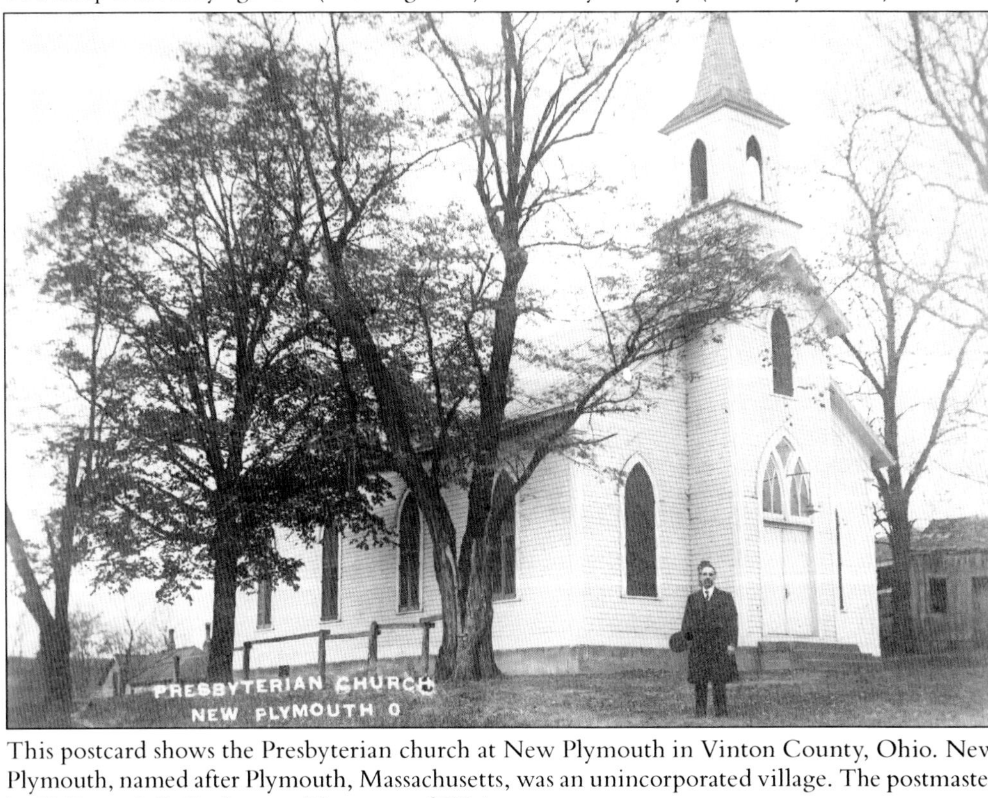

This postcard shows the Presbyterian church at New Plymouth in Vinton County, Ohio. New Plymouth, named after Plymouth, Massachusetts, was an unincorporated village. The postmaster in 1883 was J.G. Eggleston. (Courtesy of DB.)

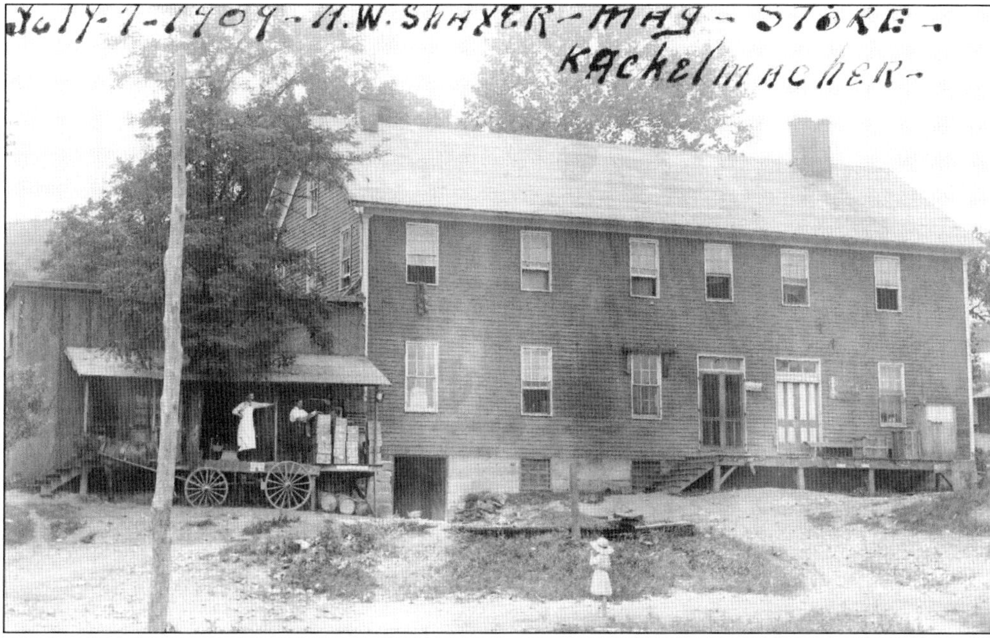

The company store at Kachelmacher in Hocking County, Ohio, is shown here. The town was originally named for its developer, Nils Kachelmacher. The name was later changed to Greendale for Green Township. The entrepreneur and his New York associates built a rug brick (ridged) plant that was said to be the largest brick plant in the world, costing $1 million. The plant was in operation from 1907 to the mid-1930s. The Depression was the direct cause of Greendale's closing. In its heyday, the plant sold brick throughout the country, supplying many hotels, schools, and factories. It was used to build the Deshler Hotel in Columbus, Ohio. (Courtesy of HH.)

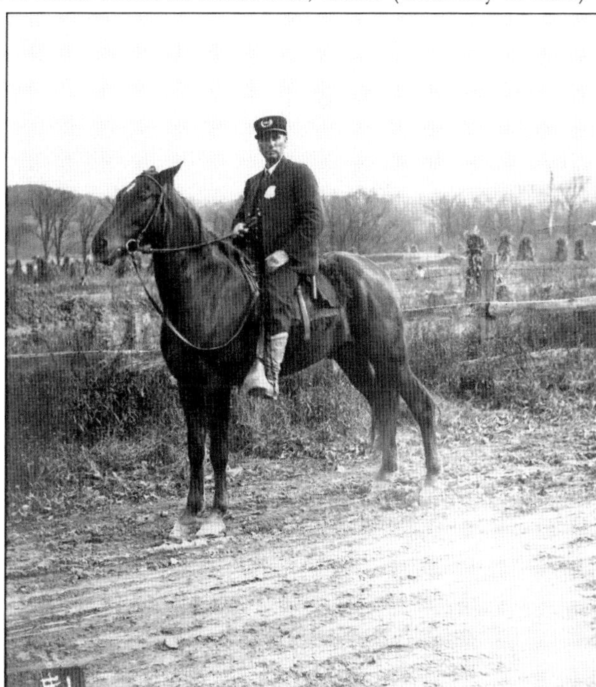

The subject of this photograph is a horse-mounted deputy sheriff who patrolled the brickyard during its construction. He was given a house to reside in, and conveniently located beside it was the town jail. The expansive area (13,000 acres) is now part of the Wayne National Forest in Hocking County. The post office, company store, kilns, houses, and other buildings are all gone; there is nothing but postcards and photographs to remind people of what once was. (Courtesy of KK.)

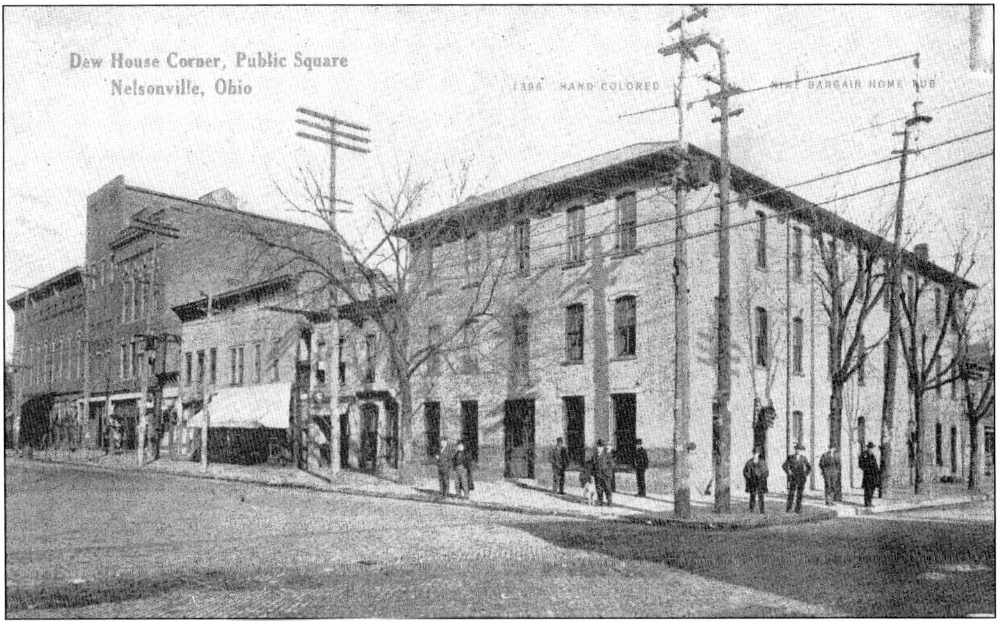

Nelsonville, in Athens County, was founded by Daniel Nelson. Thomas Dew purchased the first two lots on the public square and built a hotel, naming it the Ohio House. His descendents expanded the property 116 years later and changed the name to the Dew Hotel. These two postcards show both sides of the public square in historic Nelsonville. The Dew Hotel is on the far-right corner of the top postcard. (Above, courtesy of MT; below, JM.)

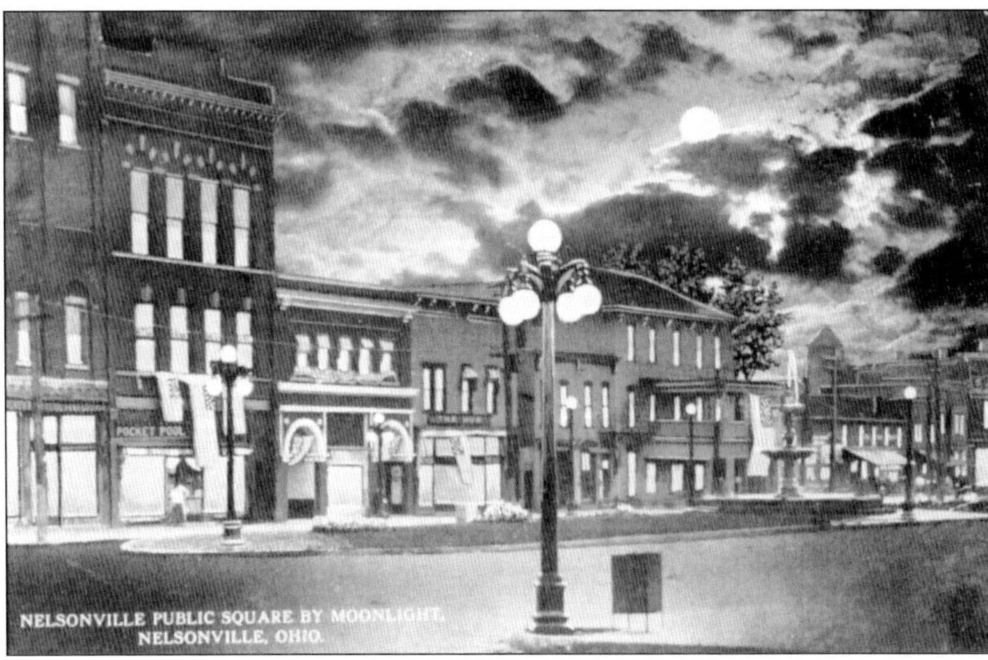

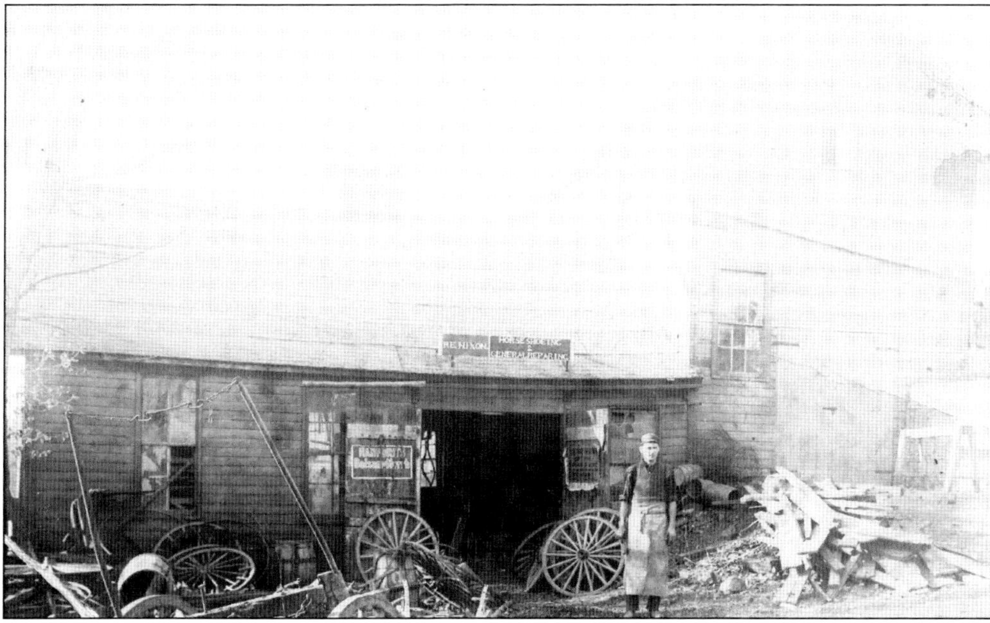

Raymond E. Nixon was the owner of a blacksmith shop in New Straitsville in Perry County. Nixon had a sign that advertised, "Horse Shoeing & General Reparing." The misspelled word on the sign did not keep customers away, and Nixon made a living smithing during the horse-and-buggy days. (Courtesy of HH.)

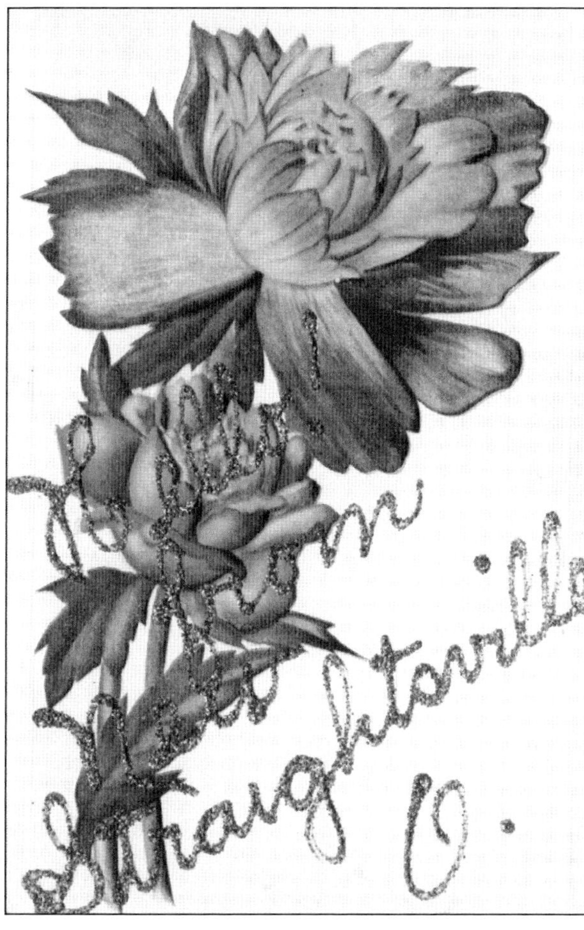

This fancy postcard is pretty to look at, but it also has a misspelled name. New Straitsville or New Straightsville? Historical information notes that the village was founded in 1870 and was named for the Straitsville and Monday Creek Coal Company that owned the mines in the area. (Courtesy of WD.)

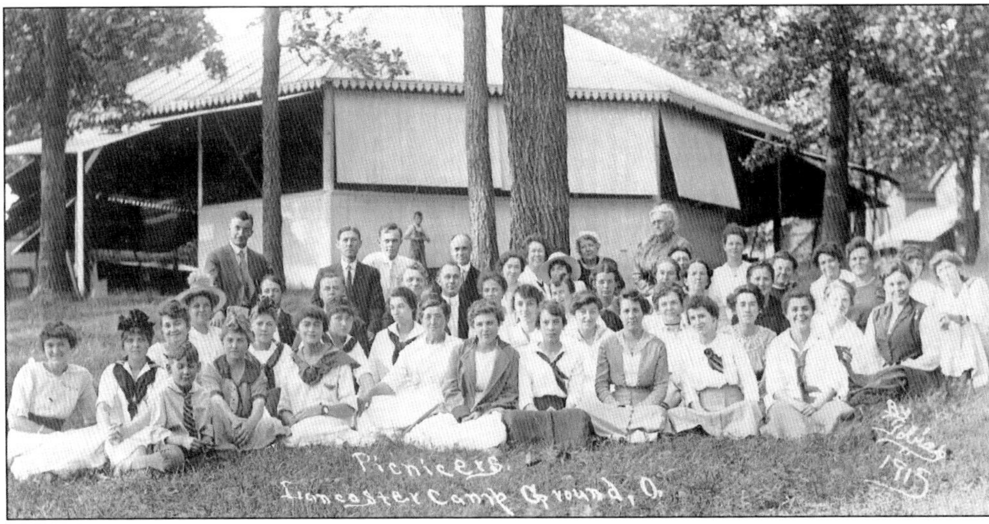

The Lancaster Camp Meeting and Church Assembly Association, Inc. (Lancaster Camp Ground) was organized in 1872, according to the group's written history. Its primary emphasis was on the Christian gospel. After a brief stay on leased land in Logan and Carroll, Ohio, organizers settled on the Hilltop in Lancaster in 1875. Many Logan families owned cottages on the grounds and spent time in the main auditorium listening to various speakers, such as Billy Sunday and Homer Rodeheaver. This postcard image was taken about 1915 and shows a part of campground life. (Courtesy of HH.)

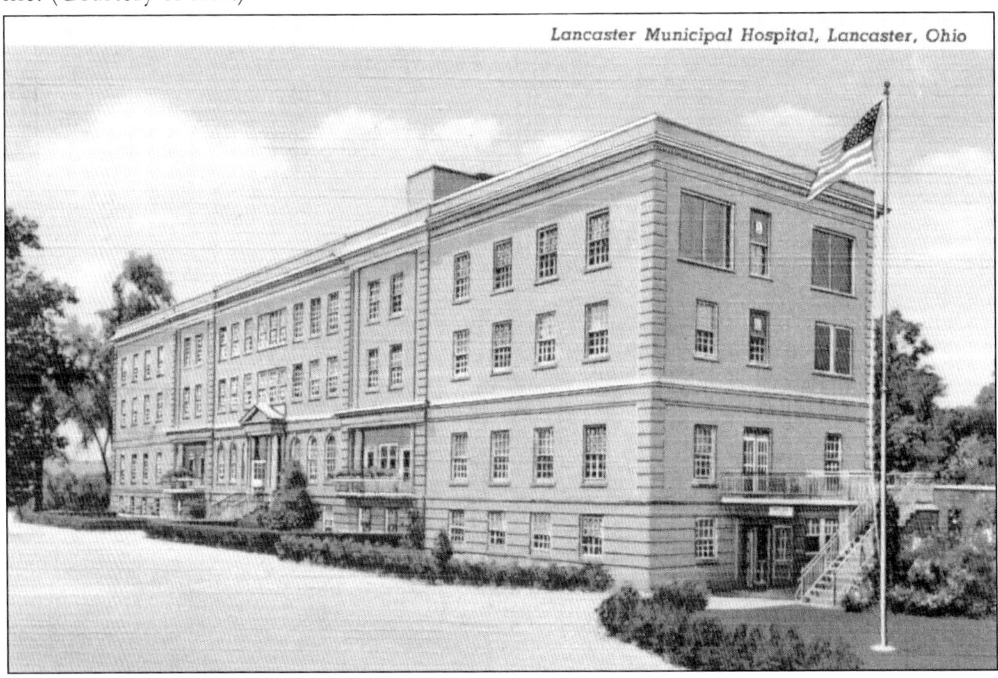

This postcard shows the Lancaster Municipal Hospital around the time of its construction in the 1920s. At one time, a nursing school was located in the hospital. Now Fairfield Medical Center, it is one of the largest employers in Lancaster. The facility has extended its services to include the latest cardiovascular surgery, has an accredited oncology department, and continues to make strides in meeting the medical needs of the surrounding community. (Courtesy of HH.)

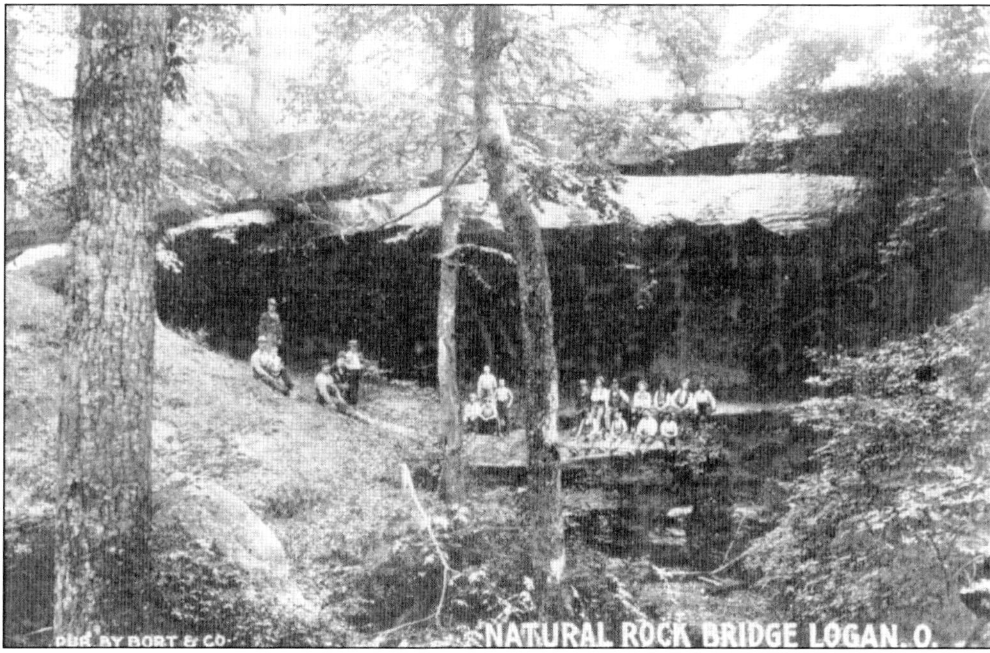

The natural Rock Bridge pictured on the postcard above is dated 1909. The bridge is an ideal place for a day's outing, as the area has many natural charms. A large group of nature lovers that has hiked to the site can be also be seen. The long rock below is in Hocking County, within walking distance from Route 33. (Both courtesy of HH.)

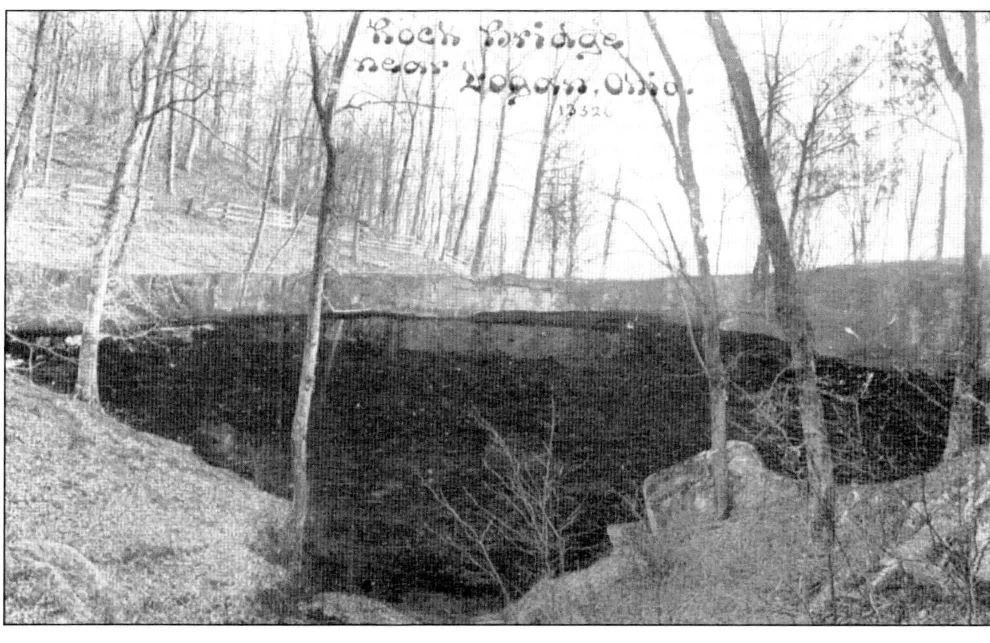

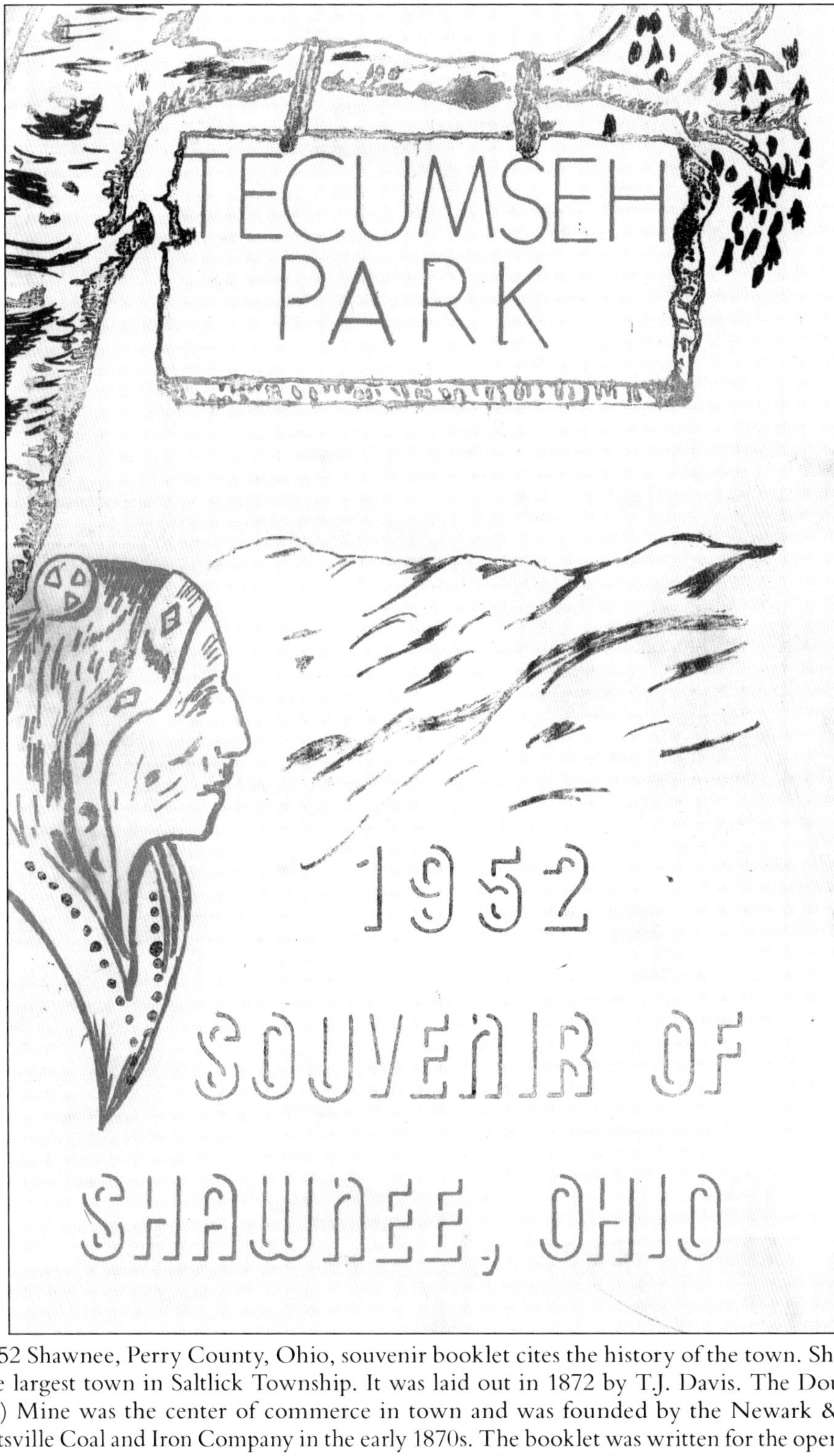

A 1952 Shawnee, Perry County, Ohio, souvenir booklet cites the history of the town. Shawnee is the largest town in Saltlick Township. It was laid out in 1872 by T.J. Davis. The Double X (XX) Mine was the center of commerce in town and was founded by the Newark & New Straitsville Coal and Iron Company in the early 1870s. The booklet was written for the opening of Tecumseh Recreation Park, built for the enjoyment of the general public. (Courtesy of JM.)

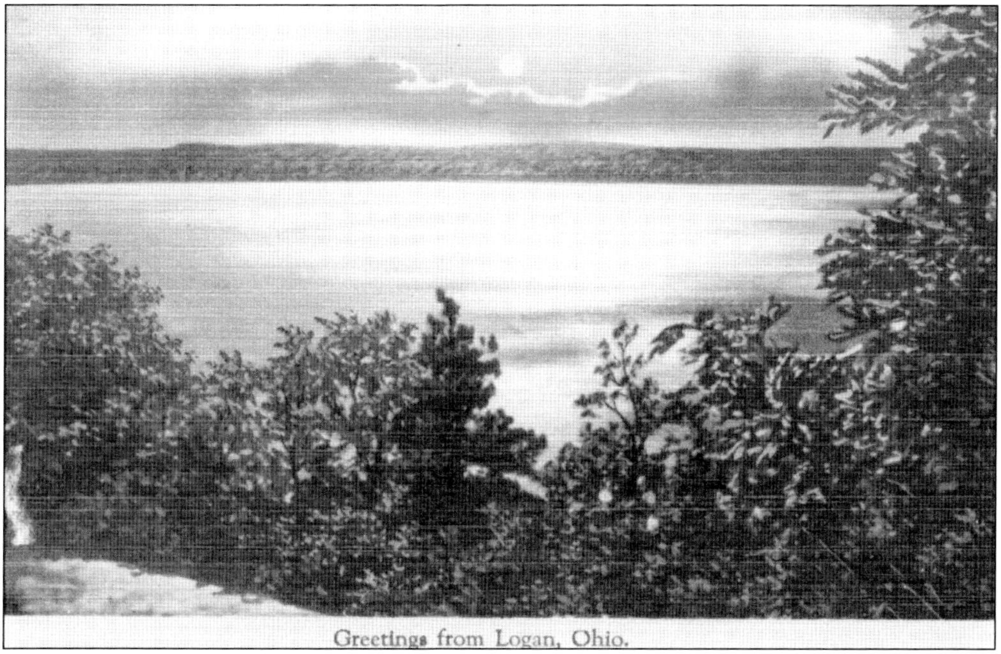

A "Greetings from" postcard shows a beautiful sunset in the Hocking Hills in Logan, Ohio. (Courtesy of CCH.)

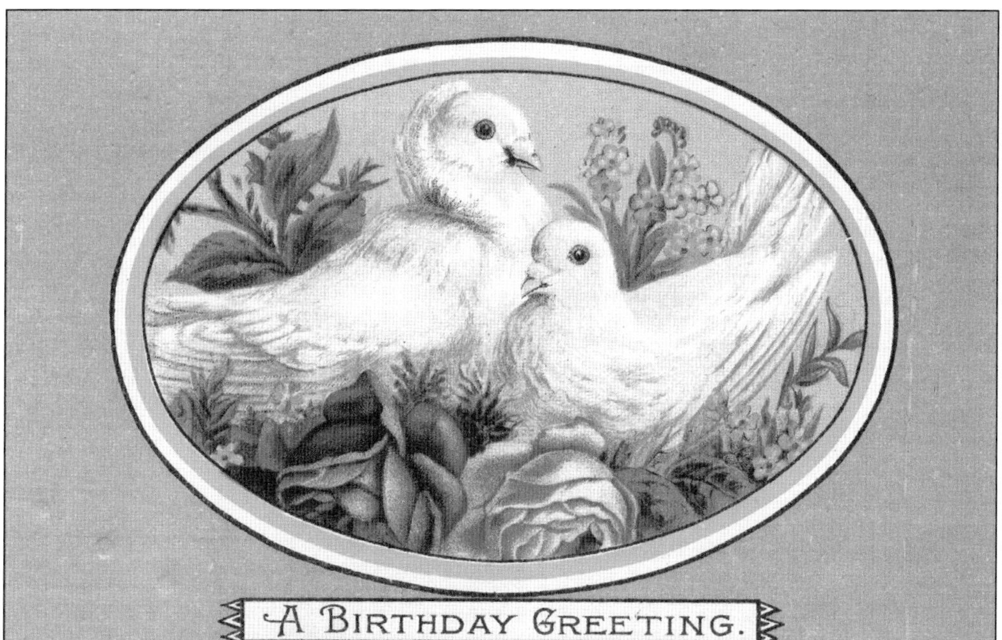

Pure-white doves send birthday greetings to the recipient of this card, which dates to 1910. (Courtesy of JM.)

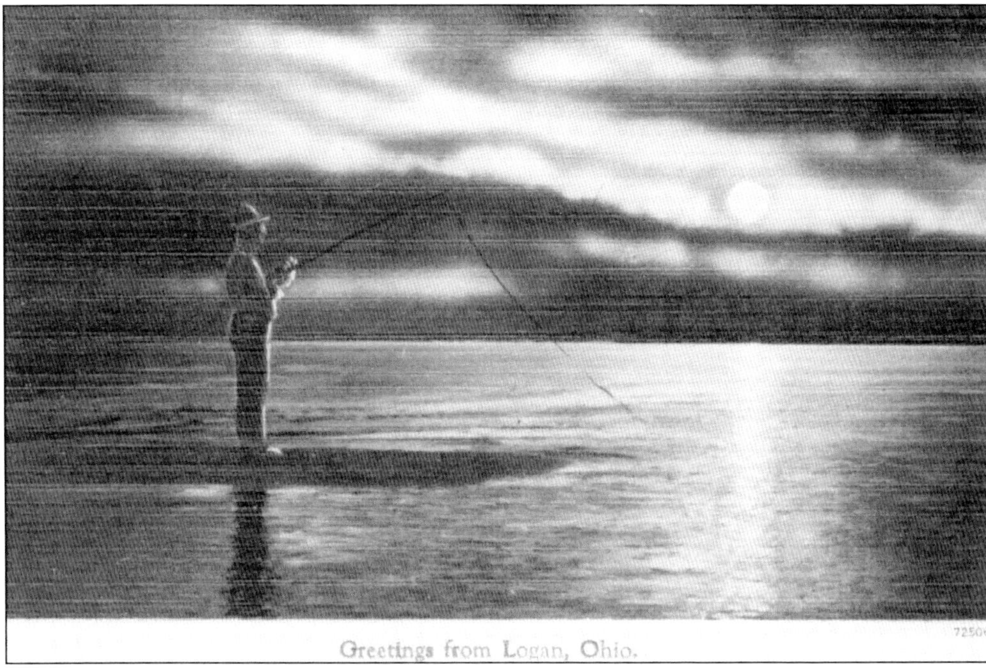

Another Hocking Hills postcard depicts a moonlit view of the Hocking River. (Courtesy of CCH.)

Roses help to say, "Be Good Darling," on a card that dates to 1909. (Courtesy of JM.)

Six

The Forgotten Few

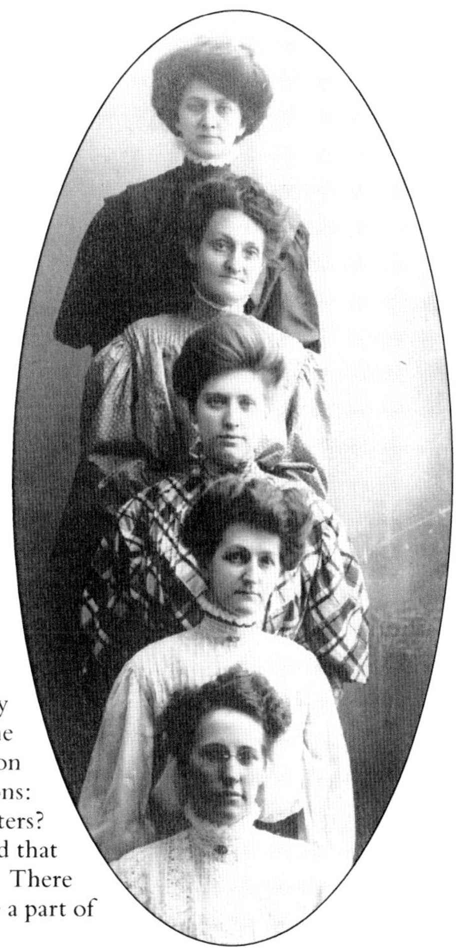

Who are the forgotten few? They are the majority of postcards and photographs that do not identify the place, date, or name of the images. The postcard on this chapter introduction page asks several questions: are these five little maids from school? Teachers? Sisters? In this cleverly posed photograph, it can be assumed that the women must have had something in common. There is nothing written on the back of the card. They are a part of this chapter's forgotten few. (Courtesy of HH.)

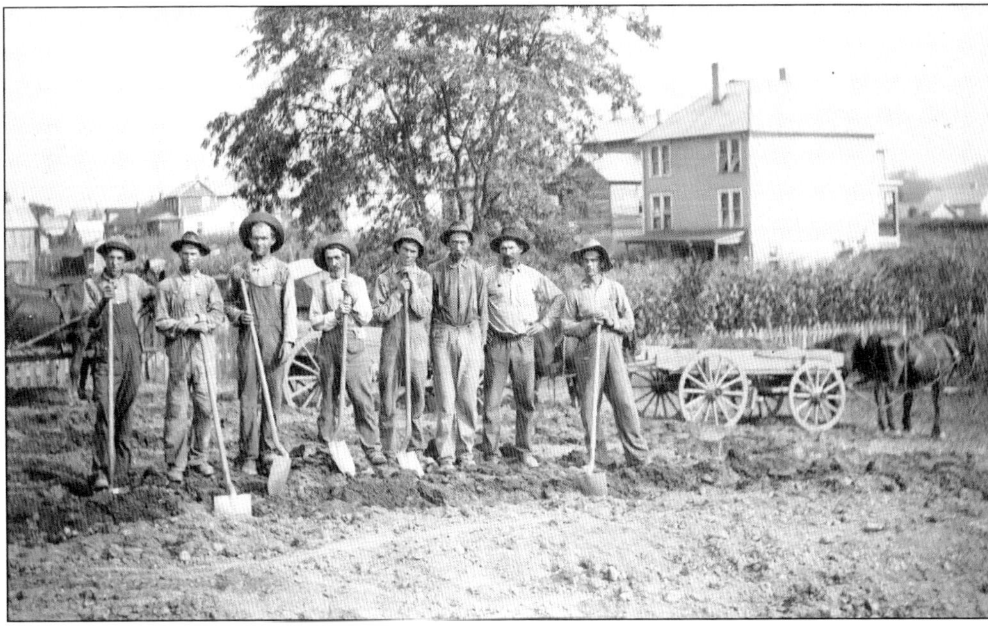

People sometimes forget that in the days prior to machinery, backbreaking work was done by hand. This work crew appears to be digging some type of ditch. Perhaps they were city laborers, but no identification or date is on the postcard. (Courtesy of HH.)

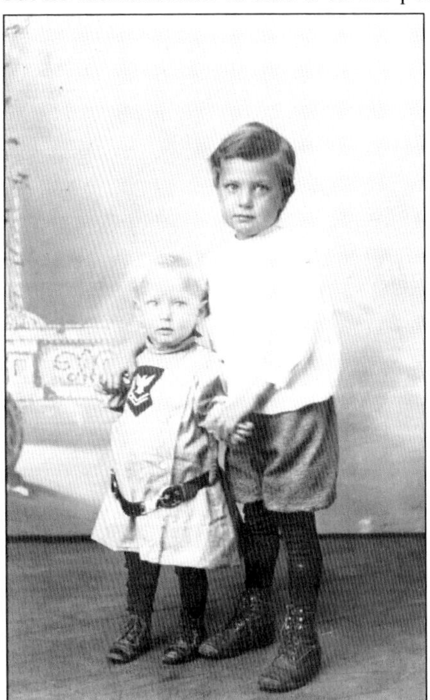

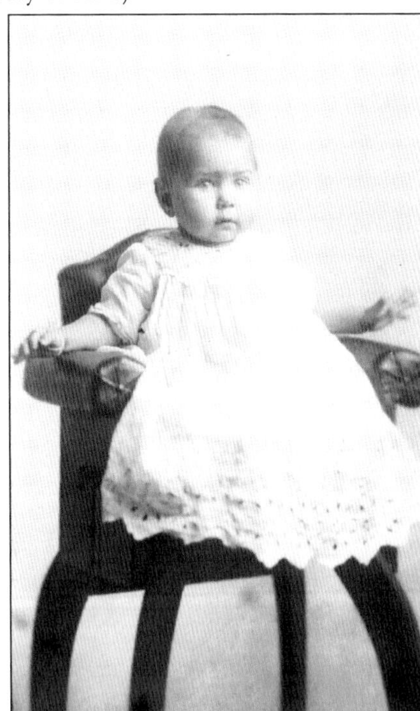

Capturing the innocence and sweetness of children on postcards helped to memorialize wonderful memories for the family. Unfortunately, the names of the children are unknown. Also, since boys were clothed in dresses during this time period, one cannot be sure if the child is a Jack or a Jill. (At left, courtesy of HH; at right, CCH.)

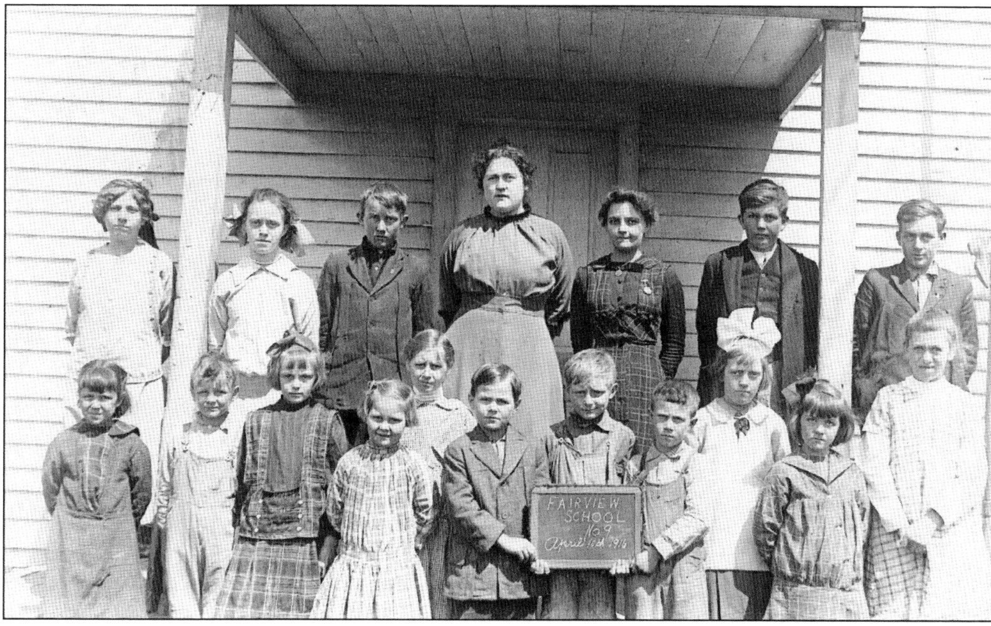

At one time, there were 100 one-room schools in the county, but by 1935 there were only 15. The following are several class-picture postcards with little information available about them. In Washington Township's Blackjack School No. 3, the photograph is dated April 20, 1917. The building was constructed in 1877 and sold at auction for $115 in 1935. (Courtesy of DB.)

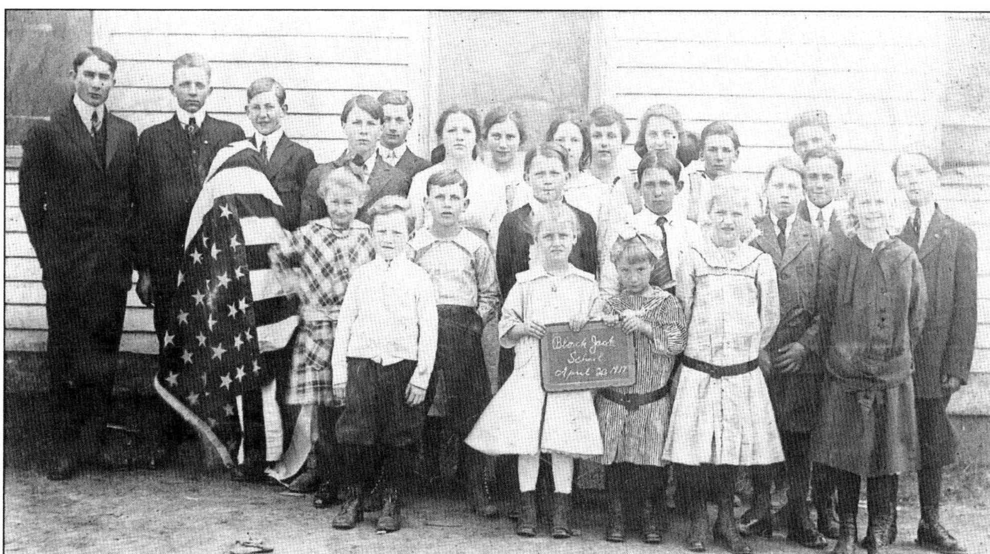

Fairview School No. 9, also in Washington Township, closed its doors about 1927. This photograph was taken in 1916 and identifies the teacher as Paul Hansel. The first record of the school is from February 17, 1840. It was closely associated with Fairview Church. (Courtesy of HH.)

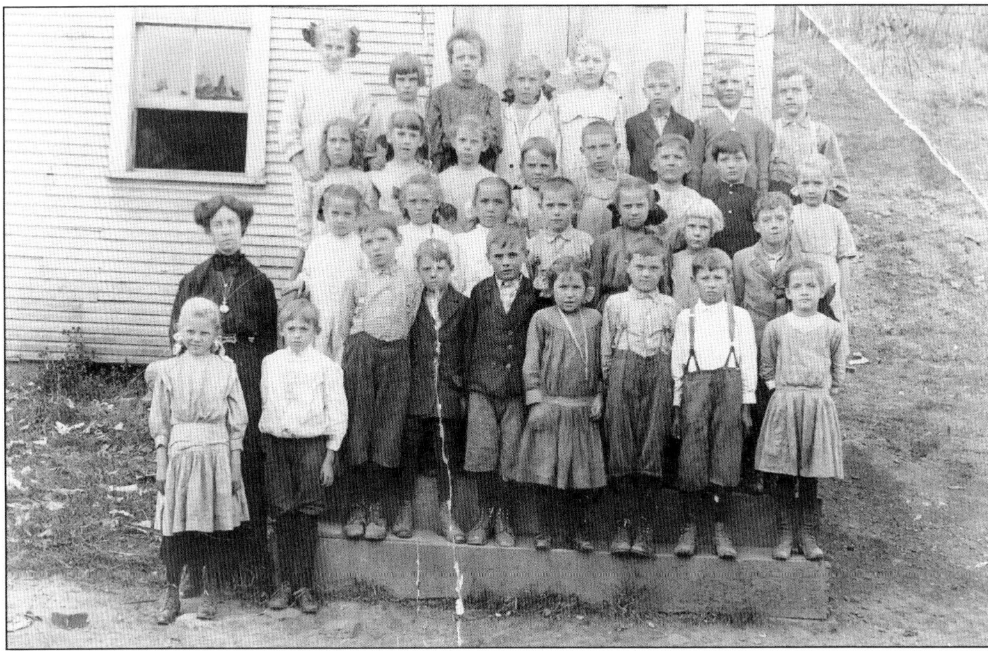

This postcard has no identification with the exception of "Murray City" printed on the back. Located in Ward Township, it was originally built of logs but later replaced by a frame structure. (Courtesy of DB.)

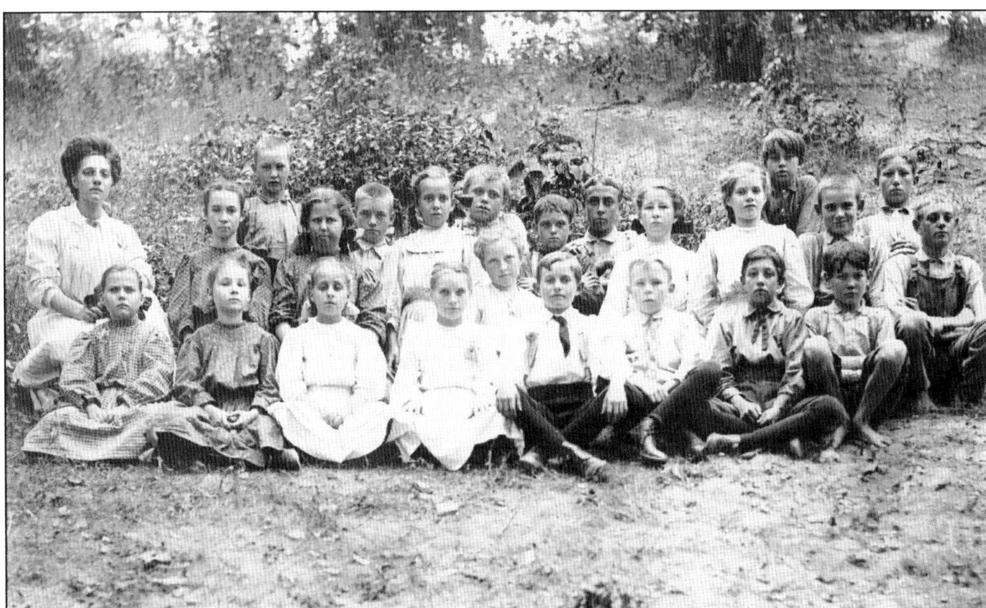

The class at the Monday School in the town of Monday, in Ward Township, poses for a photograph in 1909. The teacher's surname is identified as Reinstetle. (Courtesy of DB.)

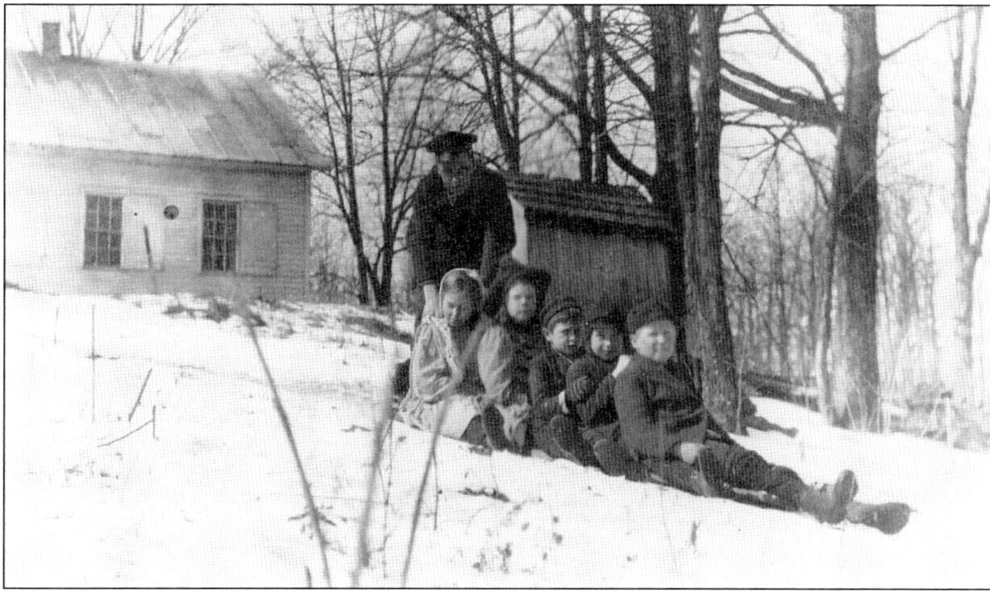

Olive Branch School No. 7 was in Starr Township near New Plymouth. The original building was constructed in 1870 of beech lumber. The last teacher at Olive Branch was Anna M. Heinlein when it closed in 1932. (Courtesy of DB.)

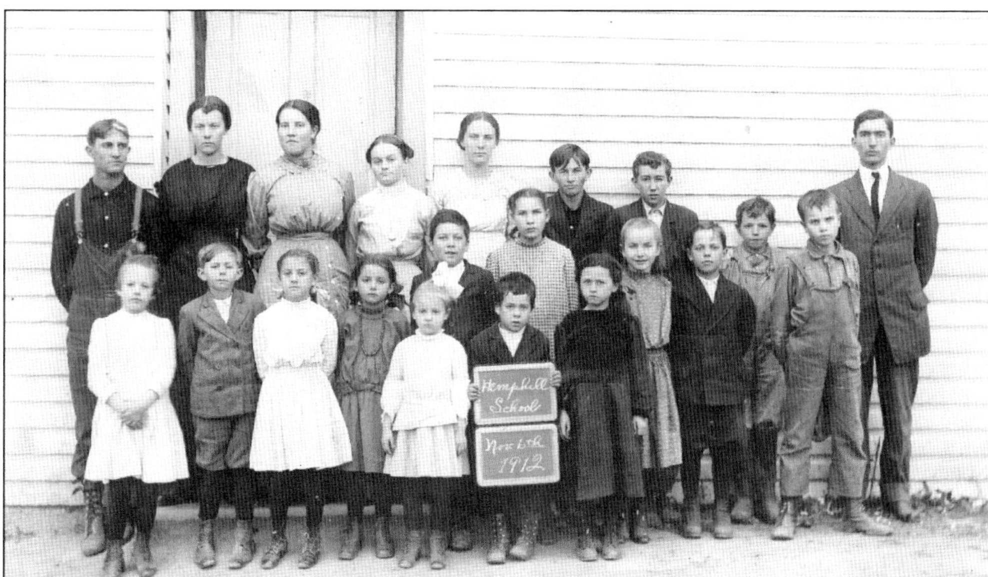

Perry Township in western Hocking County had several schools, including Hemphill School. The date of the postcard is November 1912. In 1860, Margaret Hemphill deeded land to the Perry Township School Board for school purposes, hence the name. (Courtesy of HH.)

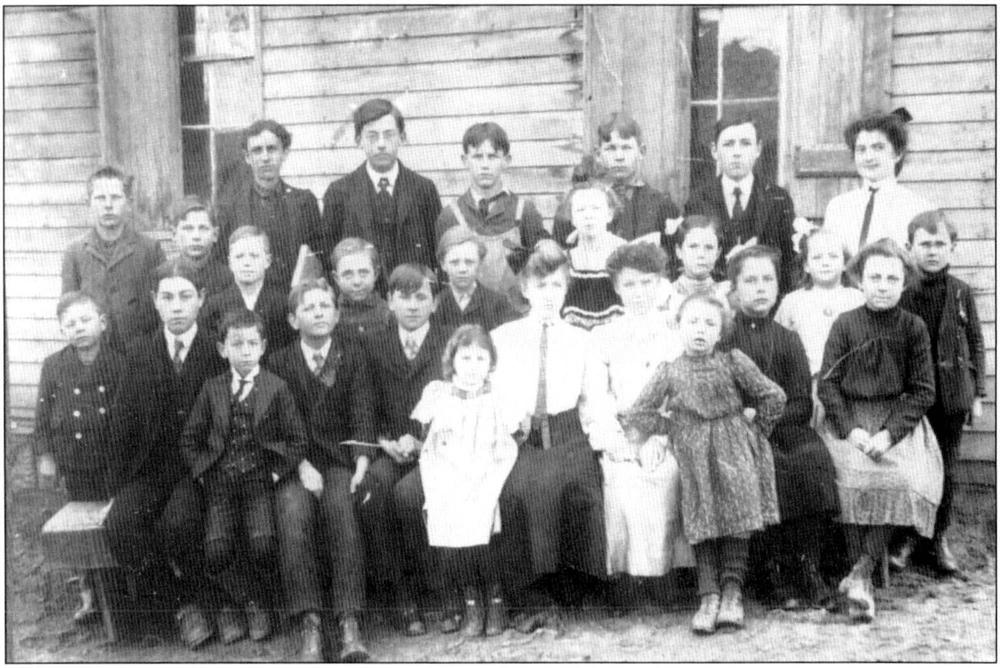

Pictured here is Strawberry Ridge School in Perry Township. The teacher is identified as Bertha Keplar, and John and Frank Coakley are mentioned as being students in the top row. (Courtesy of HH.)

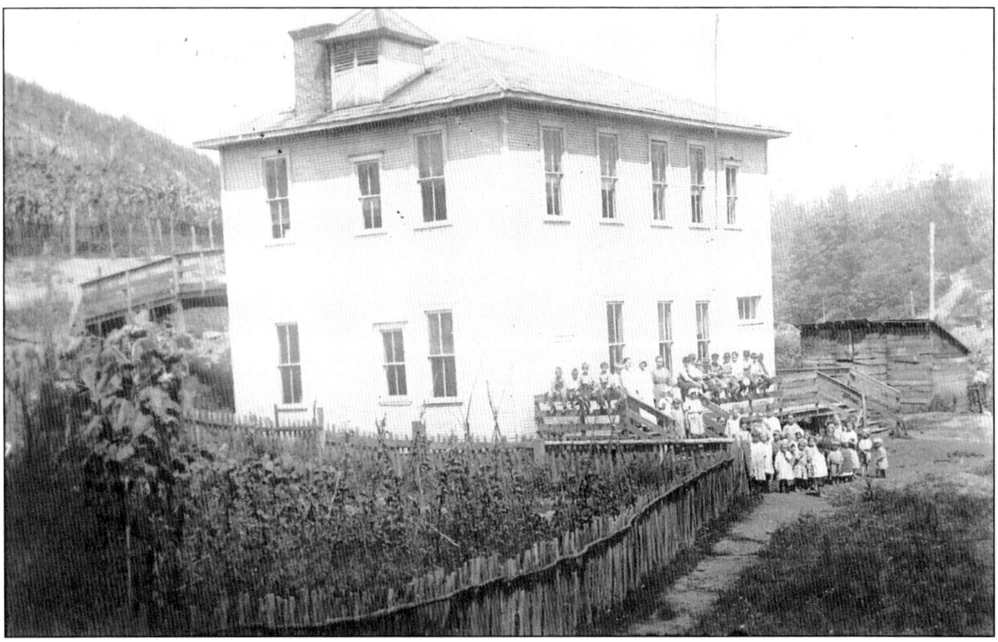

Newtown School, in Ward Township, was ordered closed by the state department of education in 1938. The closure was determined by the fact that the students could have a better education at a school just a few miles away. Newtown School remained open for the school term in 1938–1939. Other Ward Township schools closed at the same time were Orbiston, Jobs, and New Pittsburgh. (Courtesy of DB.)

These newlyweds celebrated the occasion by having postcards made for friends and family who could not attend the event. The card is addressed to William Miller. (Courtesy of JM.)

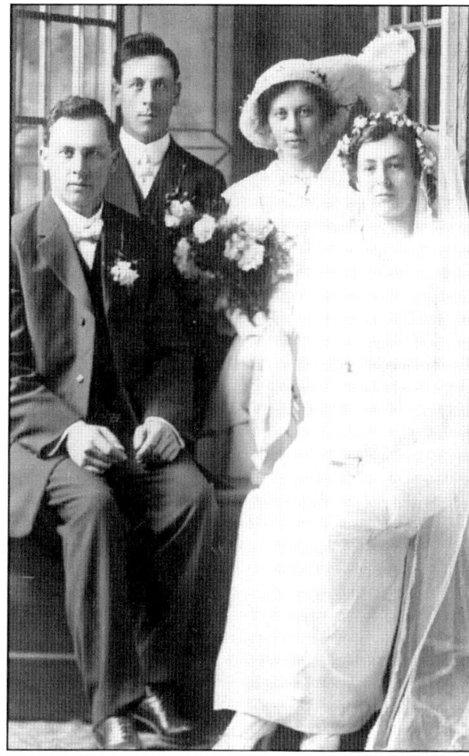

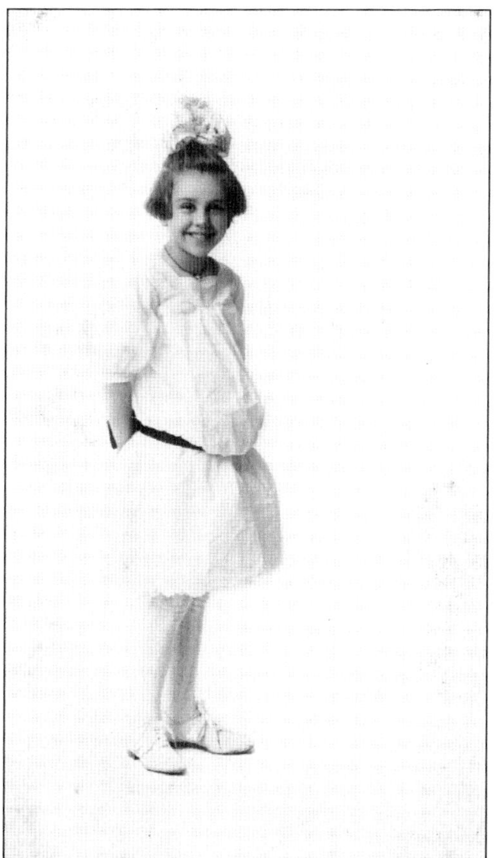

This little girl is dressed in her finest for a photograph. The occasion is unknown, but perhaps it is her birthday. The large hair bow was typical in the 1920s. (Courtesy of HH.)

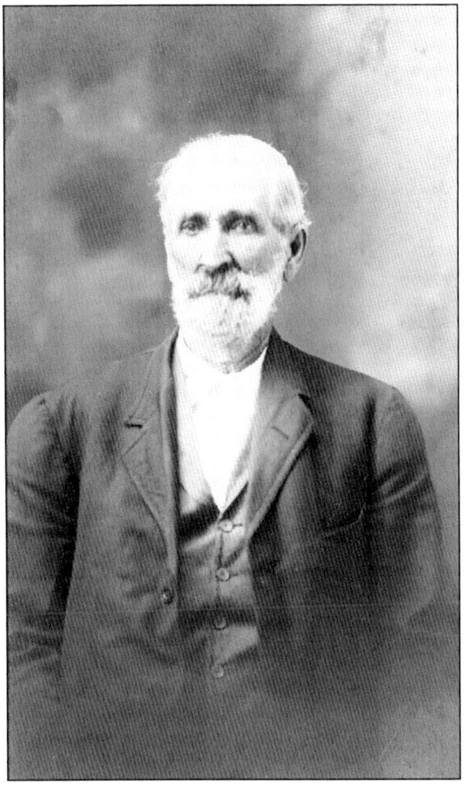

This patriarch with his weathered face was perhaps encouraged by his family to have a portrait taken in the autumn of his life. One cannot help but wonder about the joys and sorrows of his journey. (Courtesy of HH.)

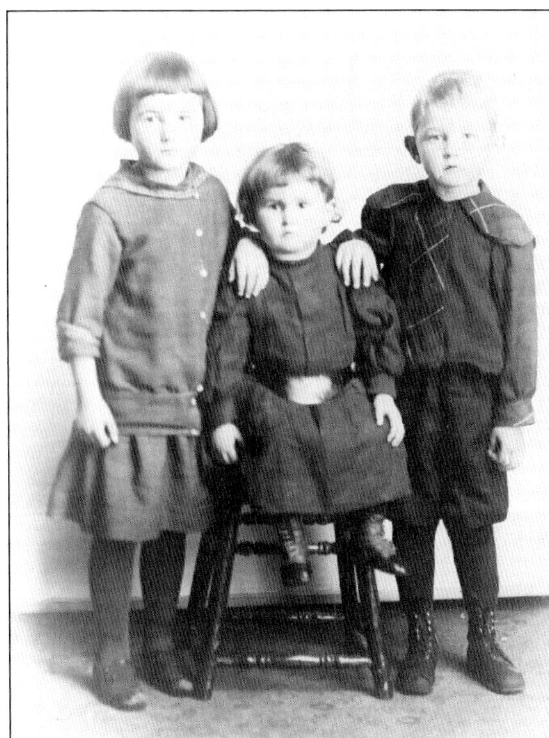

These children's mother wrote on this postcard that she has a lively family and lists their names. From left to right are Pauline (age 6), Lucille (age 3), and Richard (age 5). (Courtesy of HH.)

The "Family in Hats" or the "Hat Family"? Either title could be used for this postcard. Mother, father, and children are all obviously wearing their best for this important occasion, whatever it may have been. (Courtesy of HH.)

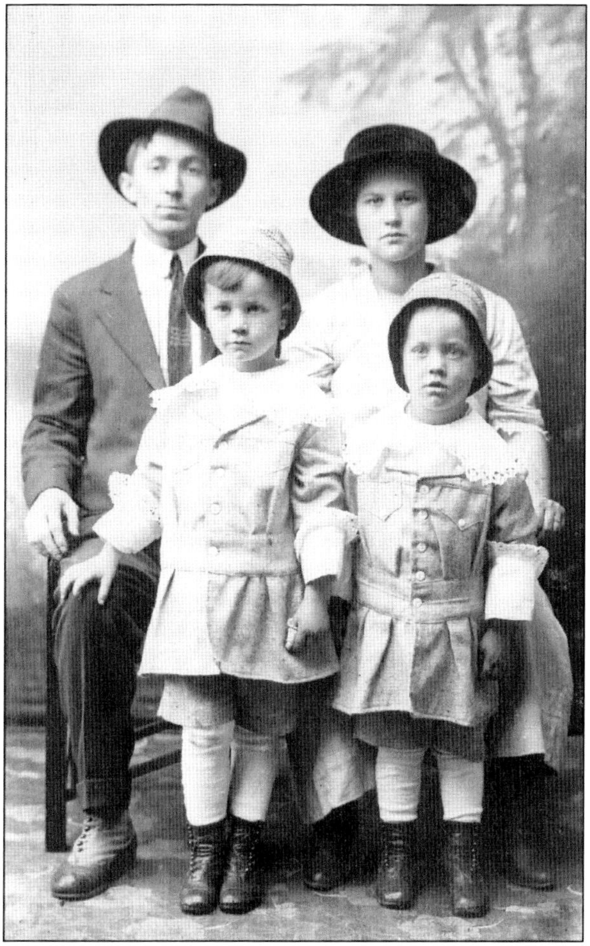

Postcards of animals, especially puppies and kittens, were best sellers, as their antics pulled at the buyers' heartstrings. This is a charming photograph with a little girl and her pet dog as they play. (Courtesy of HH.)

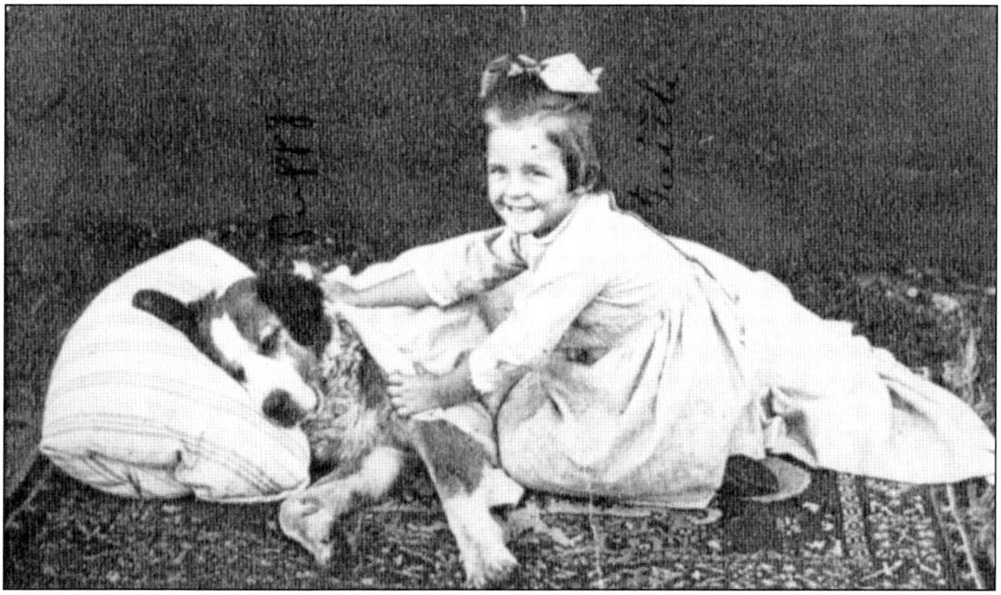

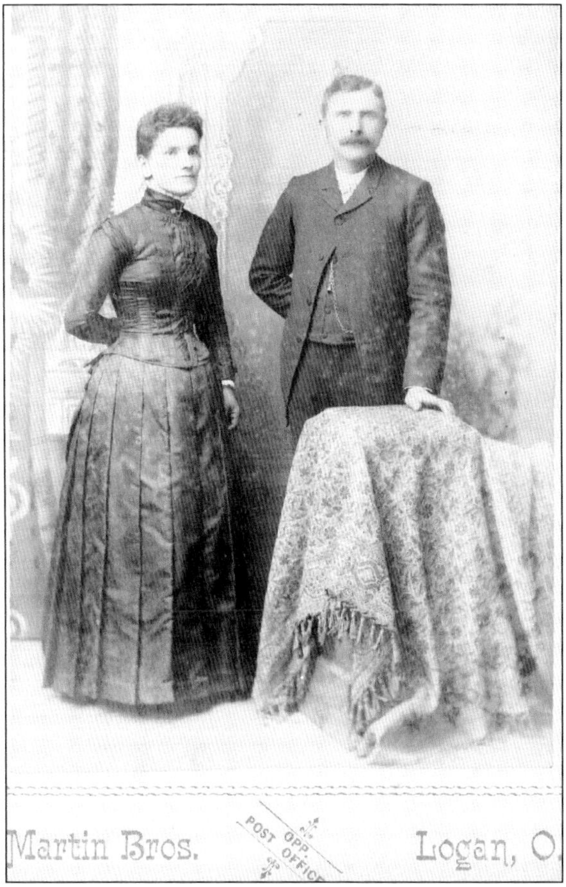

These two couples had photographs taken for posterity by Logan photographers the Martin brothers, whose address (at left) was over Harrington's Store and J.D. McLain (below), located on Gallagher Avenue. (Both courtesy of HH.)

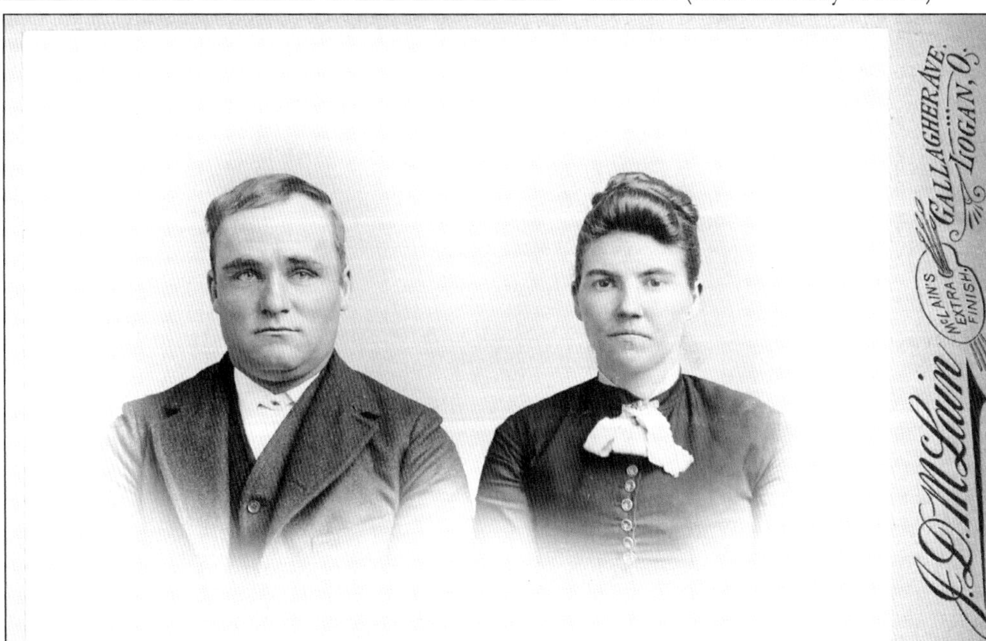

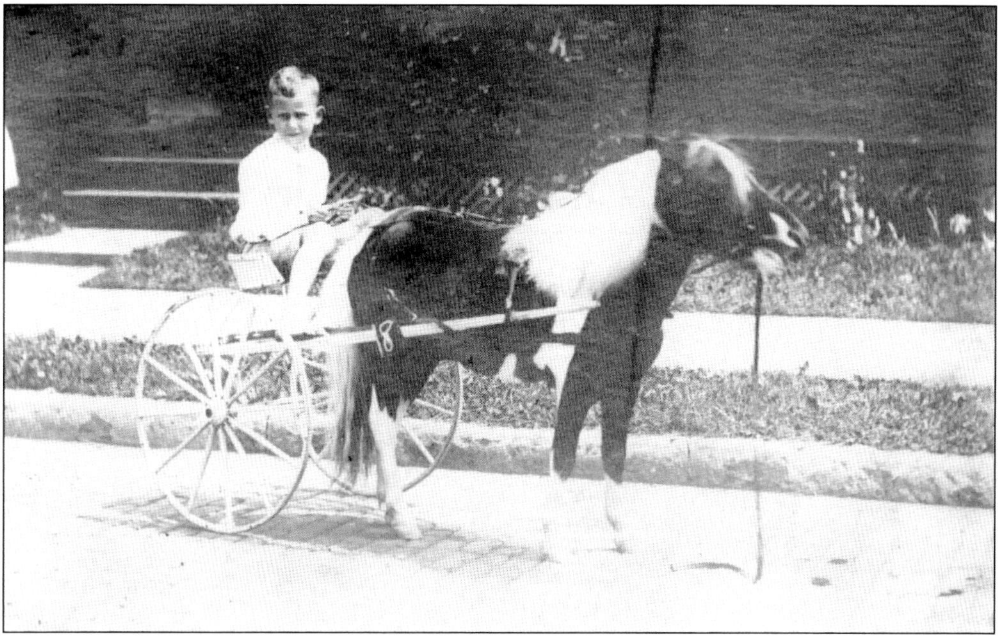

The postcard above may have been taken by an itinerant photographer. A photographer would go to a town, knock on doors, and ask residents if they would like to have a photograph taken. This little boy is shown with a pony and cart that may have belonged to the photographer. The postcard below shows a workingman pausing with his horse and wagon on an unpaved Logan street. The flag is unreadable, but note the little boy in the wagon. (Both courtesy of HH.)

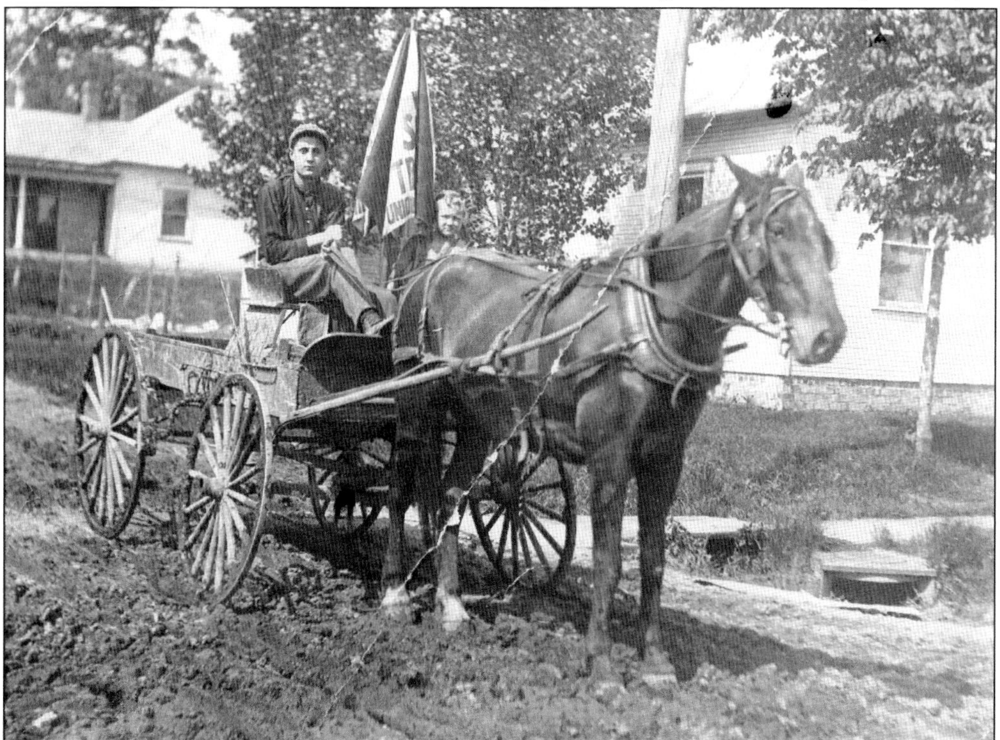

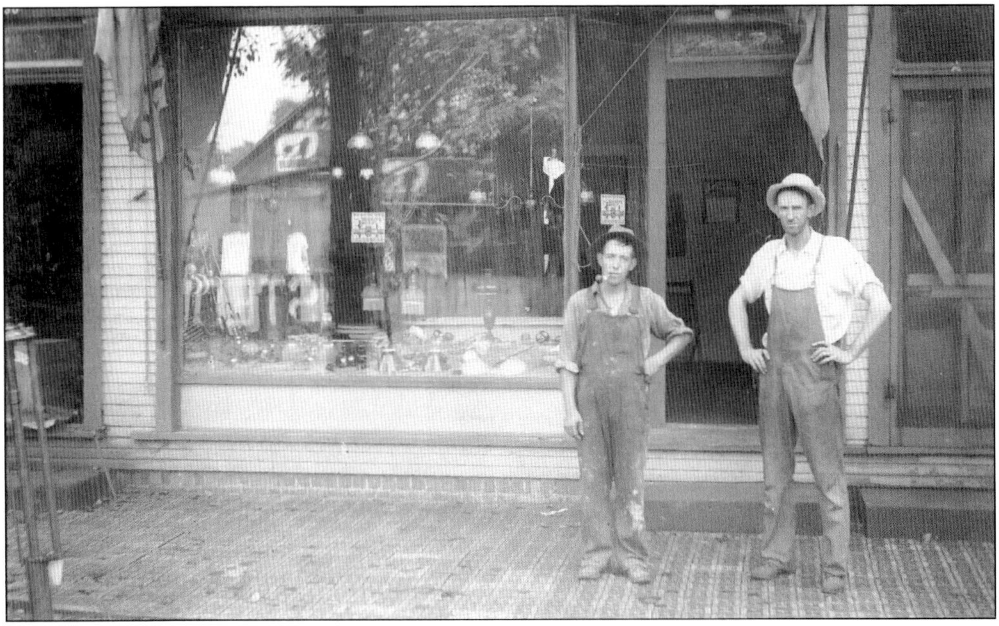

This postcard shows two farmers that have come to town to conduct their business. Saturday was the day when farm families came to sell or buy supplies. The day was highly anticipated by wives and children as a chance to visit with others in the community. The "Ladies Comfort Station" was a facility built in Logan with funds raised by local women. It was constructed to give women and children a place to rest and relax during the day while their husbands and fathers were occupied elsewhere. The comfort station has now been razed. (Courtesy of HH.)

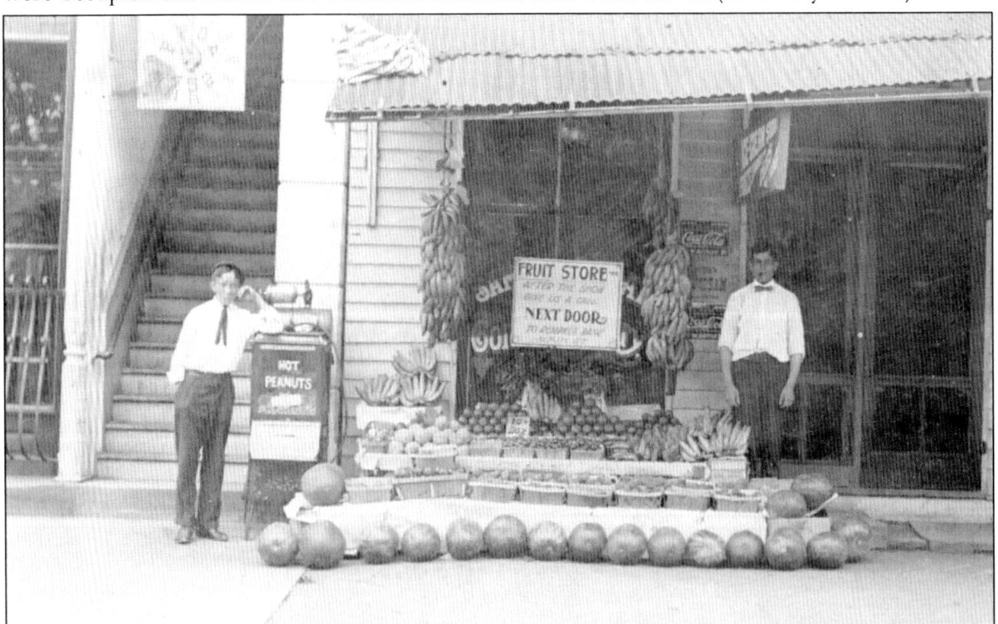

This fruit stand cannot be identified as to a place or owner, but there is a BPOE sign above the stairs to the right. Watermelons and other fresh fruits and vegetables were plentiful in the postcard image. (Courtesy of JM.)

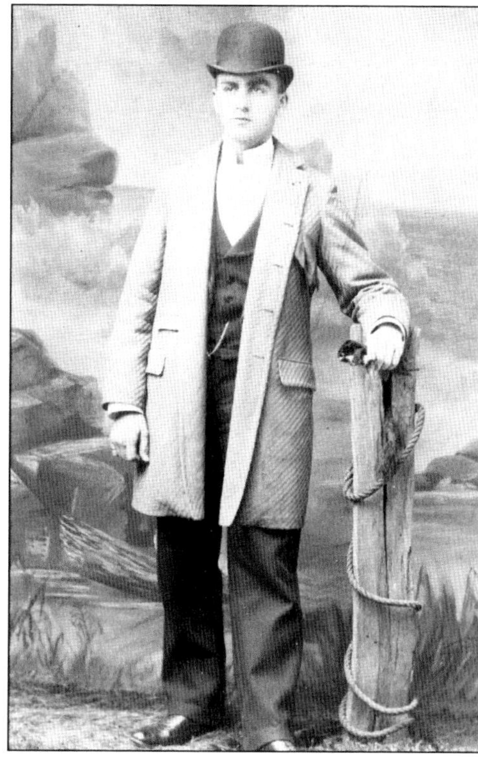

These postcards are showing two different men dressed in their best outfits. The gentleman at right has a message on the card, "New Year's 1891." No date is available for the postcard below, but this fellow may be going to woo his favorite girl. (Both courtesy of HH.)

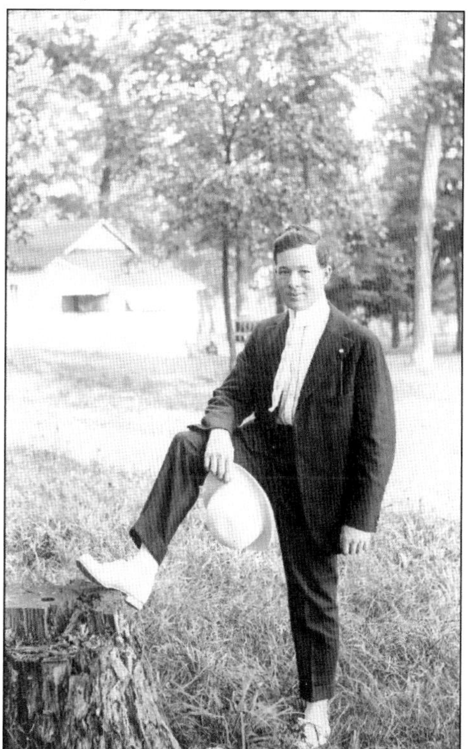

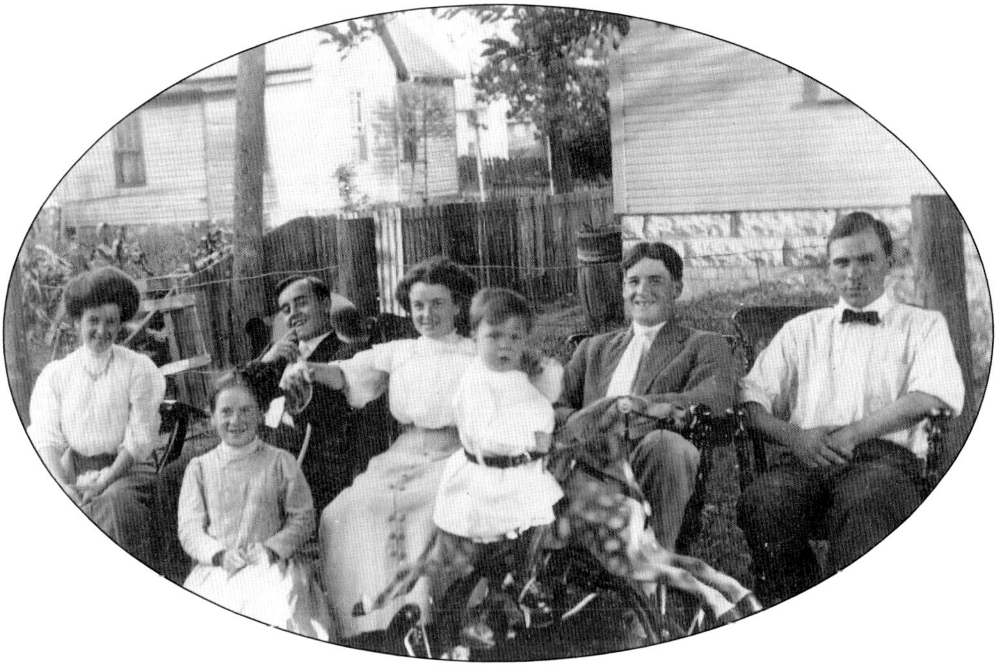

Sunday afternoons are pleasant when spent under a shade tree (above) or on the front porch with family and friends (below). These scenes bring back memories of fried chicken dinners and homemade ice cream at Grandmother's house. (Both courtesy of HH.)

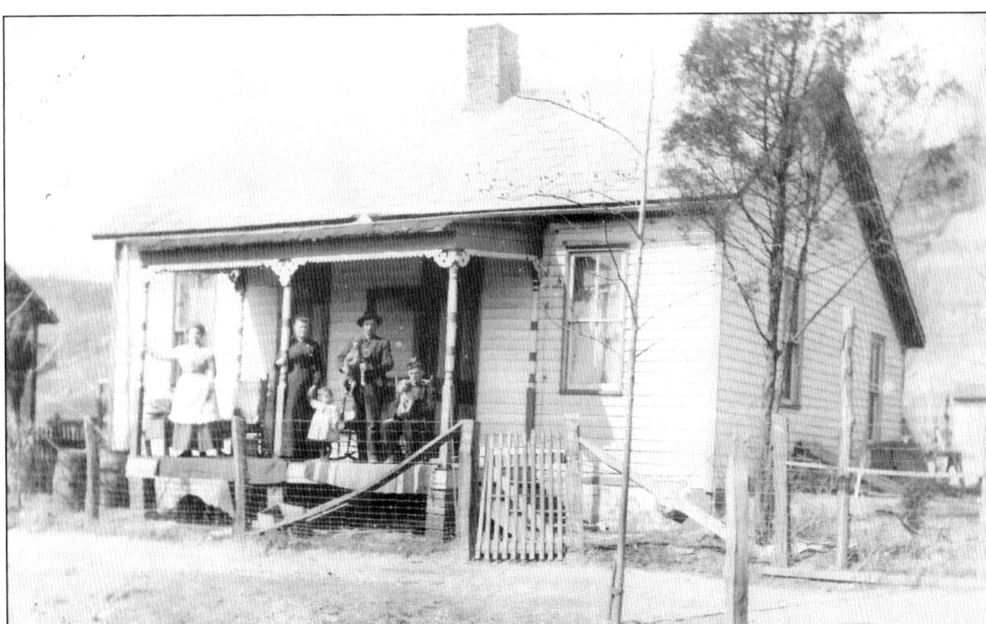

In the Golden Age (1907–1915) of the postcard, photographs were taken and then attached to a thin piece of cardboard, and no envelope was required. This young woman in a rocking chair signed the card, "Fannie," and addressed it, "Cor. Rochester and Friesner Ave's." Rochester Avenue's name was later changed to (West) Front Street. The card is dated 1911. (Courtesy of HH.)

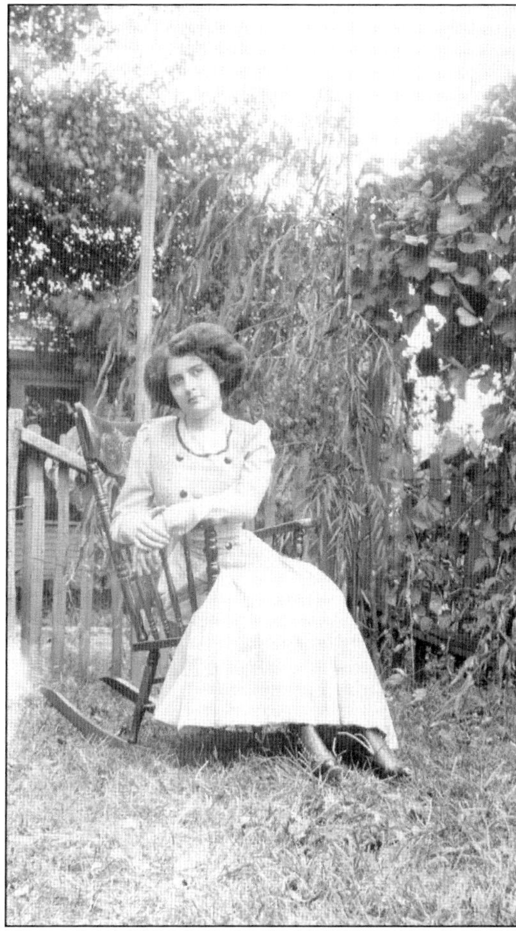

Very little information could be found about the Ladies Social Club shown here. The Nondescripts, Junia Club, Tourist Book Club, Ladies Euchre Club, and others were active among the women of Logan. Once again, a parade has brought them out to be recognized by the townspeople. (Courtesy of HH.)

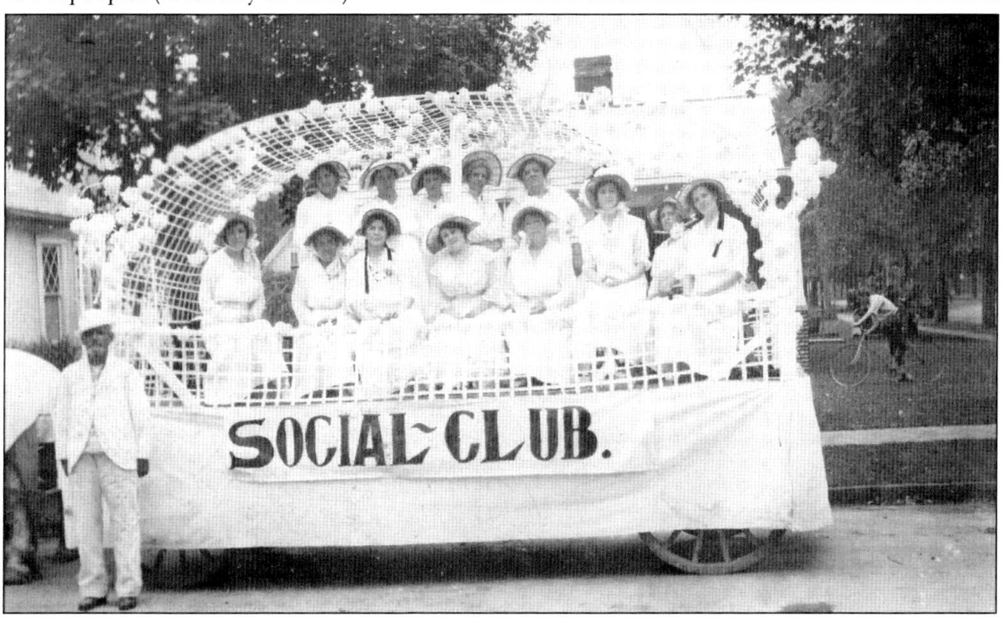

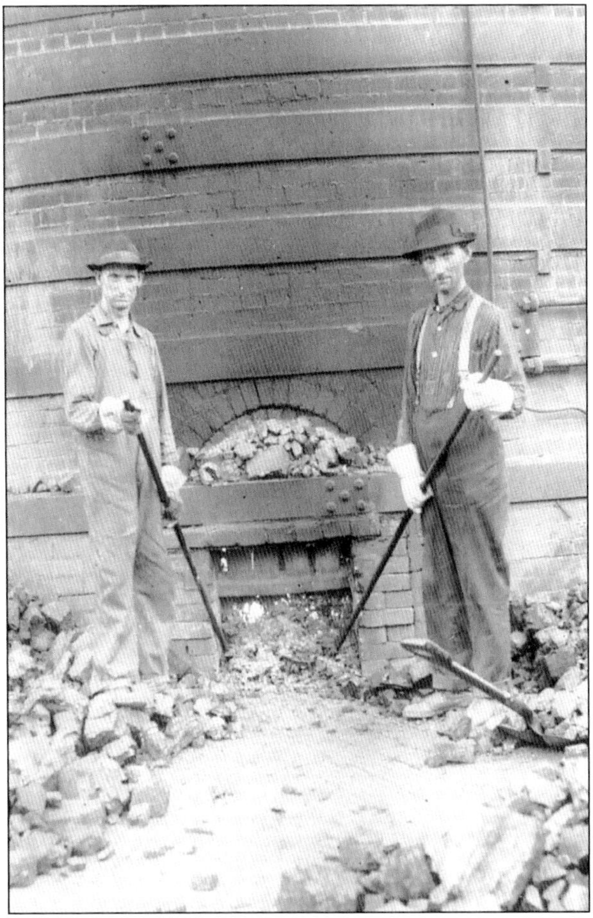

This 1914 postcard shows two men firing a kiln at the Greendale Rug Brick Plant in Green Township. Look closely at their features; they are certainly brothers and possibly twins. (Courtesy of KK.)

New Cadiz was first laid out in 1854, and the owners were James Blackburn and Melissa Butin. The name New Cadiz was not extensively used, and *Cram's World Atlas of 1900* lists only Union Furnace. These five men appear to be a work crew at the Columbus Brick and Terra Cotta (CB&TC) plant in Union Furnace. (Courtesy of HH.)

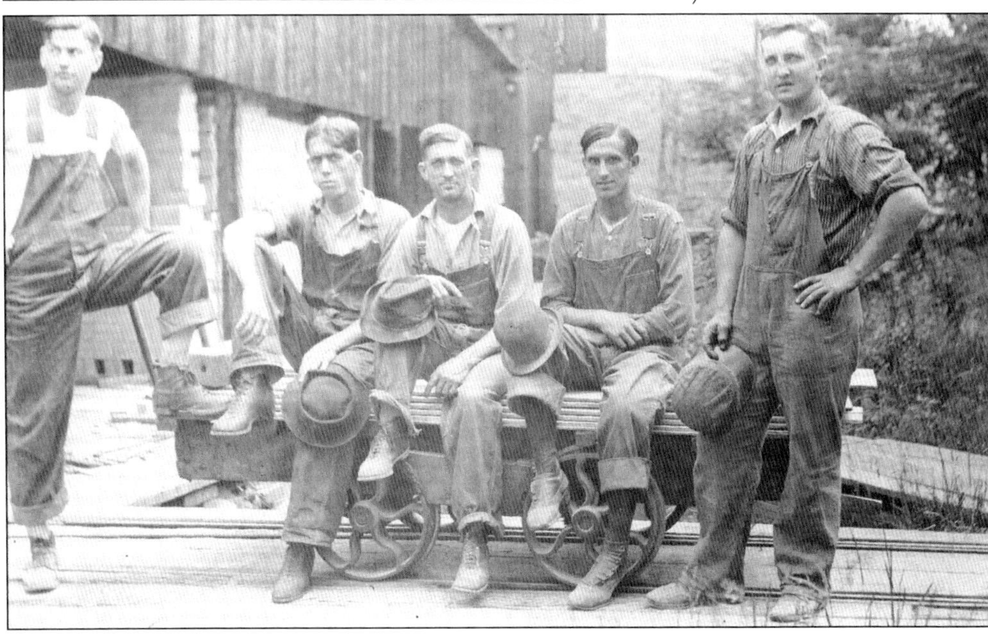

Seven

Hocking Hills Holidaze

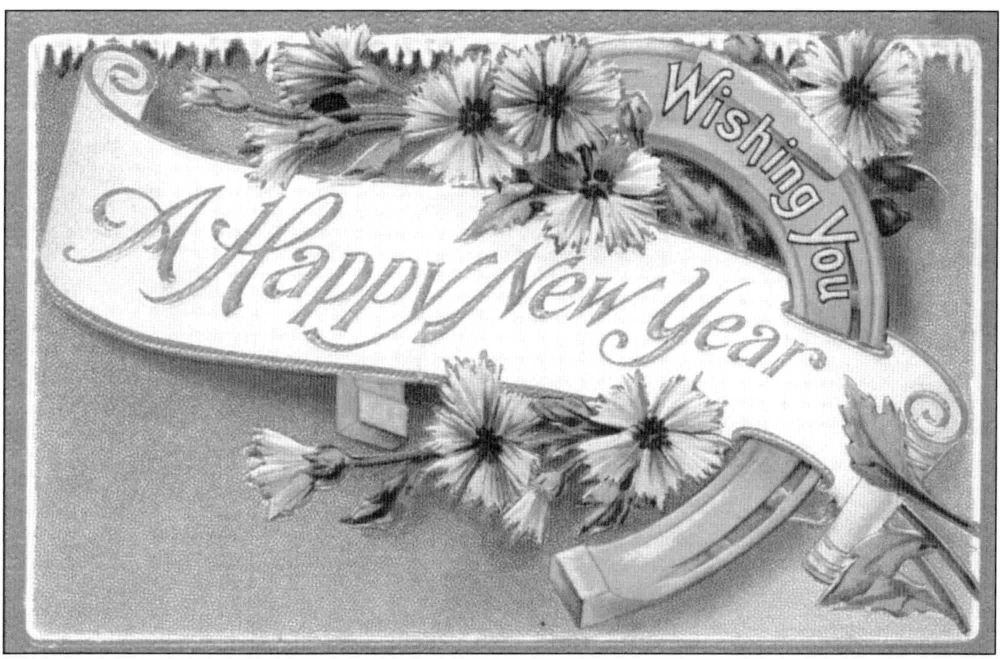

Postcard greetings were used for every occasion beginning in the early 1900s. Cards for holidays, birthdays, get well, farewell, new baby, and many others were available. One penny would relay the sender's thoughts and wishes on a card adorned with beautiful and appropriate artwork. This New Year's greeting is undated. Throughout this chapter, there are a variety of delightful holiday postcards. (Courtesy of JM.)

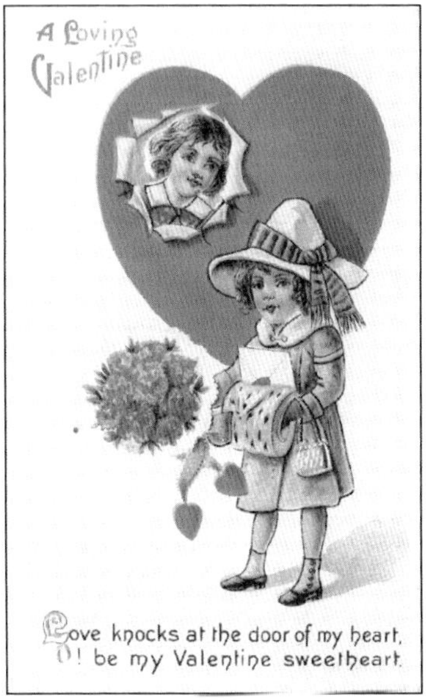

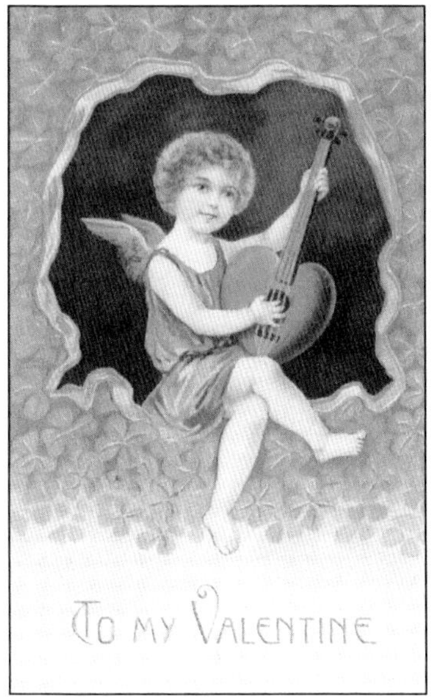

Valentine's Day seems to always brighten the winter days for Hocking Hills' schoolchildren. Homemade cards required days of coloring and pasting, which added to the excitement of this special day. Each child would also make a decorated box to hold the cards that he or she received from the rest of their classmates. The schoolteacher was a recipient of many "To My Teacher" cards embellished with lace and hearts from her favorite students. This hopeful Valentine postcard is dated 1912 and was printed in the United States. (Courtesy of JM.)

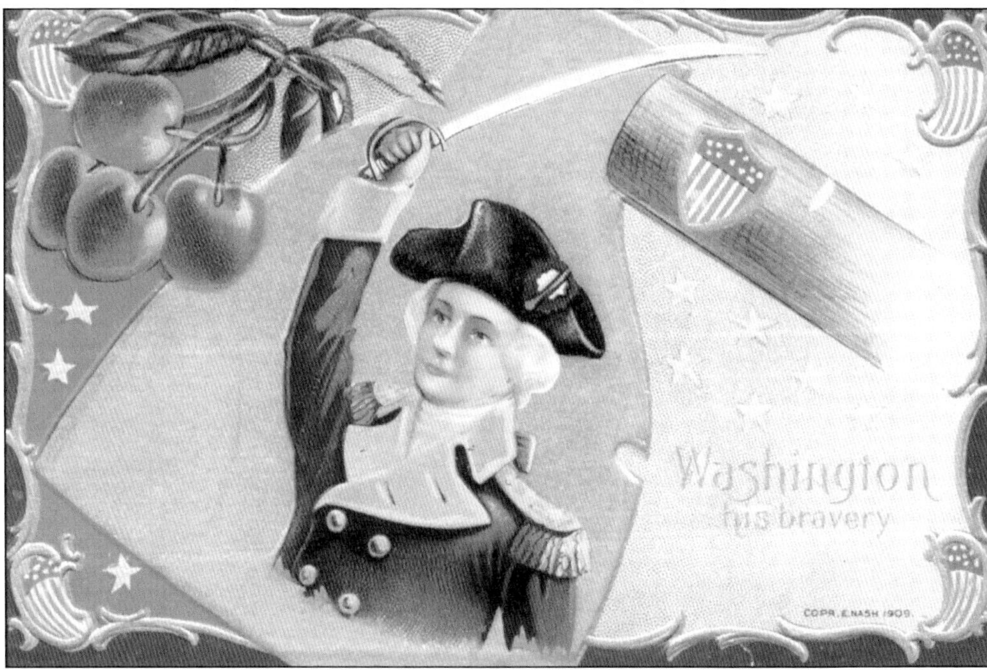

This colorful 1912 Washington's Birthday postcard honors the country's first president by featuring symbols of his life. Washington has always been remembered with great honor. Every schoolroom had an imposing portrait of Washington hanging by the chalkboard. His fabled "I shall not tell a lie" became a lesson for all good boys and girls. (Courtesy of JM.)

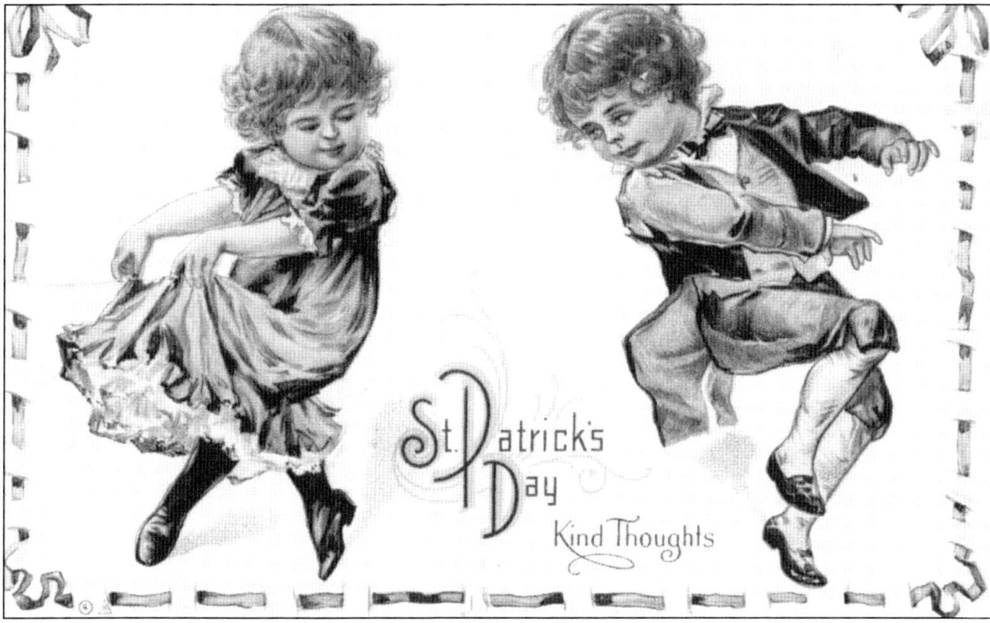

These children dancing an Irish jig sends kind thoughts to the recipient on an undated St. Patrick's Day postcard. This truly ethnic holiday celebration brought from Ireland continued in the Hocking Hills, where many Scotch Irish from the old country relocated. For many years, the late Thomas Walsh would dress in a green coat and top hat, carry his authentic shillelagh, (walking stick), and stroll the length of Logan's Main Street. He would go to each business and greet them with a hearty "top o' the mornin'." After his passing, several of his many daughters and sons carried on the tradition. (Courtesy of JM.)

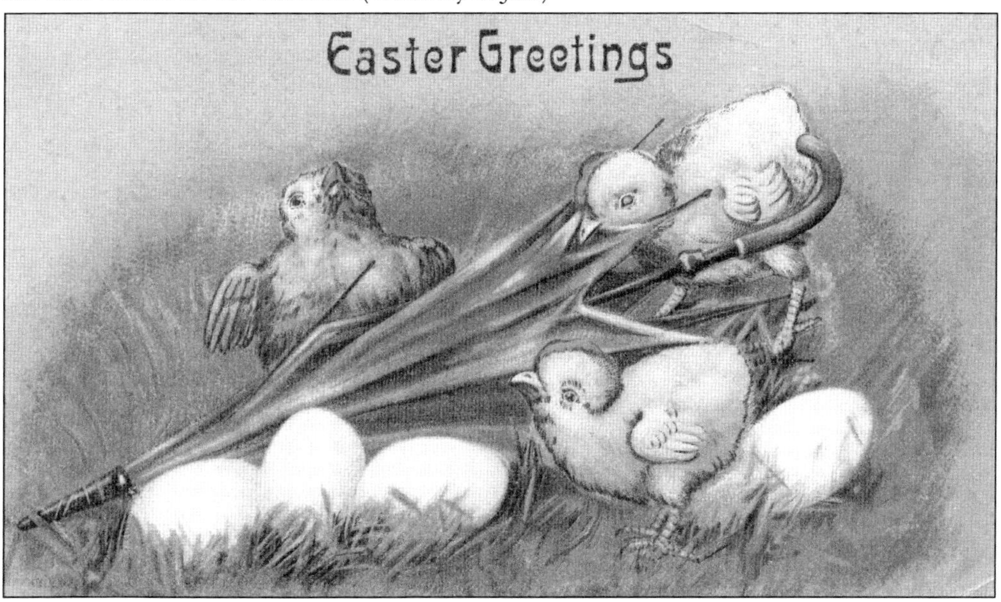

Springtime and Easter, a religious holiday, are a favorite time of year. This card is over 100 years old and marked "Made in Germany." When World War I began in 1914, the German market for postcards stopped, and in later years most cards were manufactured in the United States. (Courtesy of JM.)

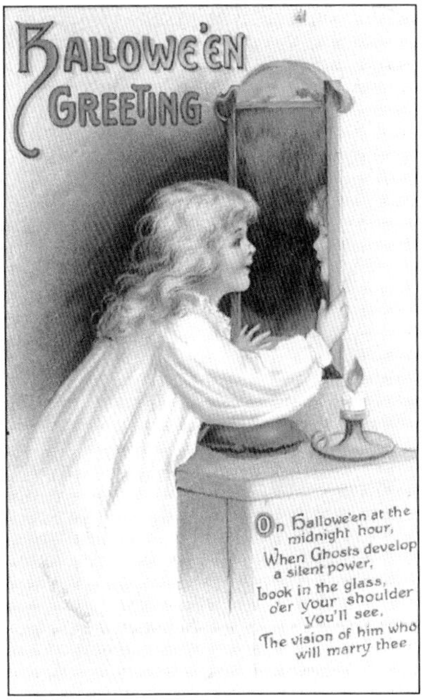

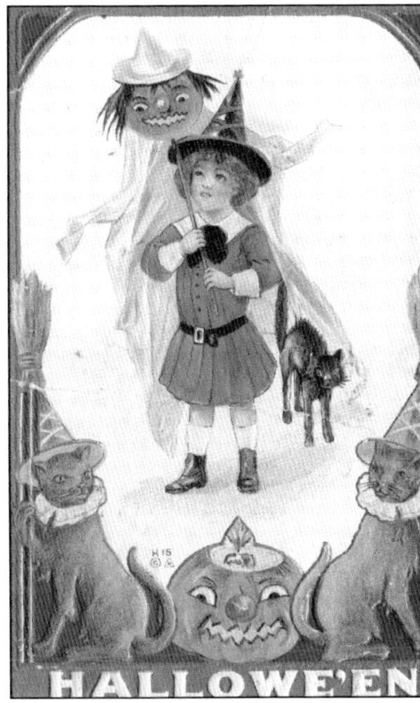

"Hallowe'en" postcards were fun rather than spooky. Costumes were part of the regalia worn by children as they went house to house begging for treats. Each little village in the Hocking Hills organizes a Hallowe'en parade or party for the children. A parade is held in Logan sponsored by a local service club, and the most beautiful, scary, and funny costumes are awarded a prize. Then it is off to the neighborhood for trick-or-treating. This holiday is a fun time for all. (Both courtesy of JM.)

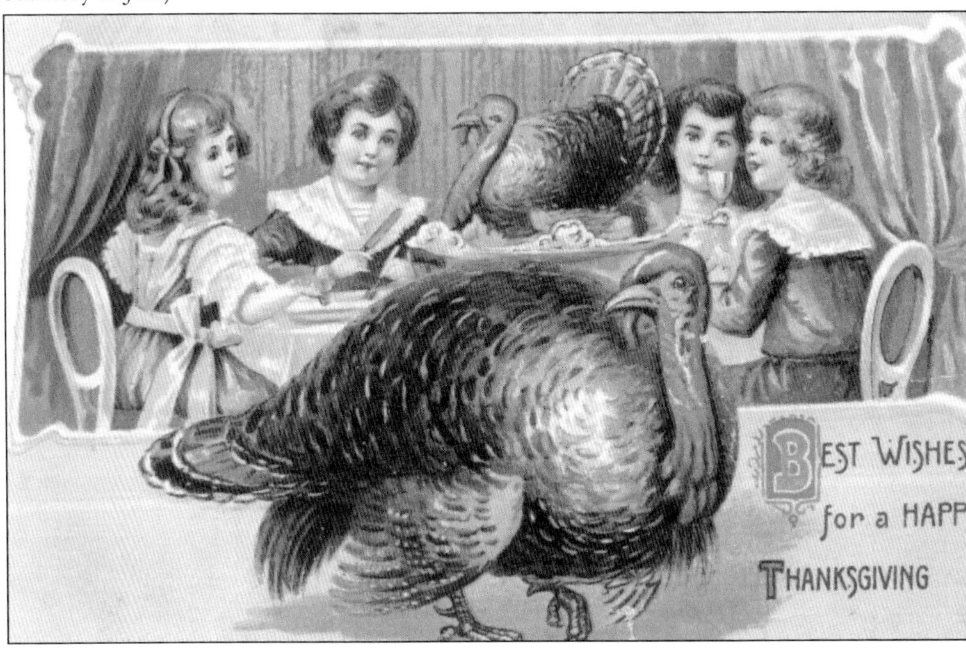

Old Tom Turkey does not know what plans the chefs have in store for him. This Thanksgiving Day postcard is dated 1910. The holiday is traditionally a family celebration with all generations joining in to give thanks for special blessings. (Courtesy of JM.)

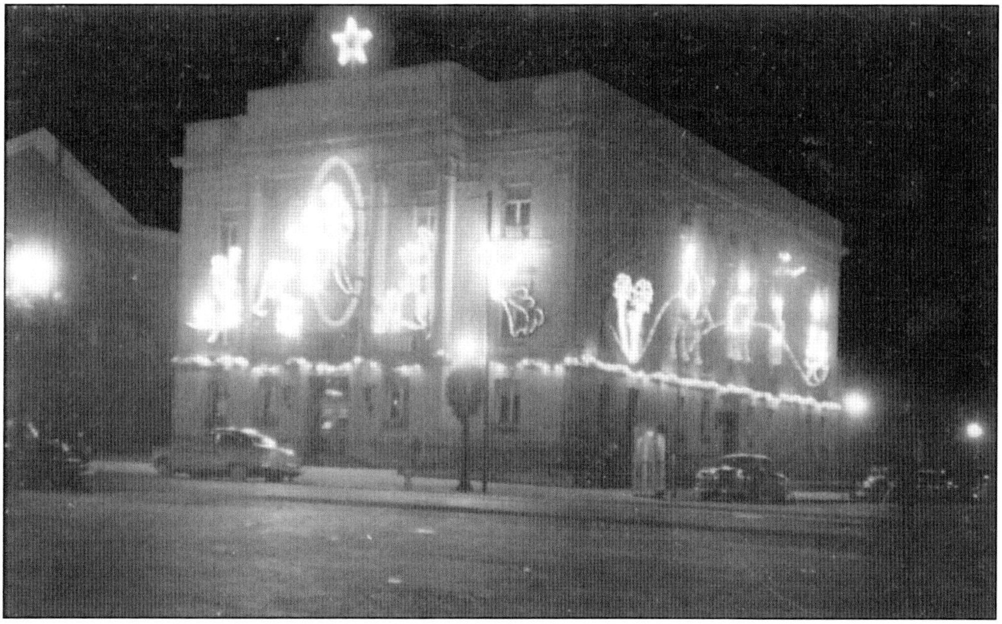

The Christmas season in the Hocking Hills always means a trip to Logan to see the famed Christmas Lights. The idea for the beautiful display came from James D. Wells (1922–1967), who designed and built the first lights about 1939. Wells used the courthouse as the centerpiece for the display (pictured) with Madonna and child, the Nativity, and the wise men. Each intersection of Main Street also has a special design, such as a poinsettia, candy cane, candle, ornament, tree, bell, cross, holly, or a star. The lights were not used during World War II but have continued every year since, cared for by the Wells family and faithful volunteers. (Courtesy of JM.)

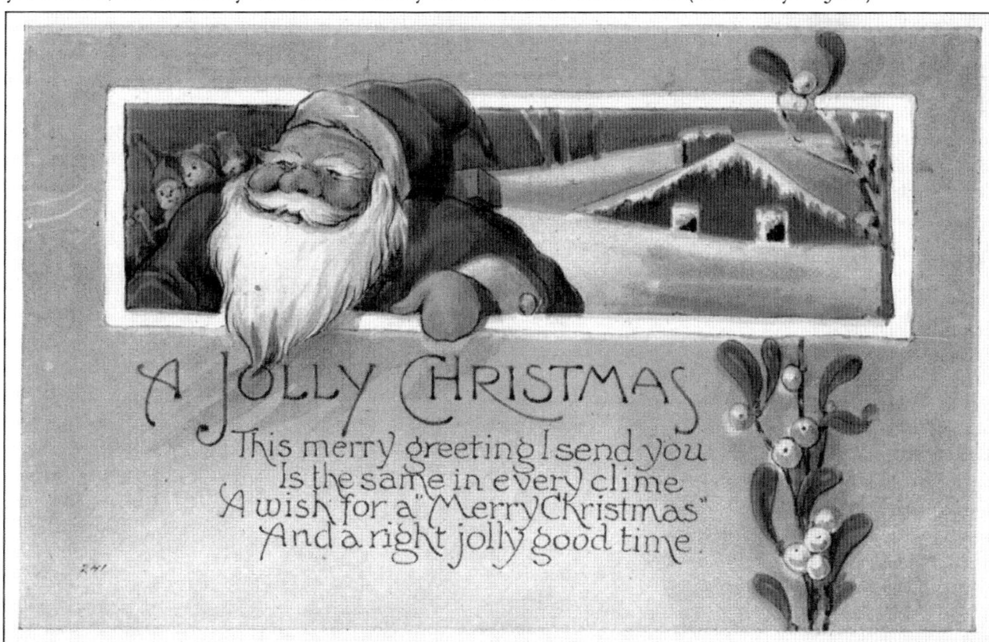

On the back of this card wishing everyone "A Jolly Christmas" is a cancelled stamp that states, "Stamp out tuberculosis." (Courtesy of JM.)